Humberto Vélez

Aesthetics of Collaboration

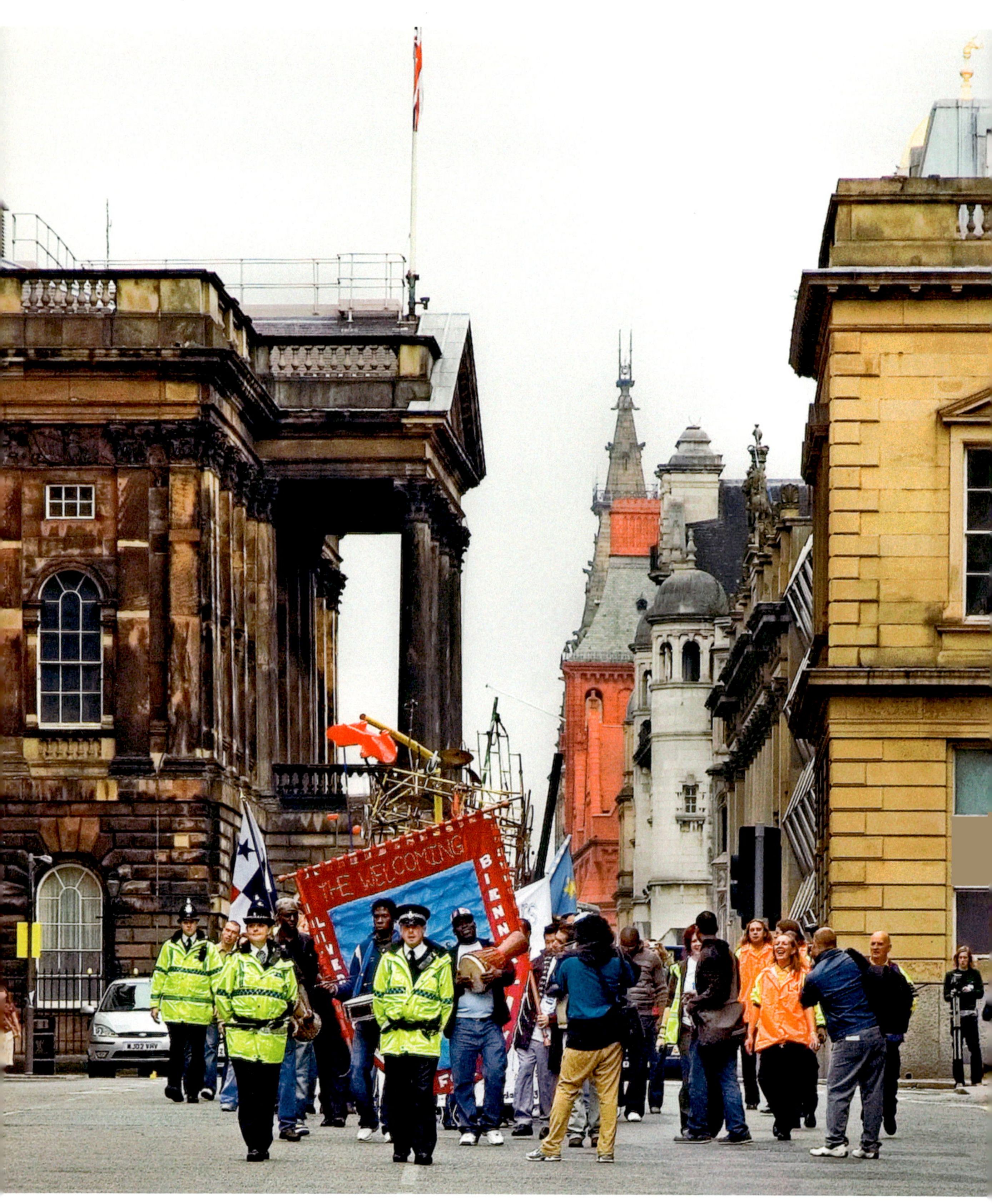

THE WELCOMING
BIENN

Humberto Vélez
Aesthetics of Collaboration

with texts by
Emelie Chhangur, Luis Camnitzer,
Hans-Michael Herzog, and Adrienne Samos

ART GALLERY OF YORK UNIVERSITY, TORONTO

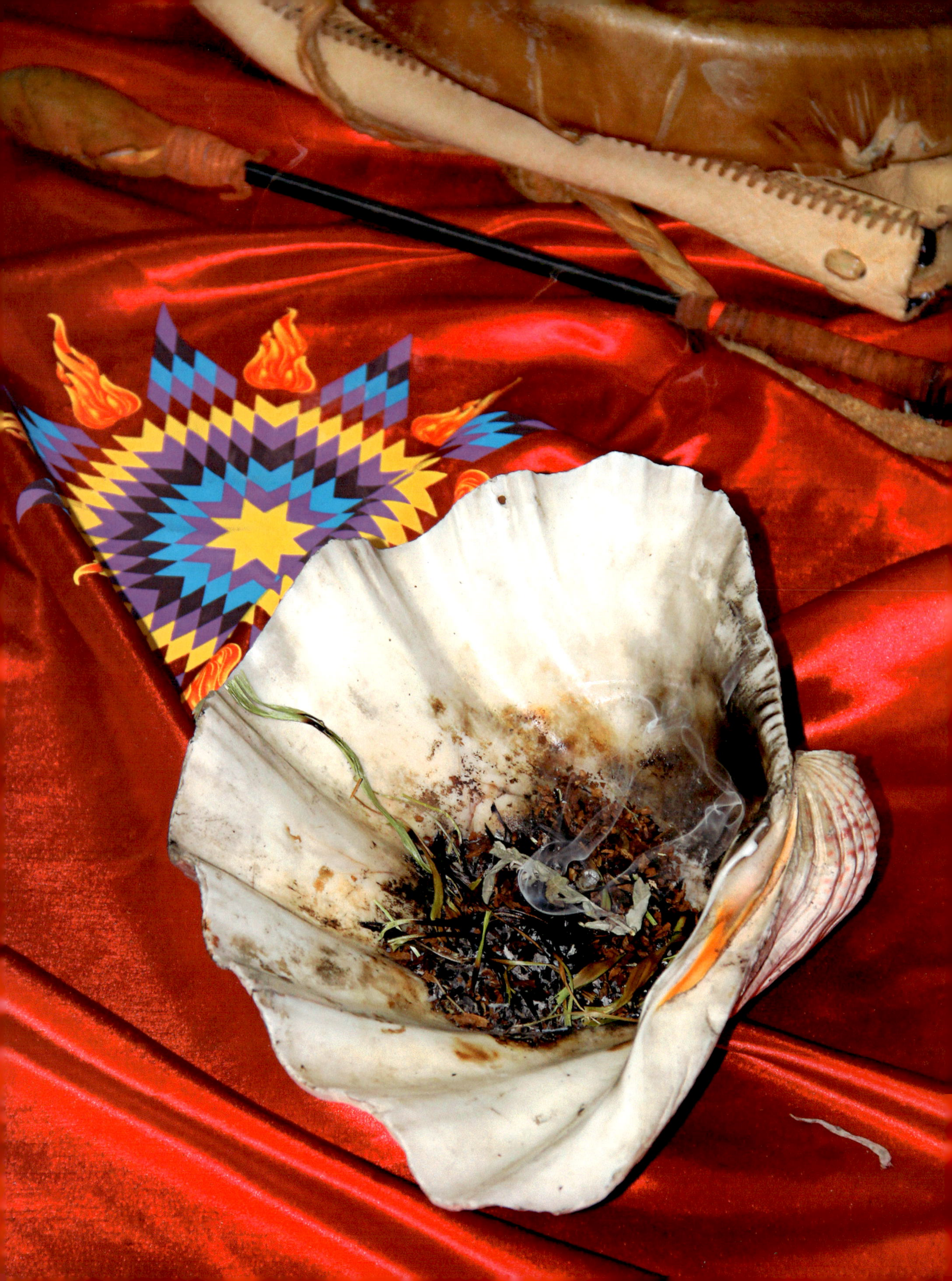

Aesthetics of Collaboration *Emelie Chhangur*   8

La estética de la colaboración *Emelie Chhangur*   13

EXHIBITION / EXPOSICIÓN   21

Works Exhibited   42

Obras expuestas   43

The Really Good-Citizen Artist *Luis Camnitzer*   46

El artista ciudadano *Luis Camnitzer*   52

PAST PROJECTS / PROYECTOS ANTERIORES   60

El grano de arena: Humberto Vélez en conversación
con *Hans-Michael Herzog*   102

At the Root: Humberto Vélez and Panama
Adrienne Samos in conversation with Humberto Vélez   106

De raíz: Humberto Vélez y Panamá
Adrienne Samos en conversación con Humberto Vélez   112

Building Bridges Not Dams: The (re) Awakening
of the Canadian Spirit *Emelie Chhangur*   118

THE AWAKENING / GIIGOZHKOZIMIN [EL DESPERTAR]   149

Contributor Biographies   172

Biografías de los contribuyentes   173

Artist Biography / Biografía del artista   174

Acknowledgements / Reconocimientos   175

Echemos a volar nuestra imaginación por un momento
e intentemos dibujar en nuestras mentes
la manera en que podríamos compartir un sueño
con la gente que vive en un país.

Imaginemos juntos imágenes auténticas que muestren
al mundo lo que realmente nos conmueve, aunque
las vayamos armando a punta de ficciones.
Soñemos *con ser parte* de la realidad de los espacios
donde vivimos a través de los marcos
imaginarios de la obra de arte.

Y a través de estos marcos de referencia, propongamos
verdaderos encuentros que tengan el poder
de redefinir el significado y el propósito del arte.

Mientras soñamos, volvamos a imaginar la ética de
los actuales modos de producción, los cuales constituyen
el mapa del mundo del arte contemporáneo y su relación
con las personas y lugares excluídos de "mapa" artístico.
Propongamos algo nuevo a los sistemas de inclusión
y exclusión del mundo del arte. Revisemos la estética,
pues en el mundo real lo que ustedes consideran bello
puede no serlo para mí o para alguien más.

Abramos las posibilidades de los discursos de belleza y arte
a formas de expresión híbridas y alternativas, así como
a diversos circuitos culturales. Asaltemos las instituciones
con nuestro nuevo poder colectivo para imaginar que
el arte puede tener un propósito real y un nuevo territorio.

Emelie Chhangur (marzo del 2011)

Let's open our imagination for a moment and picture
how we might relate to a place through
a dream we share with the people who live there.

Let's imagine real images to show the world what really
moves us—though we create them together through
fictitious situations. Let's truly *participate* in the reality of
our place through the imaginary frameworks of art projects.

And through these frameworks,
let's propose *real* encounters that have the power
to redefine the meaning and purpose of art.

While we are dreaming, let's also re-imagine the ethics
of current modes of production that constitute the map
of this contemporary art world and its relationship to
people and/or places that are not on this art "map."
Let's propose something new to the art world's systems
of inclusion and exclusion. Let's also reconsider aesthetics,
because, in the real world, your view of what is beautiful
may not be the same as mine, or someone else's.

Let's open up the possibilities of the discourses of
beauty and art to alternative, hybrid forms of expression
and diverse cultural circuits. And let's storm the institutions
with our new collective power to imagine that
art can have a real purpose and also a new territory.

Emelie Chhangur (March 2011)

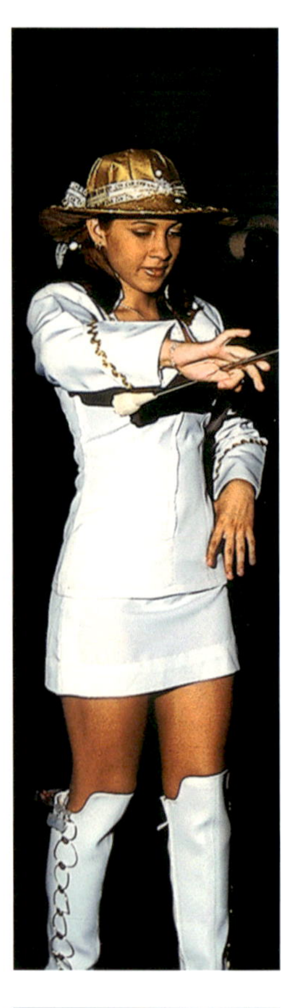
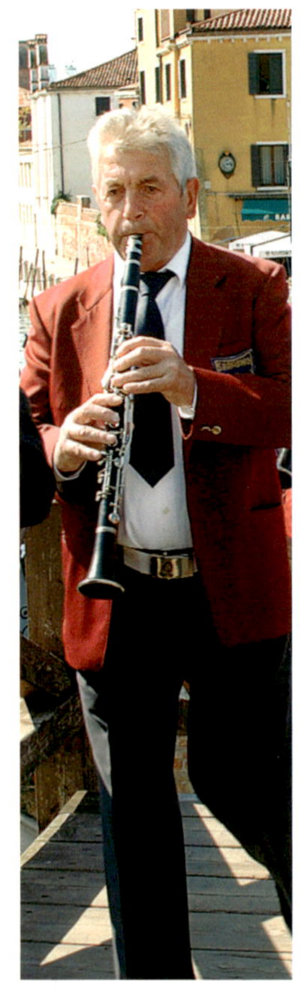
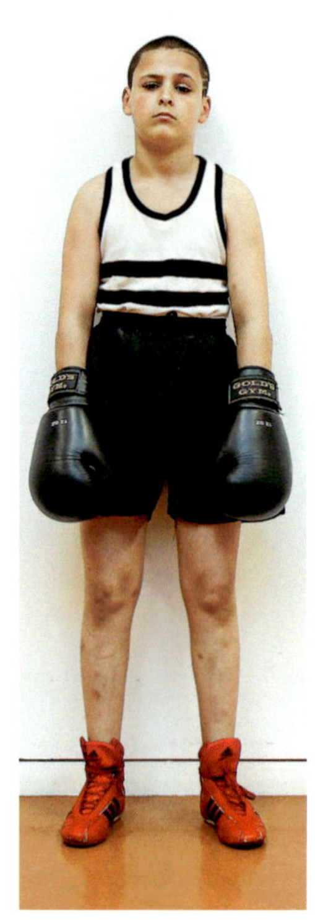
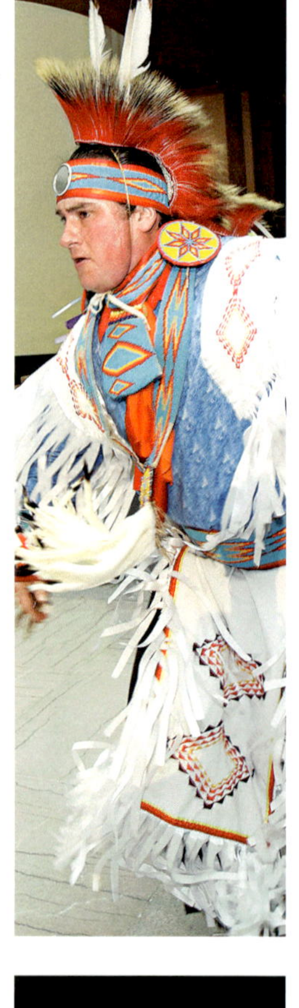
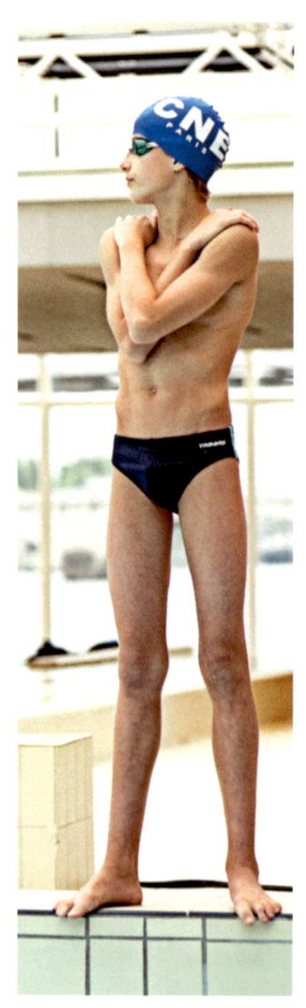
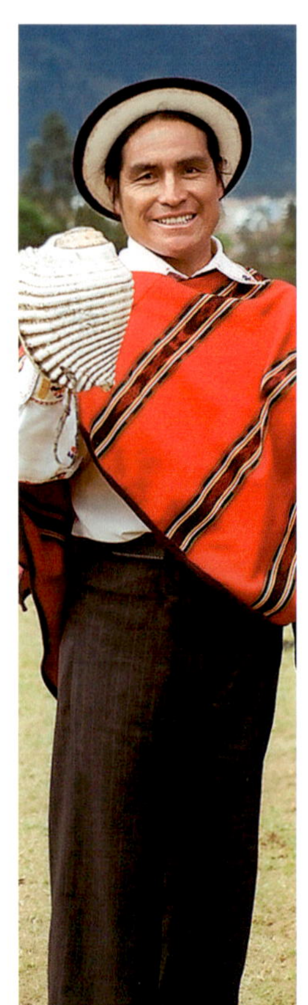
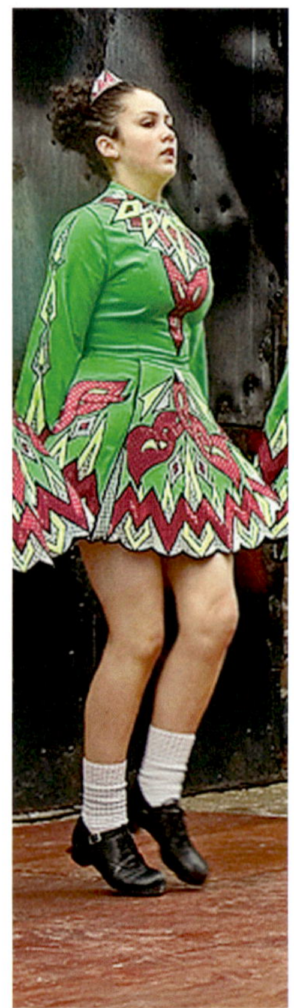
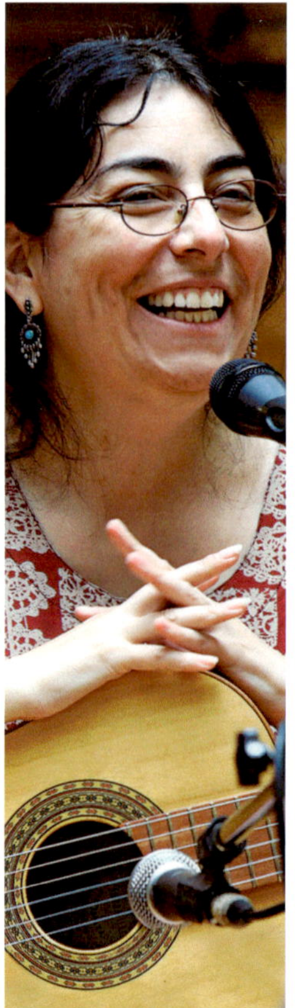
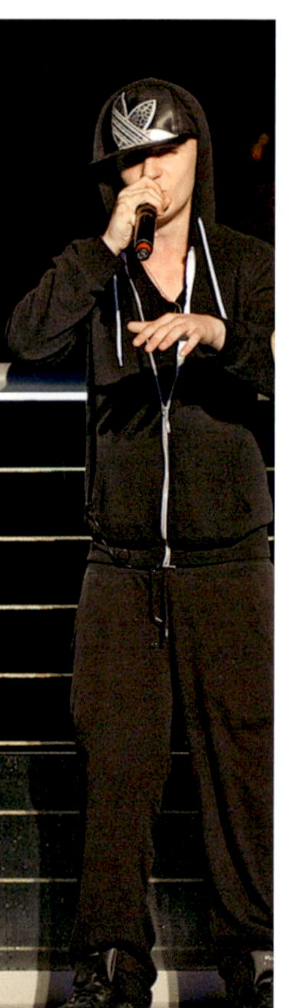
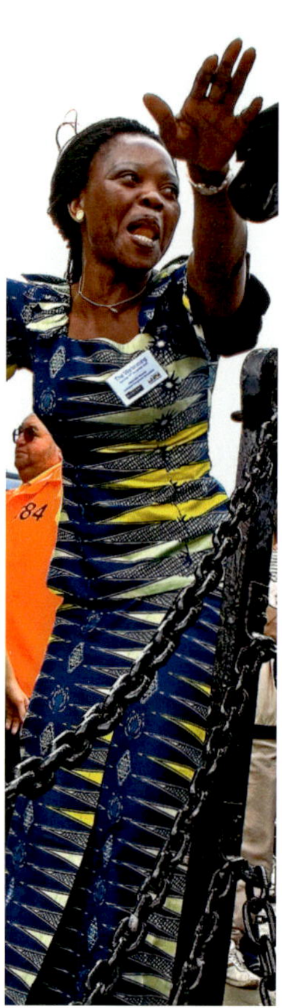

Aesthetics of Collaboration

Emelie Chhangur

Humberto Vélez's multi-faceted participatory performance practice actively explores the generative possibilities of working in collaboration with diverse groups of people brought together especially for each project in each location. In places across the world, he has collaborated with boxers, hip hop musicians, Indigenous Peoples, refugees, asylum seekers, synchronized swimmers, spoken word artists, marching bands, and bodybuilders, amongst many others. Over the past decade, these collaborations have resulted in large-scale orchestrated artistic actions as diverse as beauty contests with llamas, amateur boxing matches with youth, concerts with popular poets, and bodybuilding competitions transcending divisions of gender and class.

Collaboration is not an end in itself for Vélez; it is an operative strategy integral to questioning the role of art and aesthetics *today*. By opening up to diverse cultural input as well as to the participation of non-artists, Vélez's projects develop what he calls the collaborators' "capacity to produce aesthetics." Through extended periods of development and the final performances, his projects propose different concepts of culture, power, and ethics that counter those found in mainstream art institutions. Indeed, these collaborative performances are forms of resistance to the status quo of the Eurocentric art world.

These works re-picture the world by imagining new forms and associations of belonging—often for those who "belong" within neither society's norms nor the contemporary art world. The performances appropriate other "social" forms of organization—such as parades, sports events, and regattas—and script them otherwise (as stories of migration, identity, race, beauty, and/or class) in order to reinsert them into exclusionary symbolic institutions, art museums or otherwise, crossing many different cultural and aesthetic borders in the process. In many of these performances, Vélez doesn't necessarily show us anything different, even if the works do propose an entirely different "look" for contemporary art. Rather, he opens our eyes to why we keep seeing things the same way. By radically redefining the form and function of contemporary art, he opens new aesthetic possibilities that open *us* up to alternative forms of cultural production.

Vélez's work questions the ethics around collaboration (how we work together) and participation (who gets to participate and why) by making these questions integral to the process of art making. He makes them the *subject*, not the style, of a way of working, believing that the ethical issue of collaboration in art is not to represent politics but to enact politics. As such, his collaborative performances differ from many current participatory practices in Europe and the United States in that they are based on human relations and the inclusion of popular expressions of identity (i.e., hip hop or boxing), not institutional interests (i.e., "education outreach") or a reliance on art world references (i.e., relational aesthetics).

His are not top-down "community art" projects, either. They do have a pedagogical imperative, however: they are open-ended learning situations intended to transform the structures in which he and his collaborators live and work, not the people he collaborates with. Vélez's focus is on exposing existing cultural practices of exclusion both inside and outside the art frame by incorporating, but not *appropriating*, the cultural expressions of his collaborators into the final artwork. Through collaboration, Vélez brings new forms of social organization into the arts which changes not only how art looks but, more importantly, how it operates.

There are no hierarchies within Vélez's projects. Participants help each other to tell their stories. Though based on their particular skill sets, *together* they shape them into concrete forms and actions for others to see and experience. In a sense, Vélez's projects are based upon a very basic human impulse: to find what we have in common and, with a shared sense of urgency, move toward a mutually beneficial goal. As Caribbean spoken word artist and playwright Sonia Hughes comments, "When [Vélez] engages with his collaborators in his participative works, he walks alongside them and largely they accept him as they are rarely of the majority or with power due to their race and/or class and recognize that he is also a rara avis [rare bird]. He feels they have something to say, he also has something to say, he'd like to know how each of them could strengthen each other's statements."[1]

Never a *performer* in his own work, neither is Vélez the *subject* of his performances—even if he shares a similar "outsider" perspective. Rather, he is a catalyst for other people's stories and ideas, playing a role more akin to a conductor of an orchestra or a director of a film; he combines and shapes their collective current cultural interests and forms of expression into new narrative contexts. Through his early experiences as a lawyer working for unions and *campesinos* in the rural provinces of Panama and then as a student of documentary film at the *Escuela Internacional de Cine y TV San Antonio de los Baños* in Cuba, he has learned how to negotiate, to listen, and to bridge communities. Vélez knows through experience what it means to bring real, humanizing influences into the art world. Collaborators contribute their ideas through dialogue *with* the artist. He gently guides and steers the project through to completion. He doesn't project current trends in contemporary art onto their interests/activities/ideas as that would necessarily lead to an already pre-determined outcome. Instead, collaborators are empowered to make decisions and to take aesthetic and social action, which is then negotiated into an art context by Vélez. By opening up a space for non-artists to participate within the art-frame, Vélez seeks to change the potentiality of art and its possible new discourses as we move forward in the twenty-first century.

Vélez's performances do not generally lend themselves to conventional gallery settings as they often occur in the streets. Yet, *Humberto Vélez: Aesthetics of Collaboration,* which took place at the Art Gallery of York University (AGYU) from April 13 to June 26, 2011, brought together the first exhibition of the artist's performance works from the last decade and put them "on display." Looking to his work as a radical model, the exhibition was intended to provoke as much as the original performances. *Aesthetics of Collaboration* was an opportunity to think through new methods of representing performance work in a gallery setting, mixing aesthetics and genres within the exhibition's design, with the aim of finding ways to exhibit the work without neutralizing the political nature of this engaged, activist practice.

To view a collection of Vélez's past work is to look at an alternative mapping of the world's cities told—or re-imagined—through the dreams, aspirations, and new forms of belonging forged by people living in them. Putting these alternative stories on display inside a cultural institution meant that we, too, could participate in the creation of counter-narratives, and, like Vélez, change the typical way in which we view these "other" places in other than exoticized terms. Thus, the exhibition told the stories of places as diverse as London and Valparaíso, Paris and Cuenca, Panama City and Liverpool, Manchester and Toronto, side-by-side. In the multi-cultural context of Toronto, this made particular sense.

In the exhibition, each story took shape through different forms of documentation. Performative exhibition strategies lent a participatory agency to viewers, much as Humberto gives to his collaborators. Original performance documentation, re-edited into mini-films that unfolded cinematically, narrated the "action" of the performances themselves. For each performance, iconic moments were represented by photographs, accompanied by portraits of individual performers hung side-by-side—a strange family portrait of all of Humberto's past collaborators and friends. The videos and photographs, moreover, were framed by artifacts, such as the banners created by participants for some of the performances showing the pride that each performance elicited from its participants. When viewed together, the documentation and artifacts became testaments to the new aesthetic possibilities manifested in Vélez's performative actions.

At the AGYU, we understand that Humberto is more interested in seeing how art changes the institution than how the institution changes artworks. He knows that the history of institutions has always been to "absorb" new forms of practice while discounting their politics. For Humberto this is just moving things along to suit the interest of the art market. Nevertheless, Humberto is willing to play the institution's game in order to move things along, *on his terms*, reversing the traditional relationship institutions have to emergent art practices. He knows his performances have real effect on the institutions that commission them because he frames those institutions and their practices *from the point of view of the people he works with.*

Aesthetics of Collaboration was a way for the AGYU to bring Humberto's work *inside* our institution, complementing *The Awakening / Giigozhkozimin,* a commissioned off-site performance that spoke to the cultural context of Toronto. The exhibition was a way to highlight the profound effect Humberto's work has had on the nature of our institutional practice—indeed it has absorbed us—learning as we have from the three-year process of collaboration on *The Awakening*, one of the artist's most ambitious performances to date. At the AGYU, we share Humberto's belief that the contemporary art gallery should serve a social as well as an aesthetic function.

We have come to share Humberto's approach to art making in our curatorial projects, believing they too can simultaneously serve a pedagogical purpose as much as an artistic one. We are no longer interested in the hierarchies between curatorial and education projects, hoping to incorporate aspects of both in all that we do. Over the years of working with him, the AGYU has developed strategies of "in-reach" that counter traditional top-down outreach practices instigated by many art institutions under the auspices of "education," paralleling Humberto's desire to open the field of art to diverse perspectives. By bringing new forms of expression and different cultural practices *into* the institution, in-reach projects are designed to open up the institution, to follow paths into new territories with unexpected outcomes.

By changing the "rules of the game," *we* can govern the way we participate in the world on our *own* terms. We *can* reshape our cultural institutions from the inside, ensuring that they are positively and productively affected by *the actual cultural landscape* of our cities. Vélez teaches us that it is imperative that we incorporate the complexities of the communities that we live within.

NOTES

1. Sonia Hughes, Humberto Vélez 8th Residency Project at Persistence Works Studios at: http://www.artspace.org.uk/documents/SoniaHugesonHumbertoVelez.pdf. May 2007.

La estética de la colaboración

Emelie Chhangur

Mediante sus representaciones o *performances* participativas, Humberto Vélez explora posibilidades creativas de trabajar en colaboración con individuos reunidos especialmente para cada uno de sus proyectos. Vélez ha trabajado en muchos lugares del mundo en colaboración con boxeadores, músicos de hip hop, aborígenes, refugiados, asilados políticos, nadadores sincronizados, escritores, bandas musicales y culturistas físicos. Durante la última década, estas colaboraciones se han convertido en representaciones artísticas organizadas a gran escala, tales como concursos de belleza de alpacas, peleas entre jóvenes boxeadores aficionados, conciertos con poetas populares y competencias de fisicoculturismo que trascienden las divisiones de género y clase.

Para Vélez la colaboración no es un fin en si mismo, sino una estrategia operacional integral para cuestionar el papel del arte y la estética de *hoy*. La apertura a diversas influencias culturales, así como la participación de no-artistas, da lugar a que los proyectos de Vélez desarrollen lo que él llama la "capacidad de producir estética". A lo largo de extensos períodos de gestación y de la *performance* final, sus proyectos proponen diferentes conceptos de cultura, poder y ética opuestos a los de las instituciones artísticas tradicionales. De hecho, estas representaciones participativas son una manera de desafiar el statu quo del arte eurocéntrico.

Estas obras construyen un mundo diferente, imaginando nuevas asociaciones de pertenencia, a menudo para aquellos que no tienen voz ni en la sociedad convencional, ni en el mundo del arte contemporáneo. Sus *performances* se apropian de otras formas sociales de organización, tales como desfiles, eventos deportivos y regatas, y las presentan de una manera diferente (por ejemplo, historias de migración, identidad, raza, belleza y clase), reinsertándolas en instituciones excluyentes, museos y otras, y cruzando en el proceso muchas fronteras culturales y estéticas. En muchas de estas *performances* Vélez no nos muestra algo fuera de lo común, aun si la obra propone una visión completamente diferente del arte contemporáneo. Con esta estrategia logra abrirnos los ojos y preguntarnos por qué seguimos viendo las cosas de la misma manera. Al cambiar radicalmente la definición de la forma y función del arte contemporáneo, Vélez presenta nuevas posibilidades estéticas que nos muestran formas alternativas de producción cultural.

El trabajo de Vélez también cuestiona la ética de la colaboración (cómo trabajamos unos con otros) y la participación (quién participa y por qué), integrando estas preguntas en el proceso de la creación artística. Él las convierte en el *sujeto* y no en el estilo de su manera

"

de trabajar, convencido de que la ética de la colaboración en el arte no es representar la política sino vivirla. Las *performances* de Vélez difieren de muchas de las prácticas participativas actuales en Europa y los Estados Unidos, pues se basan en las relaciones humanas y en la inclusión de formas populares de expresión de la identidad (tales como el hip hop o el boxeo) en vez de basarse en intereses institucionales (como el "alcance de la educación") y la dependencia de referencias del mundo artístico (como la estética relacional).

Aunque poseen un impulso pedagógico, sus representaciones tampoco son proyectos de arte comunitario: son situaciones abiertas de aprendizaje, destinadas a transformar las estructuras en las que Vélez y sus colaboradores viven y trabajan, y no a las personas con quienes él colabora. El enfoque de sus proyectos es exponer las prácticas culturales de exclusión que existen actualmente, dentro y fuera del marco artístico, mediante la incorporación (más no la *apropiación*) de las formas de expresión cultural de sus colaboradores. Mediante la colaboración, Vélez establece nuevas formas de organización social en el arte, cambiando no solamente la forma como se ve el arte, sino, más importante aún, como funciona.

Dentro de los proyectos de Vélez no existen las jerarquías. Los participantes se ayudan unos a otros a contar sus historias. Aunque basadas en las habilidades particulares de cada uno, entre todos las convierten en conceptos y acciones concretas para que otros las puedan ver, experimentar y apreciar. En cierto sentido, los proyectos de Vélez se basan en un impulso humano muy básico: encontrar lo que tenemos en común y con un sentido compartido de urgencia, avanzar hacia un objetivo de beneficio mutuo. La escritora y dramaturga caribeña, Sonia Hughes, comenta sobre el método de creación del artista: "Cuando [Vélez] se involucra en los trabajos participativos con sus colaboradores, camina a su lado y ellos en gran medida lo aceptan, pues rara vez pertenecen a un grupo mayoritario, carecen de poder debido a su raza y/o clase social, y reconocen que él también es una *rara avis* [ave rara]. Él tiene algo que decir, siente que ellos también tienen algo que decir y le gustaría saber cómo podrían, unidos, fortalecer sus respectivas declaraciones."[1]

Vélez nunca actúa en sus representaciones artísticas ni se convierte en su tema principal, aunque comparte una perspectiva de "forastero" similar a los participantes de sus proyectos. Él sirve más bien como catalizador de las historias e ideas de otros, jugando un papel similar al de director de orquesta o de cine, que combina y da forma a las formas de expresión e intereses colectivos culturales, para transformarlos en nuevos contextos narrativos. Sus primeras experiencias como abogado, trabajando para los sindicatos y campesinos en las provincias rurales de Panamá, y después como estudiante de cine documental en la *Escuela Internacional de Cine y TV de San Antonio de los Baños* en Cuba, le han enseñado cómo negociar, escuchar, y crear diálogo entre varias comunidades.

Sabe por experiencia lo que significa traer influencias reales y humanas al mundo del arte. Los colaboradores de sus proyectos aportan sus propias ideas a través del diálogo *con* el artista, y él suavemente guía y dirige la obra hasta su finalización. Vélez no proyecta las tendencias actuales del arte contemporáneo en sus intereses, actividades o ideas, ya que esto conduciría a un resultado pre-determinado. Más bien, los colaboradores son incentivados a tomar sus propias decisiones y a adoptar medidas estéticas y sociales, utilizadas por Vélez para diseñar un contexto artístico. Al abrir un espacio de participación para personas que no son consideradas artistas dentro del mundo del arte contemporáneo, Vélez busca expandir las posibilidades del arte e introducir nuevos discursos artísticos a medida que avanzamos en el siglo XXI.

Por lo general sus obras no se exhiben en galerías de arte convencionales, pues casi siempre se producen en las calles. Sin embargo, *Humberto Vélez: Aesthetics of Collaboration* [Humberto Vélez: La estética de la colaboración], que tuvo lugar en la *Art Gallery of York University* (AGYU) de abril 13 a junio 26 del 2011, fue la primera exposición que reunió los proyectos participativos del artista a partir de la última década y los puso "en exhibición". Al observar la colección de sus obras como un modelo radical, podemos concluir que la exposición fue diseñada para provocar y cuestionar tanto como las *performances* originales mismas. *Aesthetics of Collaboration* nos dio la oportunidad de pensar en nuevos métodos de exhibir este medio artístico en una galería, mezclando estética y género en el diseño de la exposición, con el fin de buscar formas de exhibir el trabajo, sin neutralizar el carácter político de esta comprometida práctica activista.

Observar reunidas las obras anteriores de Vélez es como mirar una cartografía de las ciudades del mundo, ilustradas e imaginadas a través de los sueños, aspiraciones y nuevas formas de pertenencia forjadas por las personas que viven en ellas. Poner estas historias alternativas en exhibición dentro de una institución cultural, significa que nosotros también podemos participar en la creación de estas contra-narrativas, y al igual que Vélez, cambiar la asociación típica que estos lugares tienen como "otros" y verlos en términos no-exóticos. De esta manera, la exposición contó en forma yuxtapuesta historias de lugares tan diversos como Londres y Valparaíso, París y Cuenca, ciudad de Panamá y Liverpool, y Manchester y Toronto. El contexto multicultural de Toronto fue un escenario particularmente natural para esta presentación.

En la exposición cada historia fue presentada por un medio diferente de documentación. Sus estrategias de presentación "actuantes" promovieron la participación por parte de los espectadores, tal como la que Humberto da a sus colaboradores. Los videos que documentaron las representaciones fueron editados y convertidos en cortometrajes que narran la "acción" de las interpretaciones originales. Fotografías que capturaron los momentos más importantes de cada representación, acompañadas por retratos de los artistas que participaron en cada proyecto, colgados lado a lado, crearon un extraño retrato familiar de todos los colaboradores y amigos de Humberto. Además de los videos y fotografías, se exhibieron artefactos tales como estandartes creados por los participantes para algunas de las actuaciones, que mostraban el orgullo que cada representación significó para sus participantes. Vistos en conjunto, la documentación y los artefactos son un testimonio de las nuevas posibilidades estéticas que se manifiestan en las obras colaborativas de Vélez.

En la AGYU entendemos que Humberto está más interesado en ver cómo el arte cambia la institución que en cómo la institución cambia las obras de arte. Él sabe que tradicionalmente las instituciones han ido incorporando nuevas expresiones artísticas, ignorando su mensaje. Para Humberto esto solamente satisface el interés del mercado artístico. Sin embargo, él está dispuesto a jugar el juego de la institución, pero en *sus propios términos,* invirtiendo la relación tradicional de las instituciones con las nuevas prácticas artísticas. Él sabe que sus obras tienen un efecto real en las instituciones que las encargan porque enmarca tanto las instituciones como sus prácticas desde *el punto de vista de los individuos que participan en cada proyecto.*

Aesthetics of Collaboration fue una manera de traer la obra de Humberto al interior de la AGYU, como un complemento de *The Awakening / Giigozhkozimin* [El despertar], una representación colaborativa llevada a cabo fuera de las instalaciones y dirigida al contexto cultural de Toronto. La exposición fue una manera de destacar el gran efecto que el trabajo de Humberto ha tenido sobre la forma como realizamos nuestros proyectos. Aprendimos mucho a través de un proceso de colaboración de tres años en *The Awakening,* una de las representaciones más ambiciosas del artista hasta la fecha. En la AGYU compartimos la creencia de Humberto de que las galerías de arte contemporáneo deben cumplir tanto una función social, como una función estética.

Hemos venido a emplear el enfoque de Humberto en la creación artística en nuestros propios proyectos curatoriales, con la convicción de que ellos también pueden cumplir un propósito tan pedagógico como artístico. Ya no nos interesa la jerarquía entre los proyectos curatoriales y educativos, pues tenemos la esperanza de incorporar ambos aspectos en todo lo que hacemos. Durante los años de trabajo con él, nuestra galería ha desarrollado estrategias *in-reach,* es decir, opuestas a la práctica tradicional de muchas instituciones artísticas que las auspician como proyectos educativos. Compartimos con Humberto el deseo de expandir el campo artístico explorando perspectivas diferentes. Al incorporar nuevas formas de expresión y diferentes prácticas culturales, estos proyectos *in-reach* están diseñados para ampliar la forma de pensar de la institución, con el fin de abrir caminos hacia nuevos territorios en busca de resultados inesperados.

Al cambiar las "reglas del juego", *podemos* controlar la forma en que participamos en el mundo en *nuestros* propios términos. *Podemos* reformar nuestras instituciones culturales desde adentro, para asegurarnos de que el *panorama cultural actual* de nuestras ciudades las afecte en forma positiva y productiva. Vélez nos enseña que es imprescindible incorporar en el arte las complejidades de las comunidades en las que vivimos.

NOTAS

1. Sonia Hughes, Octavo proyecto de residencia de Humberto Vélez en Persistence Works Studios en: http://www.artspace.org.uk/documents/SoniaHugesonHumbertoVelez.pdf. Mayo de 2007.

Mis proyectos no son sólo acerca de mí,
sino también acerca de la gente con que trabajo
para realizar un proyecto. En ese momento es
cuando la ética entra en juego. Dejo que las
personas hagan lo que tienen que hacer como
profesionales y luego observo qué sucede.
Analizo cómo se involucran en el proyecto,
y eso a veces es muy positivo. Pero una institución
es una institución. Así, que desde el comienzo
dejo que ésta muestre su interés en el proyecto.
Cuando veo algun problema intervengo y hablo
con las personas de la institución para ponernos
de acuerdo sobre la manera de ver el proyecto.
Creo que la única limitación es la ética.
Tanto mi ética como artista, que me puede
limitar en lo que creo que puede ser el resultado
artístico, como la ética de la institución en cuanto
a su manera de relacionarse con la gente.
Creo que las instituciones no están acostumbradas
a ser cuestionadas, pero algunas veces tengo
que decirles que, desde mi punto de vista,
sus estrategias no son éticas.

Humberto Vélez (diciembre del 2009)

My projects are not only about me,
they are about the people I am working with
and those I get involved with to make the project.
This is when ethics comes into play. I let people
do what they're supposed to do as professionals...
and then I see what happens. I observe how
people engage with the project and sometimes
it is really positive. But an institution is
an institution. I let the institution show their
willingness to be a part of the project right away.
And when I see that there's a problem
I talk to some of the people at the institution
and try to establish an understanding and a
diplomatic view for the project. I think that
the only limit is ethics, and it is ethics in terms
of both me as an artist, restricting me in
what I think could be the artistic result, and also
how the institution wants to treat people.
I think institutions aren't used to being
challenged. Sometimes I just have to say,
"listen, the strategies you are using
are not ethical in my view."

Humberto Vélez (December 2009)

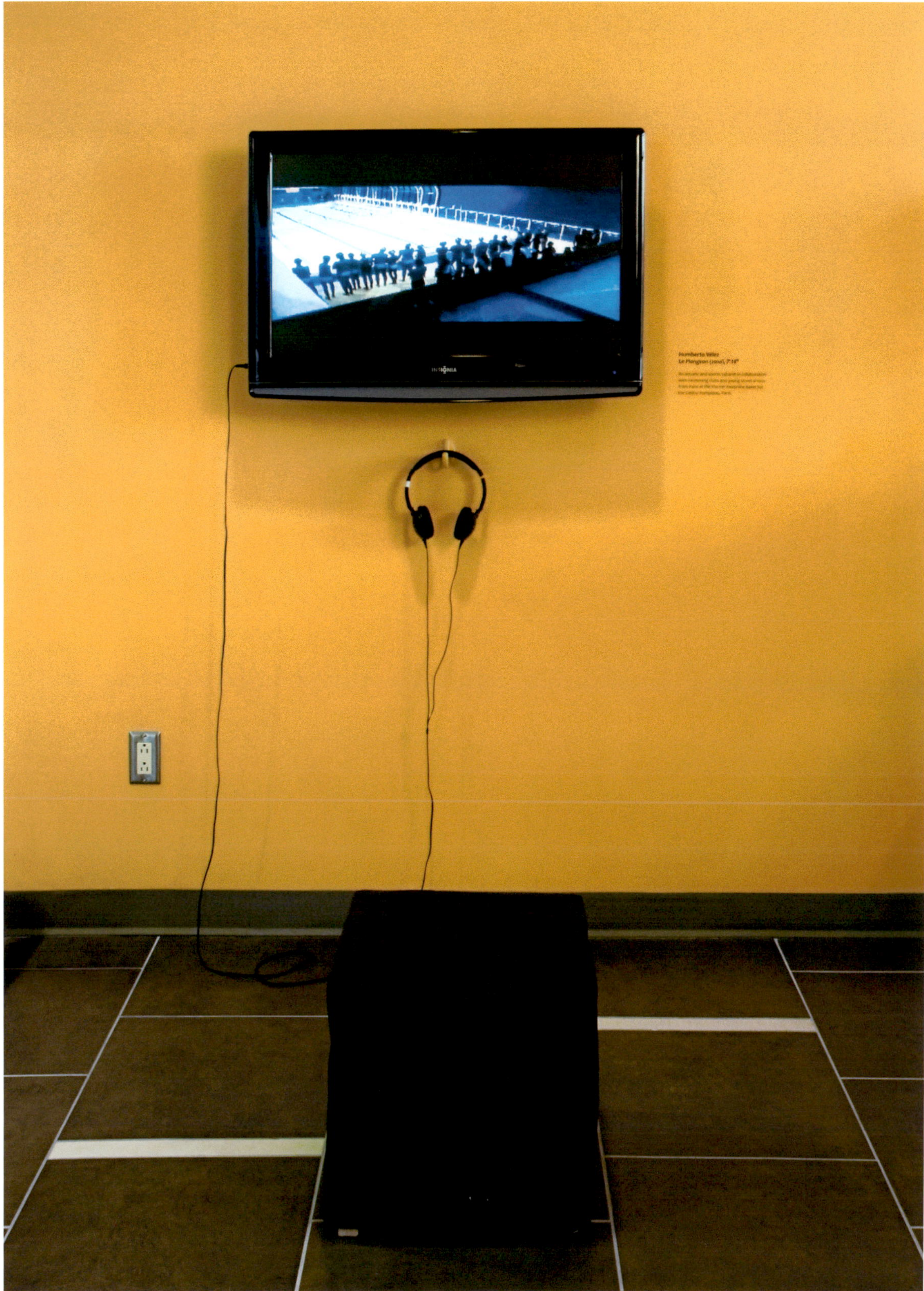

Humberto Velez
Le Plongeon (2010), 7'14"
An artistic and sports cabaret in collaboration
with swimming clubs and young street artists
from Paris at the Piscine Josephine Baker for
the Centre Pompidou, Paris.

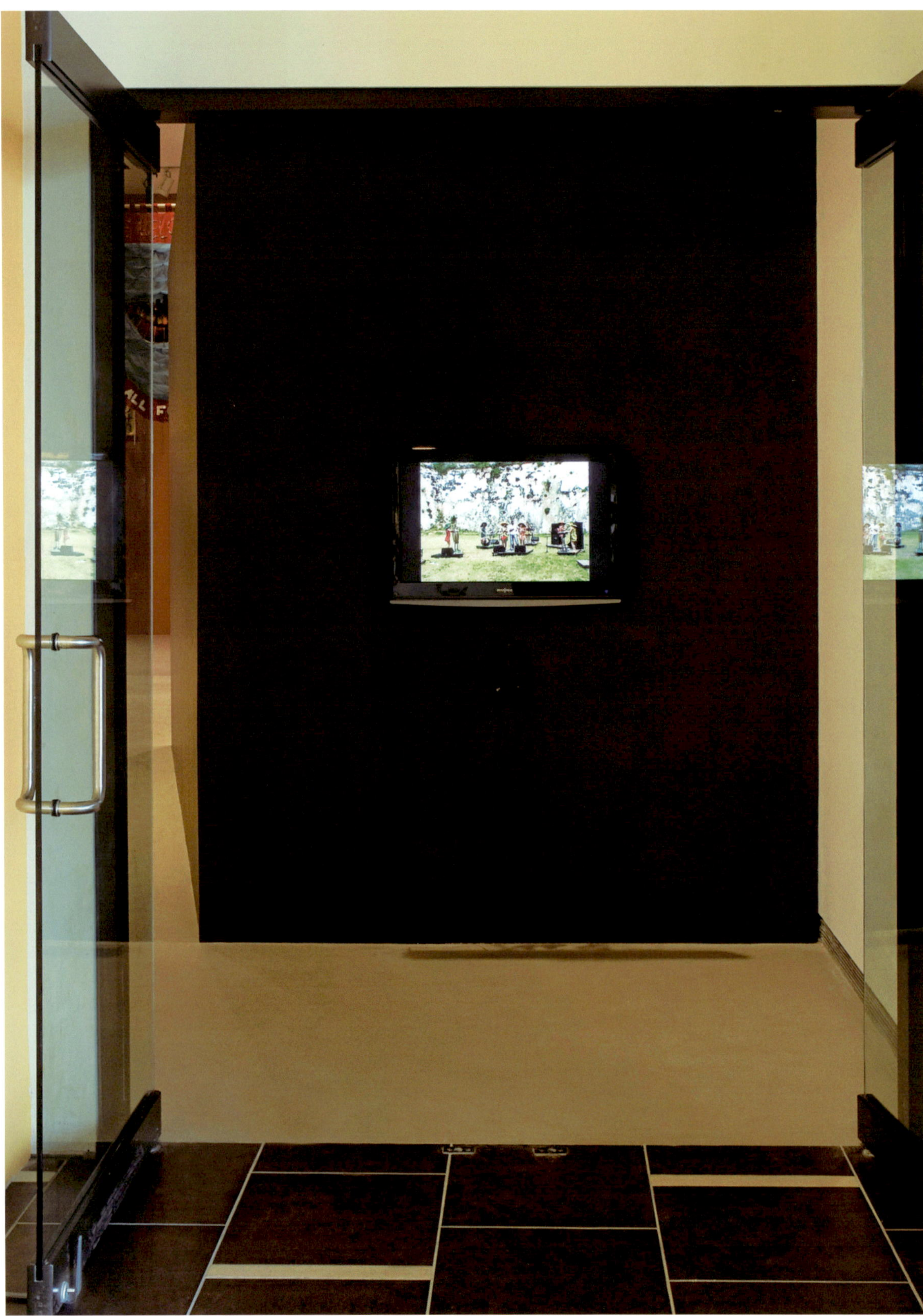

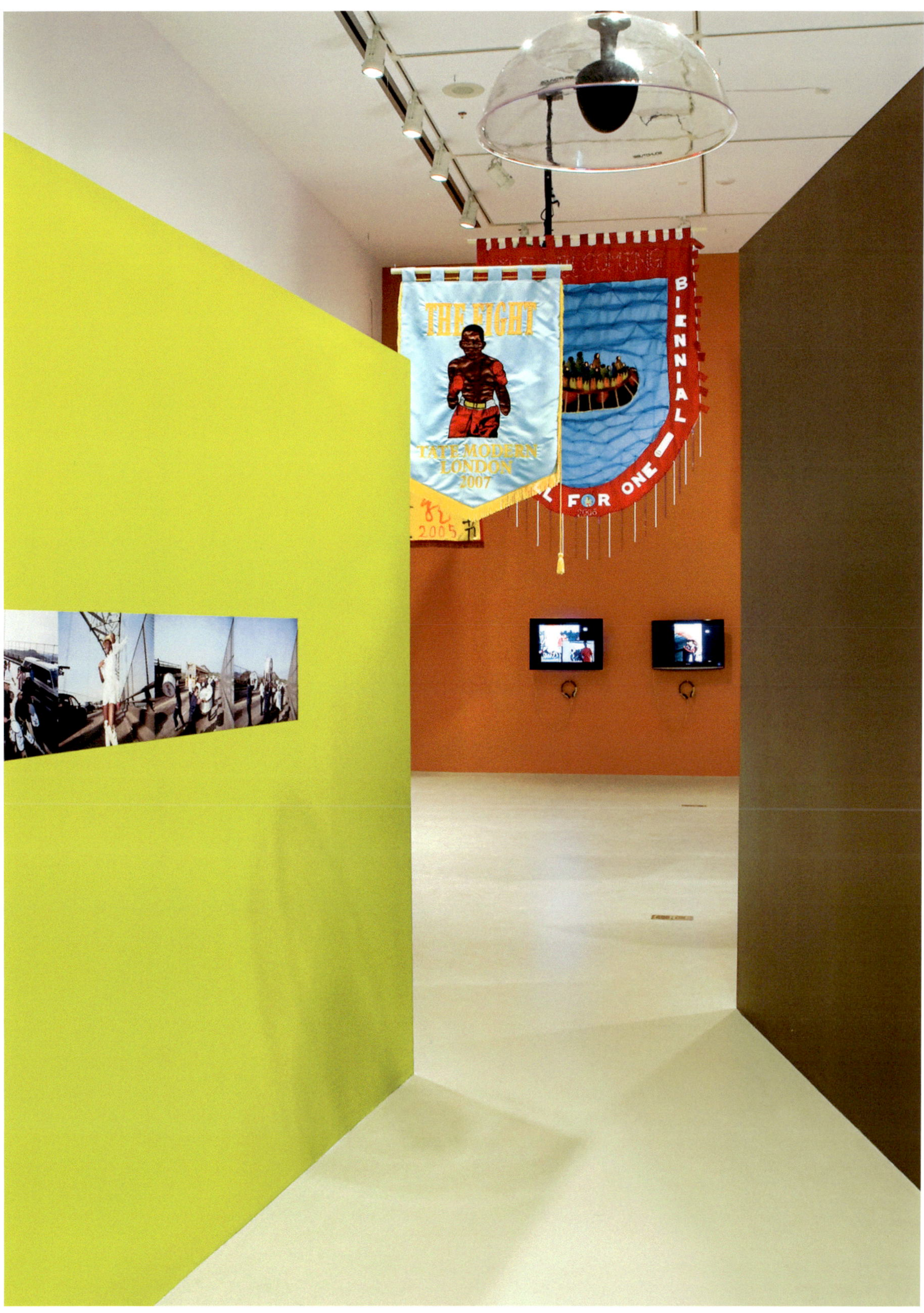
THE FIGHT
TATE MODERN
LONDON
2007
2005
BIENNIAL
FOR ONE

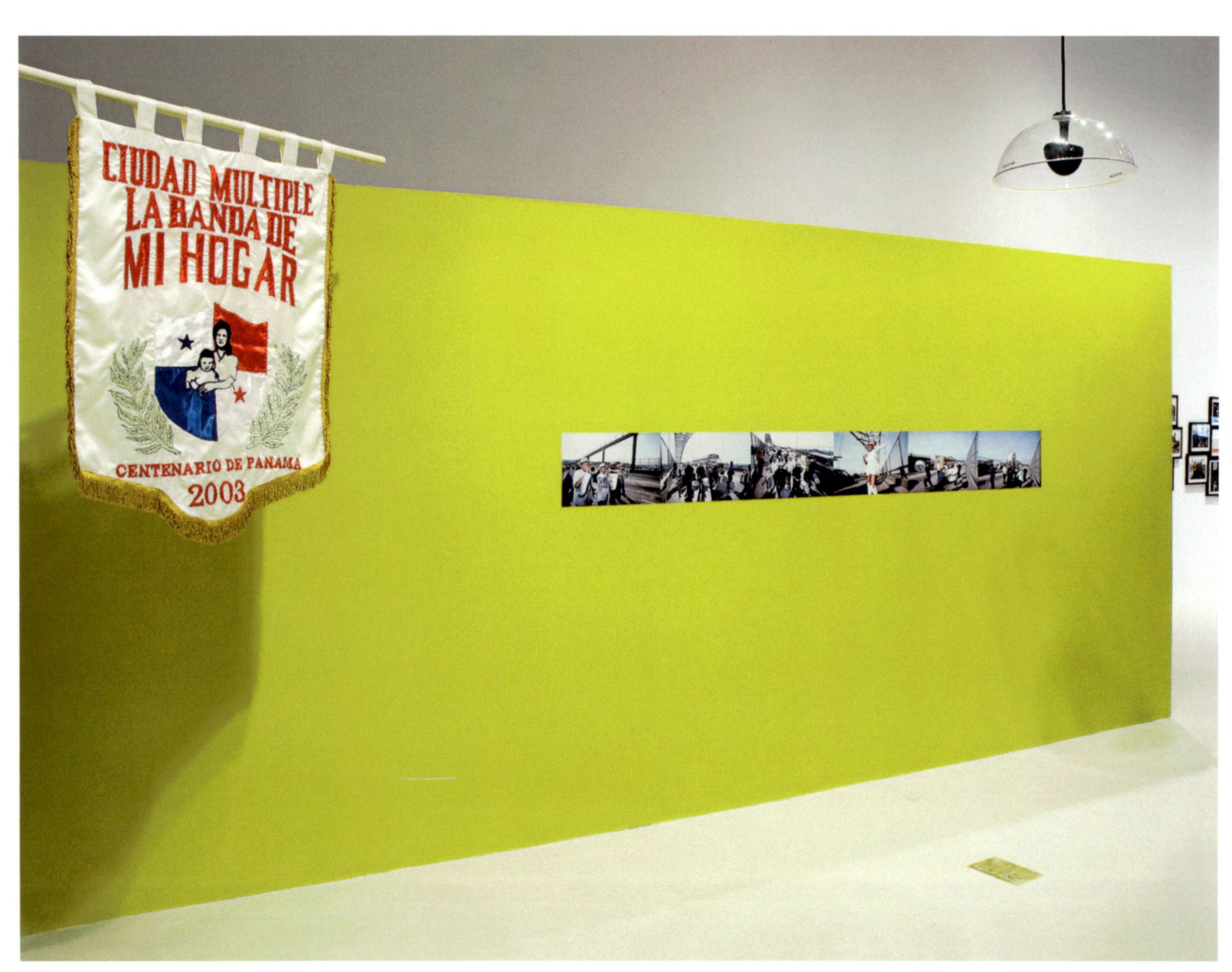
CIUDAD MULTIPLE
LA BANDA DE
MI HOGAR
CENTENARIO DE PANAMA
2003

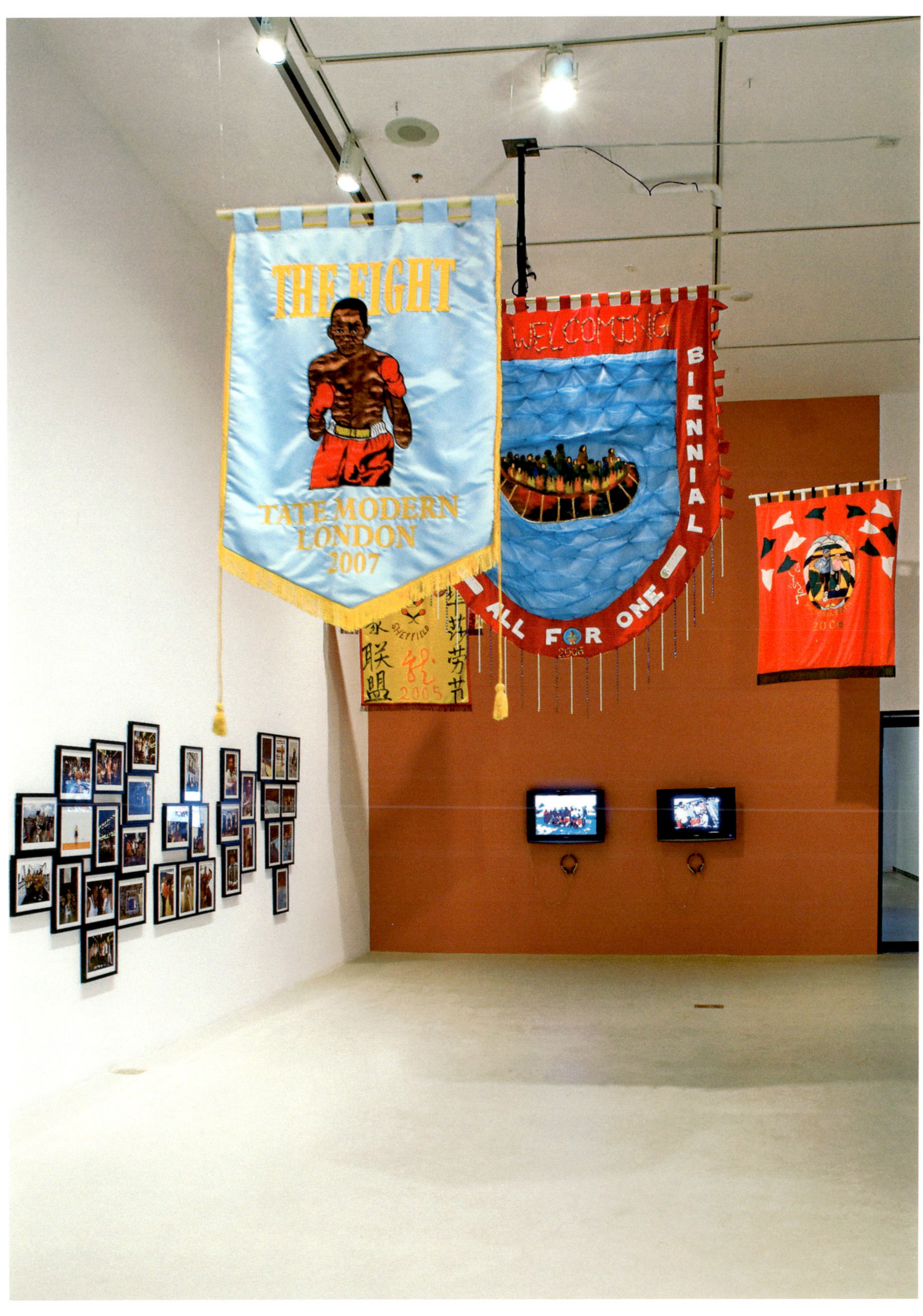

THE FIGHT
TATE MODERN
LONDON
2007
WELCOMING
BIENNIAL
ALL FOR ONE
2005

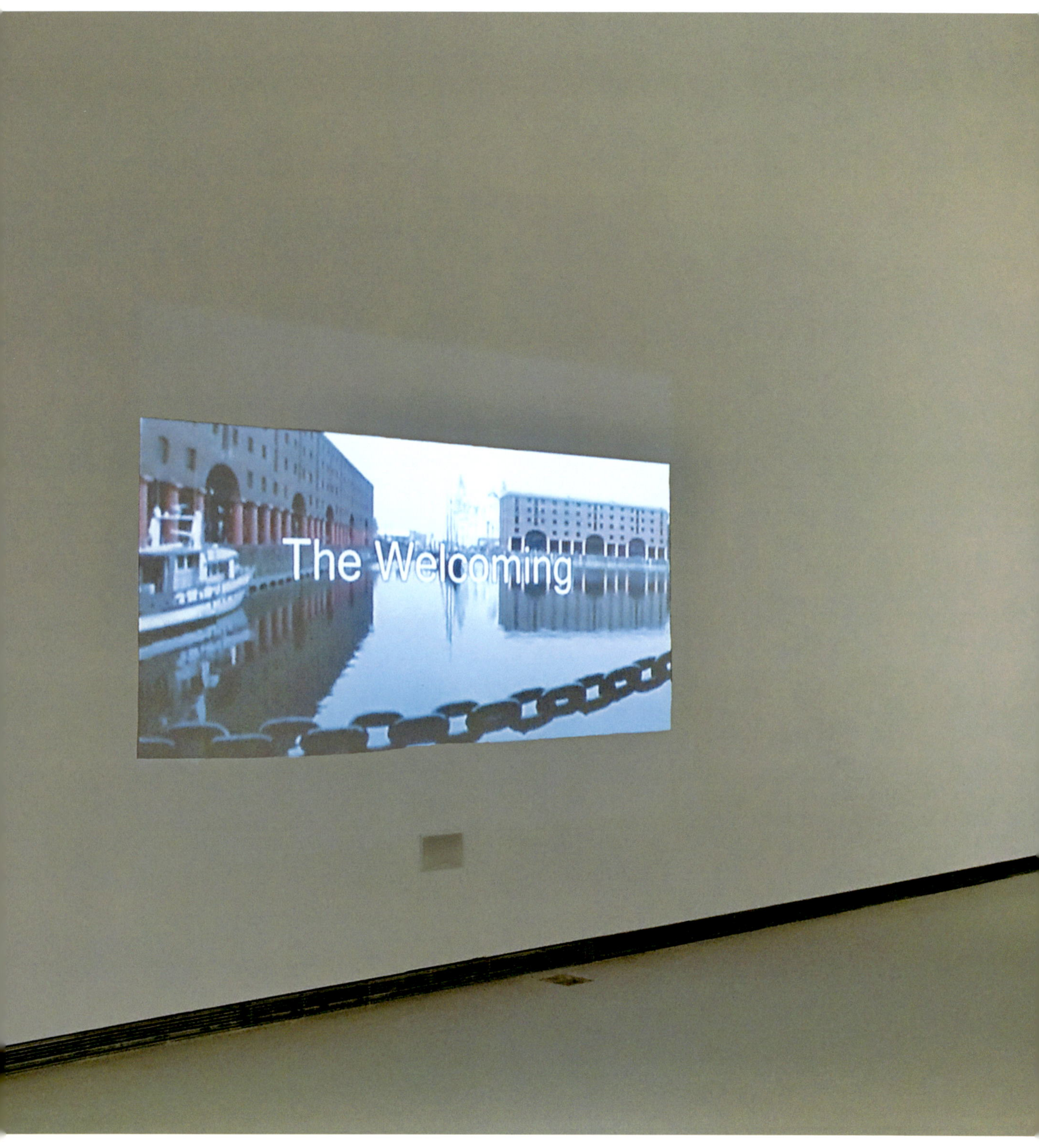
The Welcoming

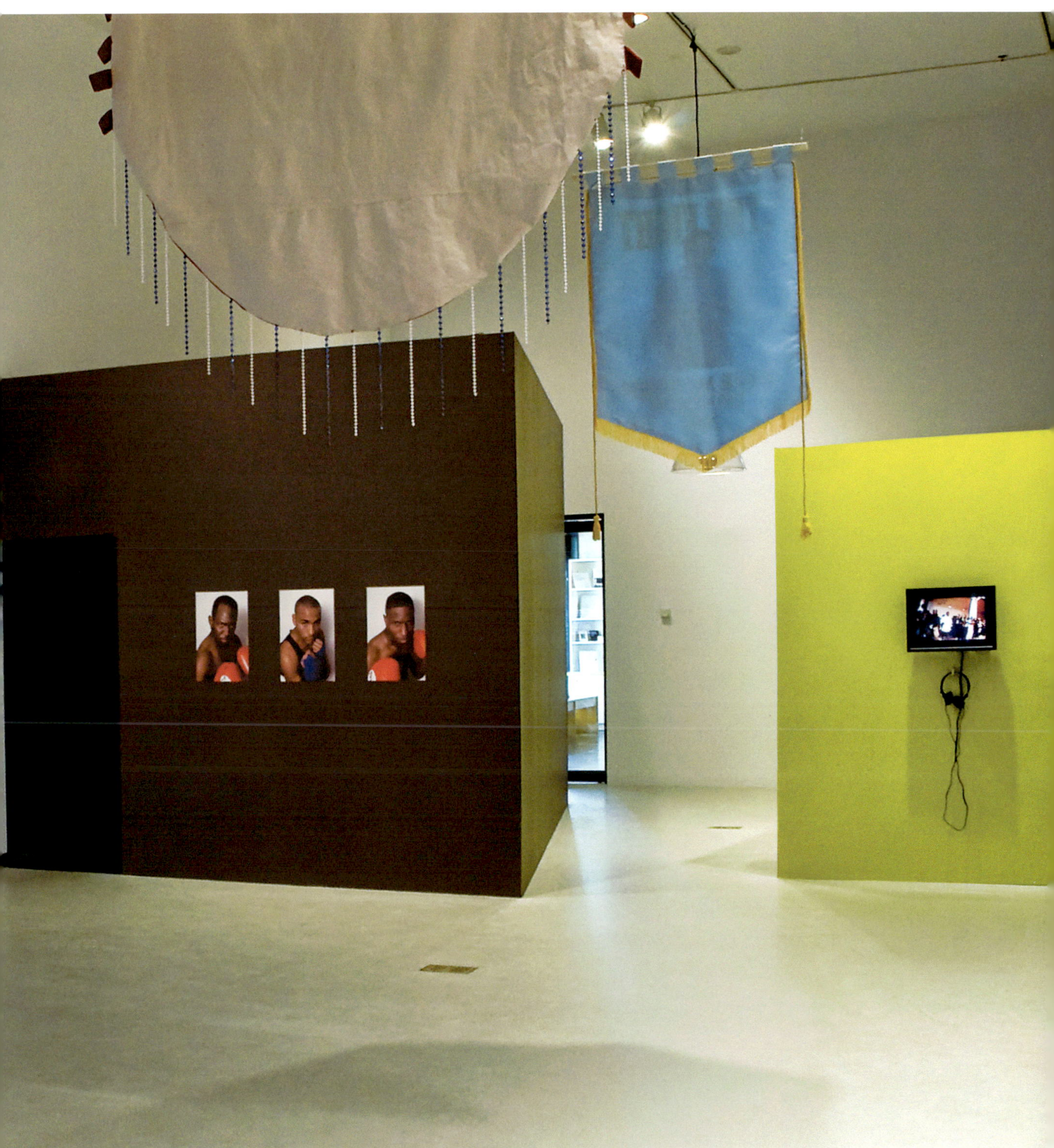

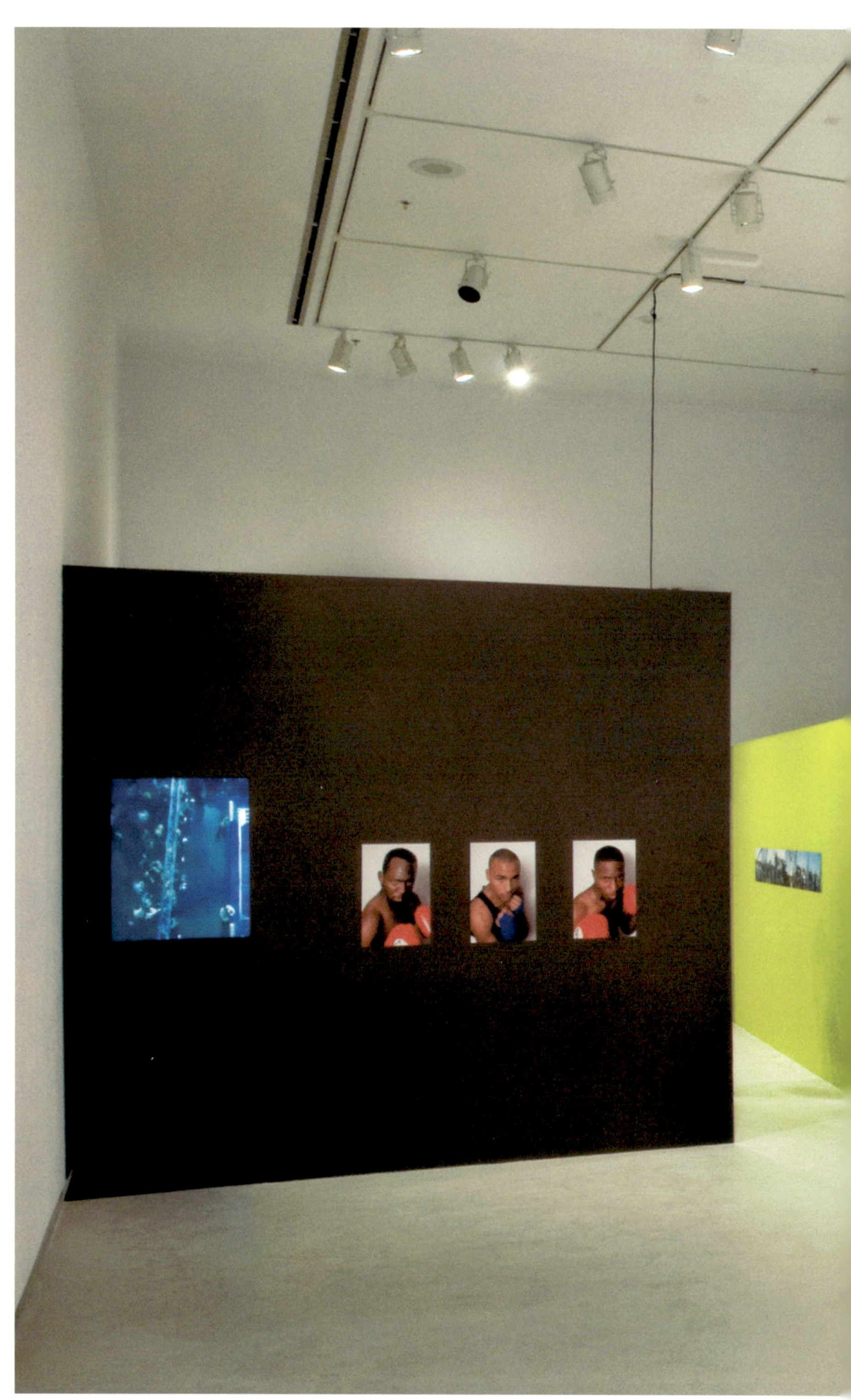

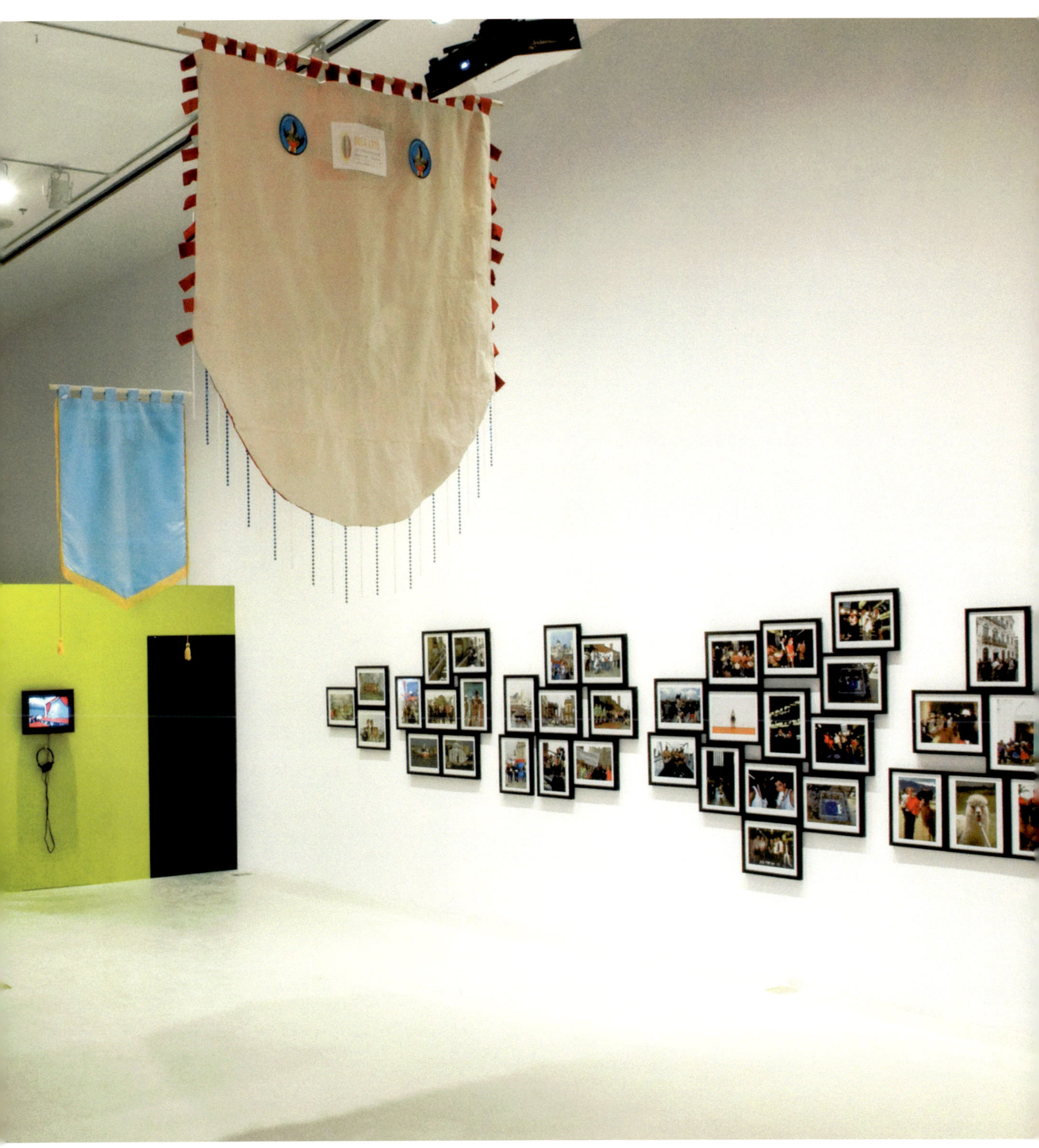

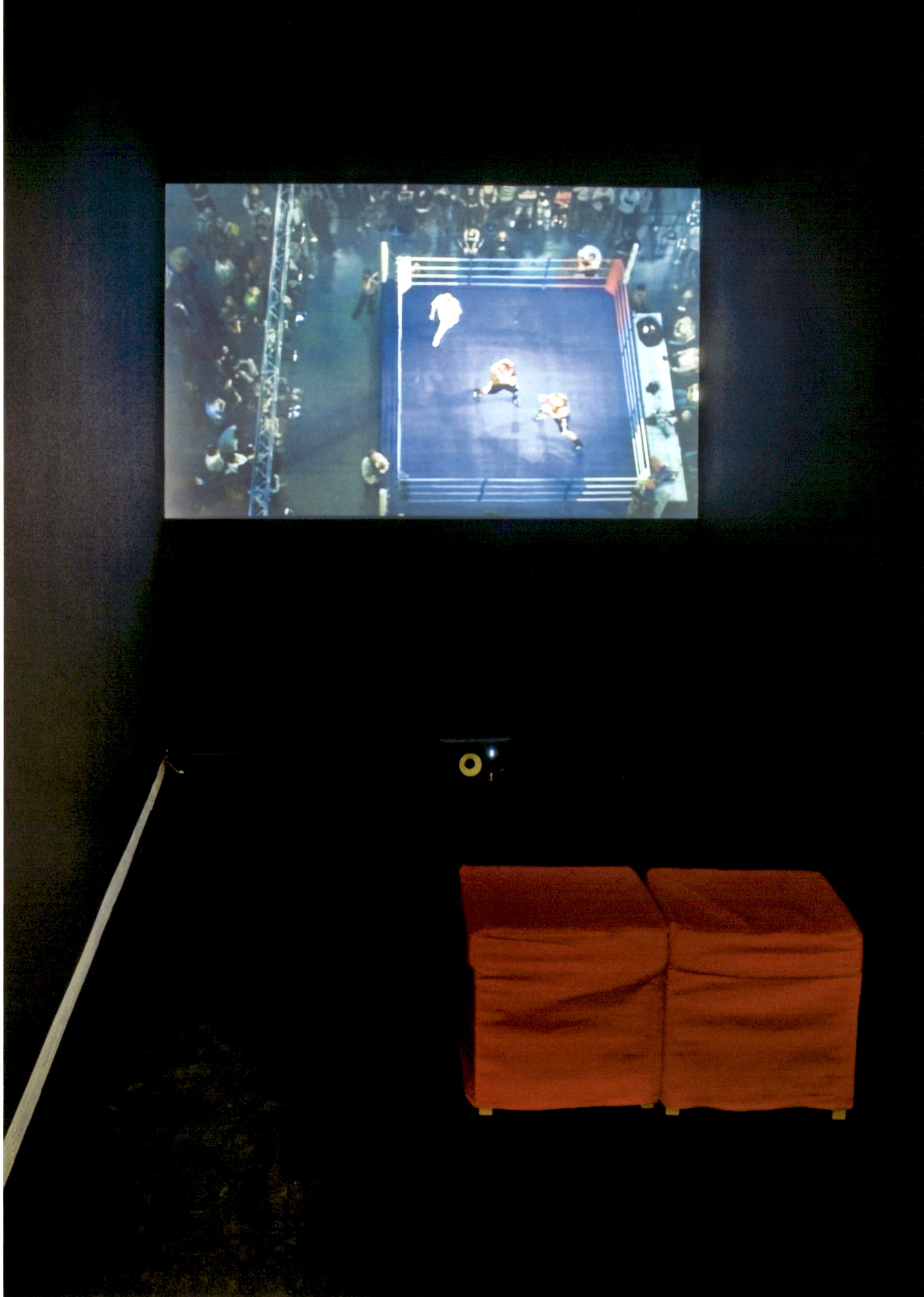

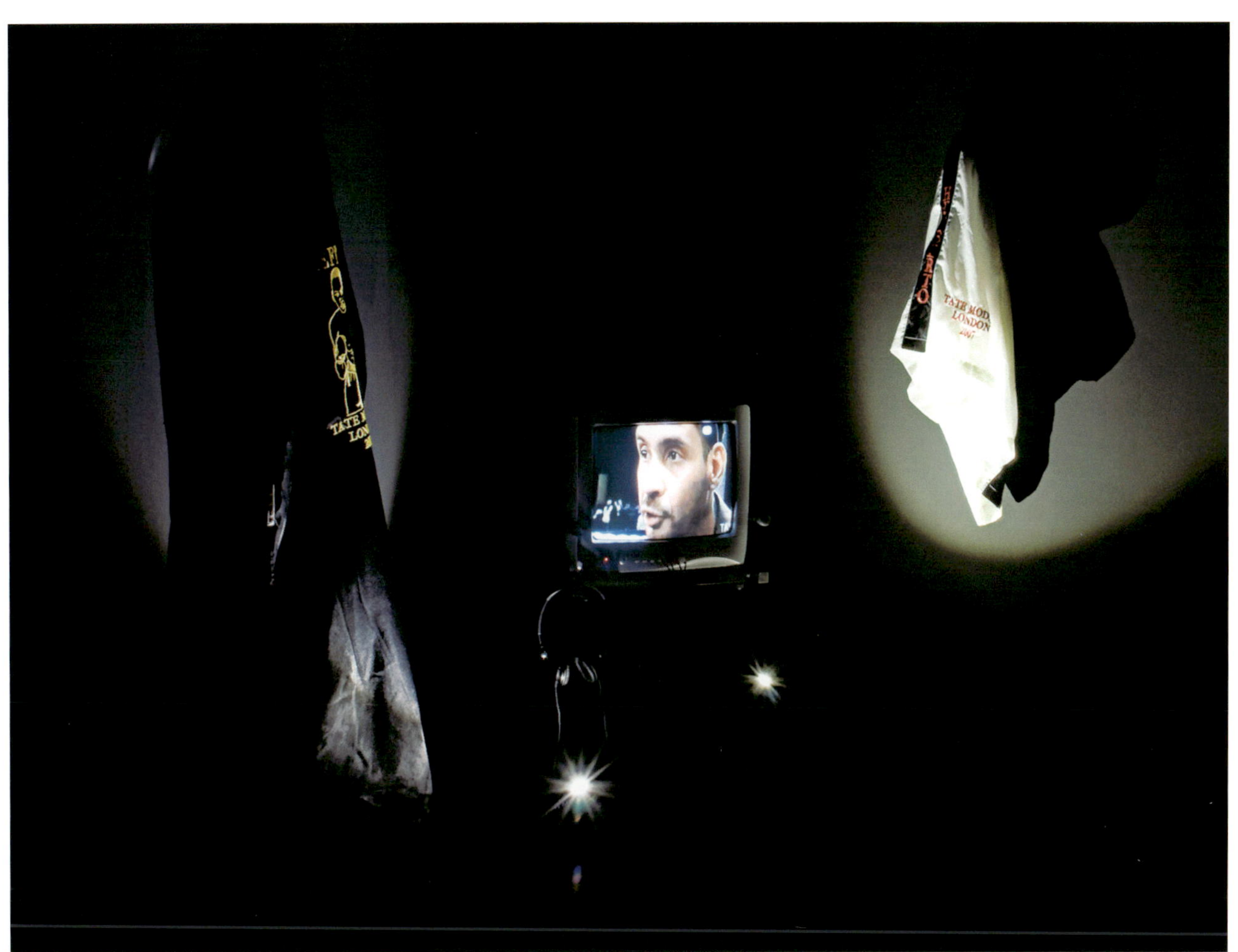
TATE MOD
LONDON

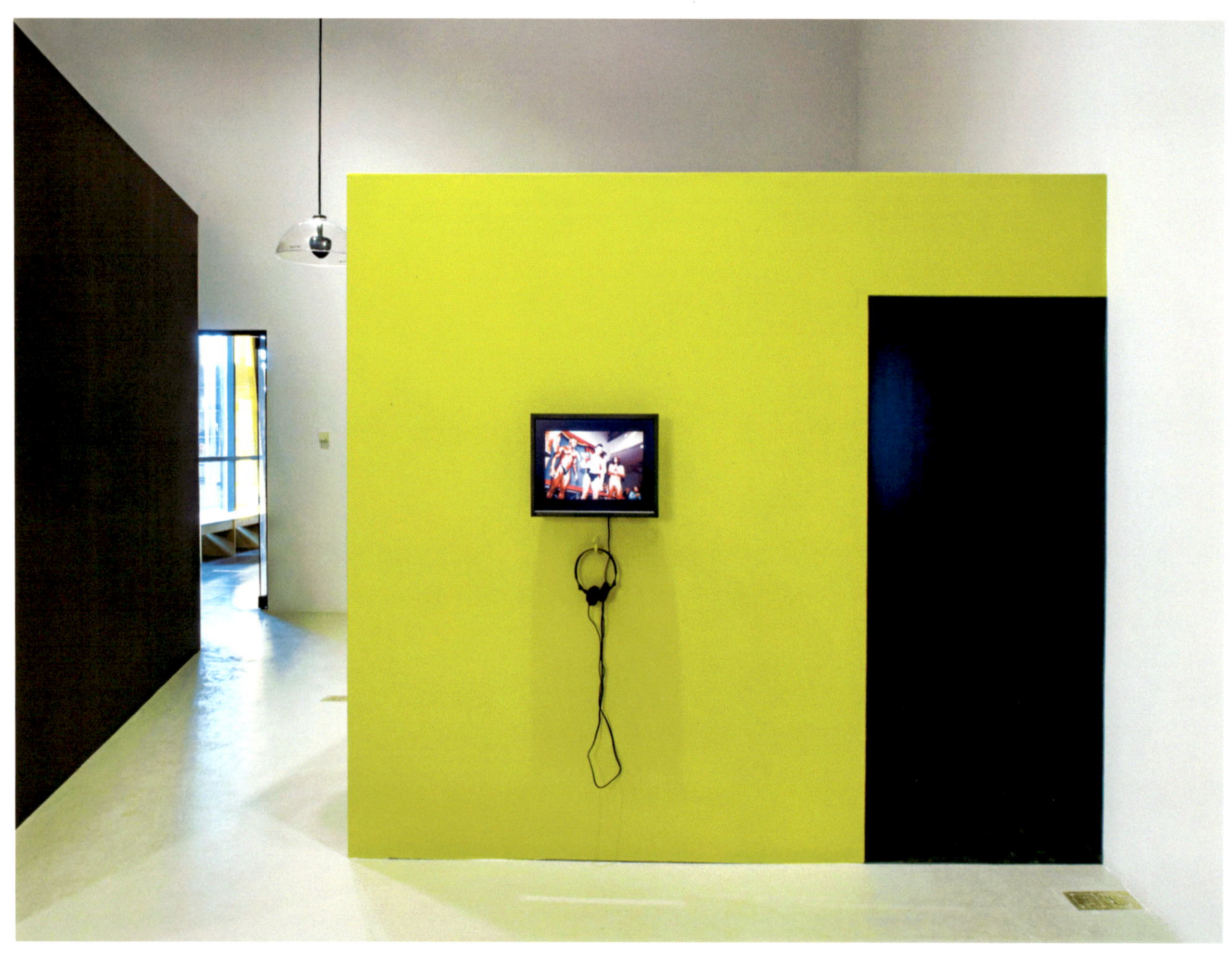

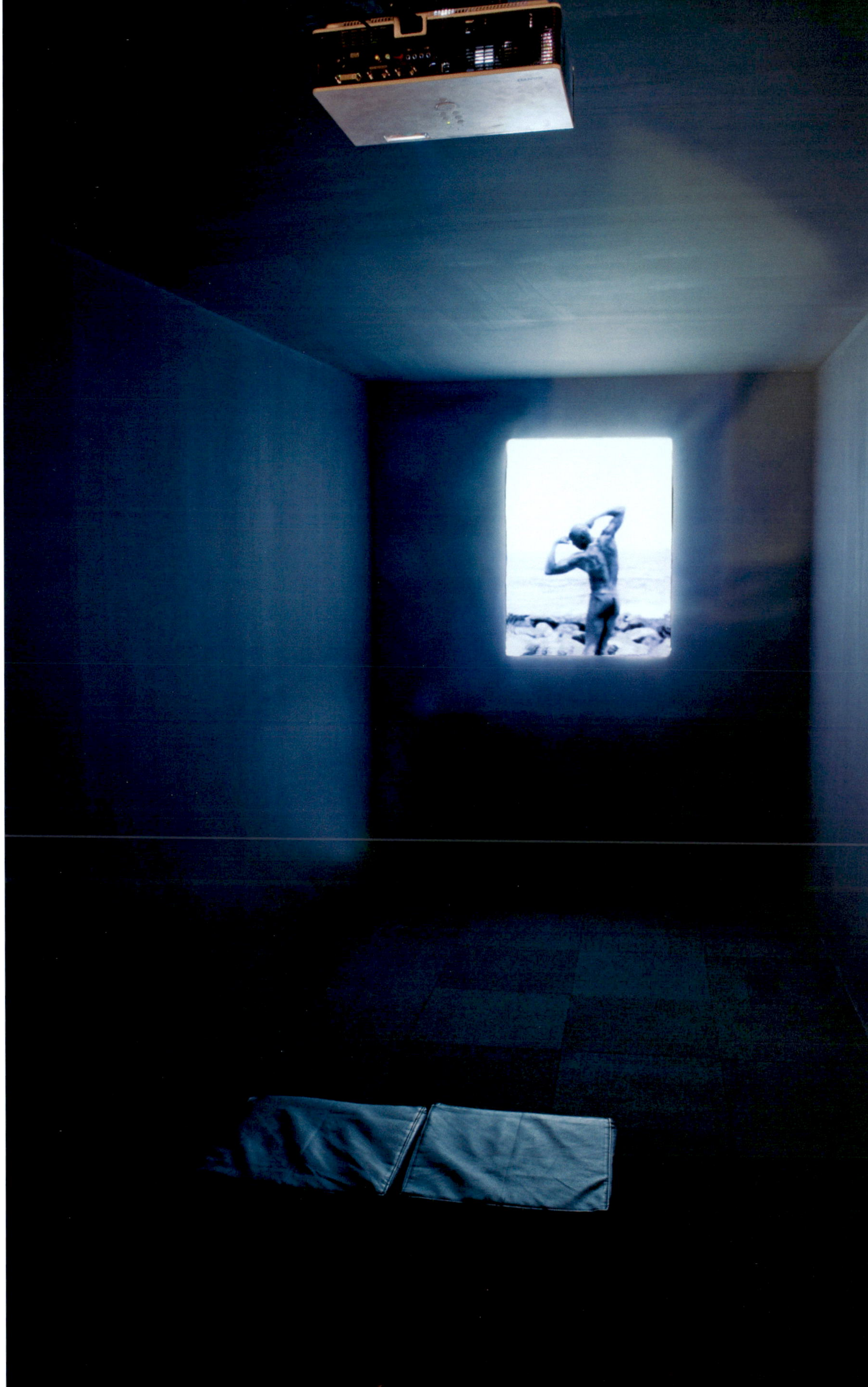

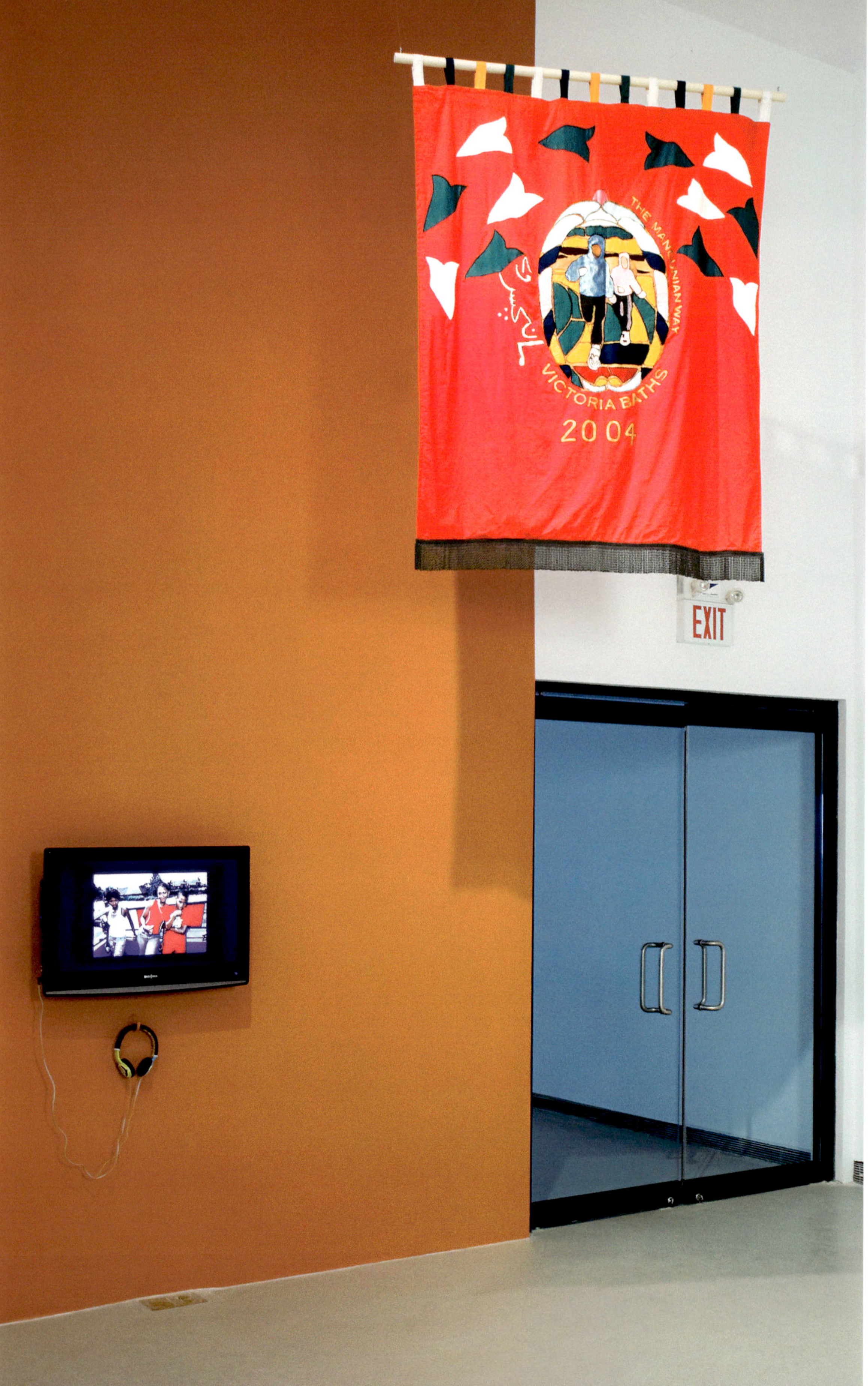
THE MANCUNIAN WAY
VICTORIA BATHS
2004
EXIT

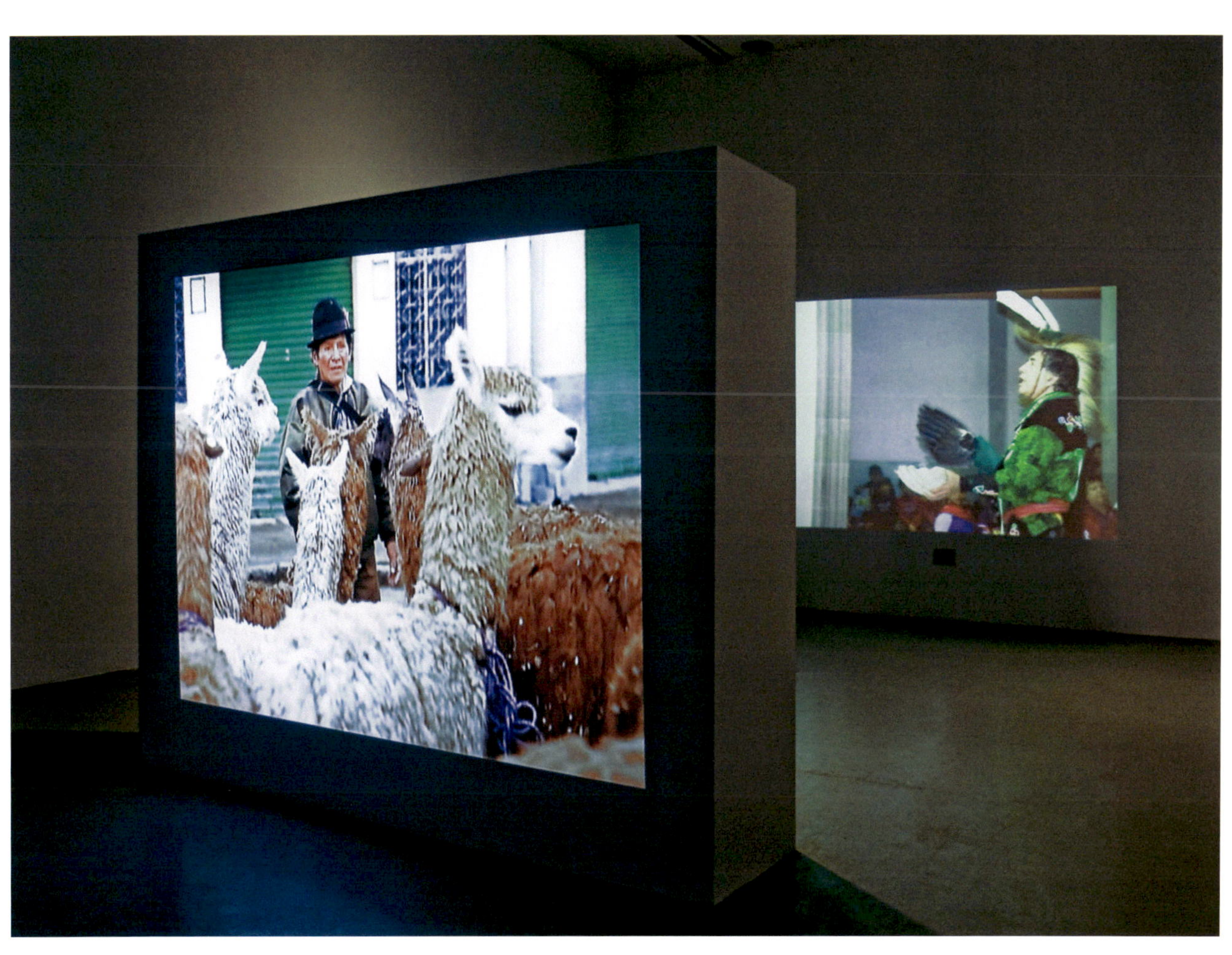

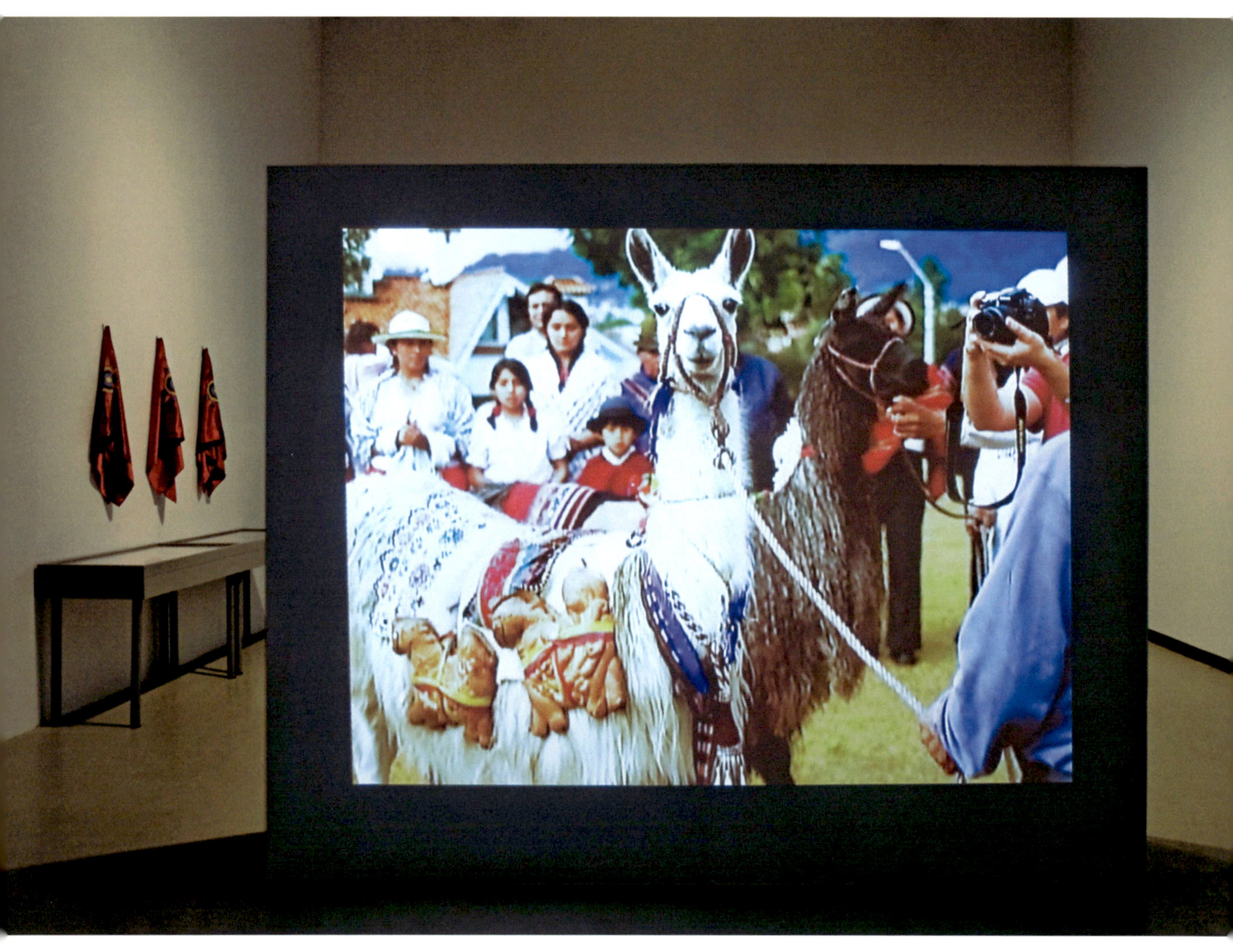

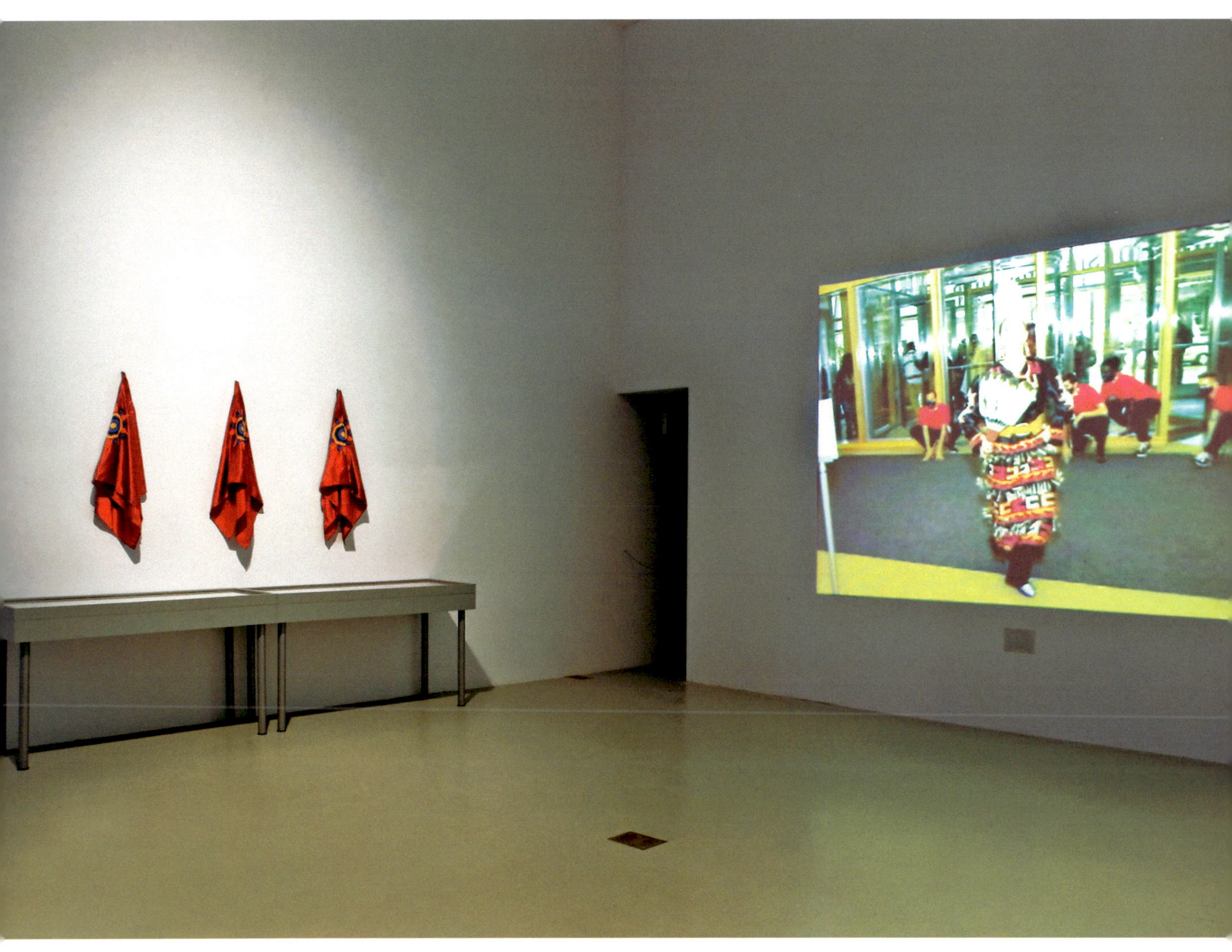

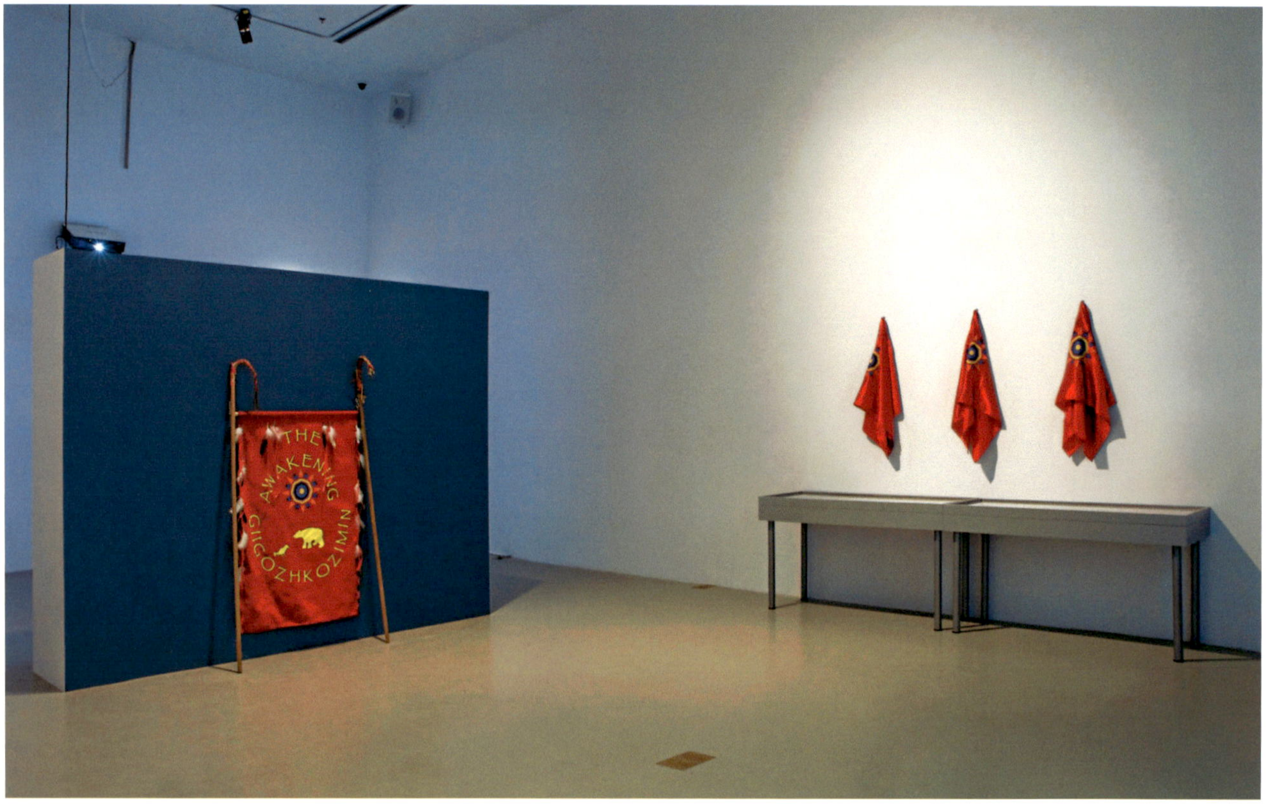

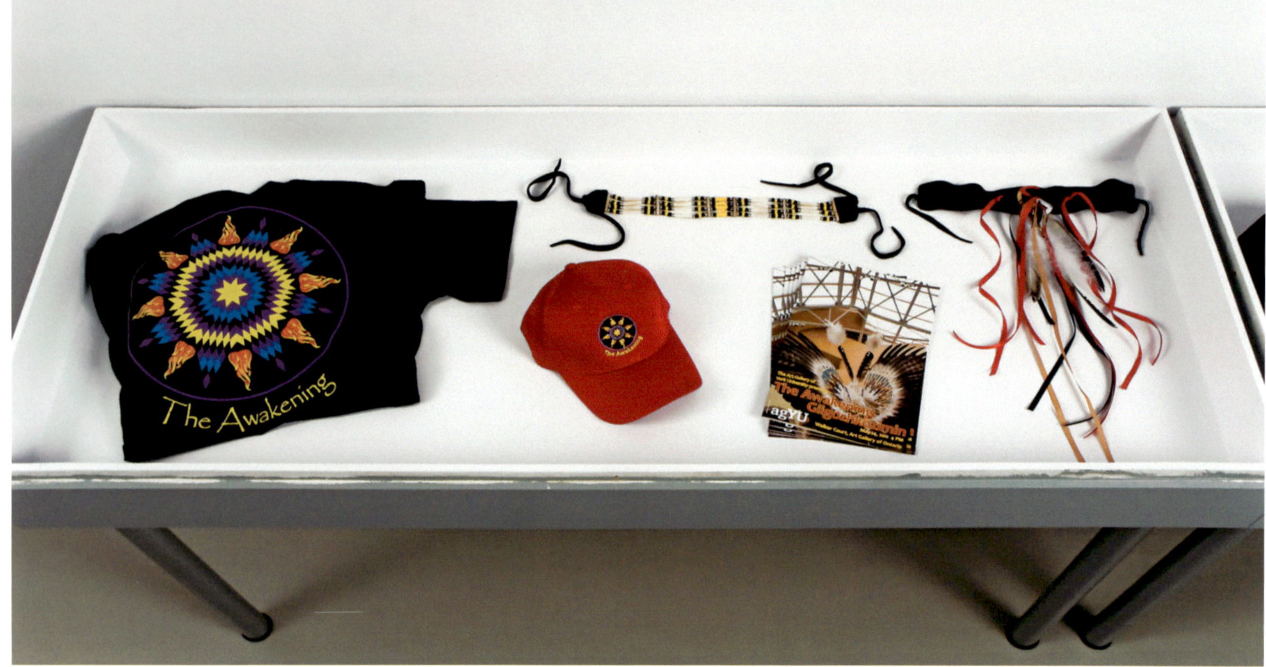

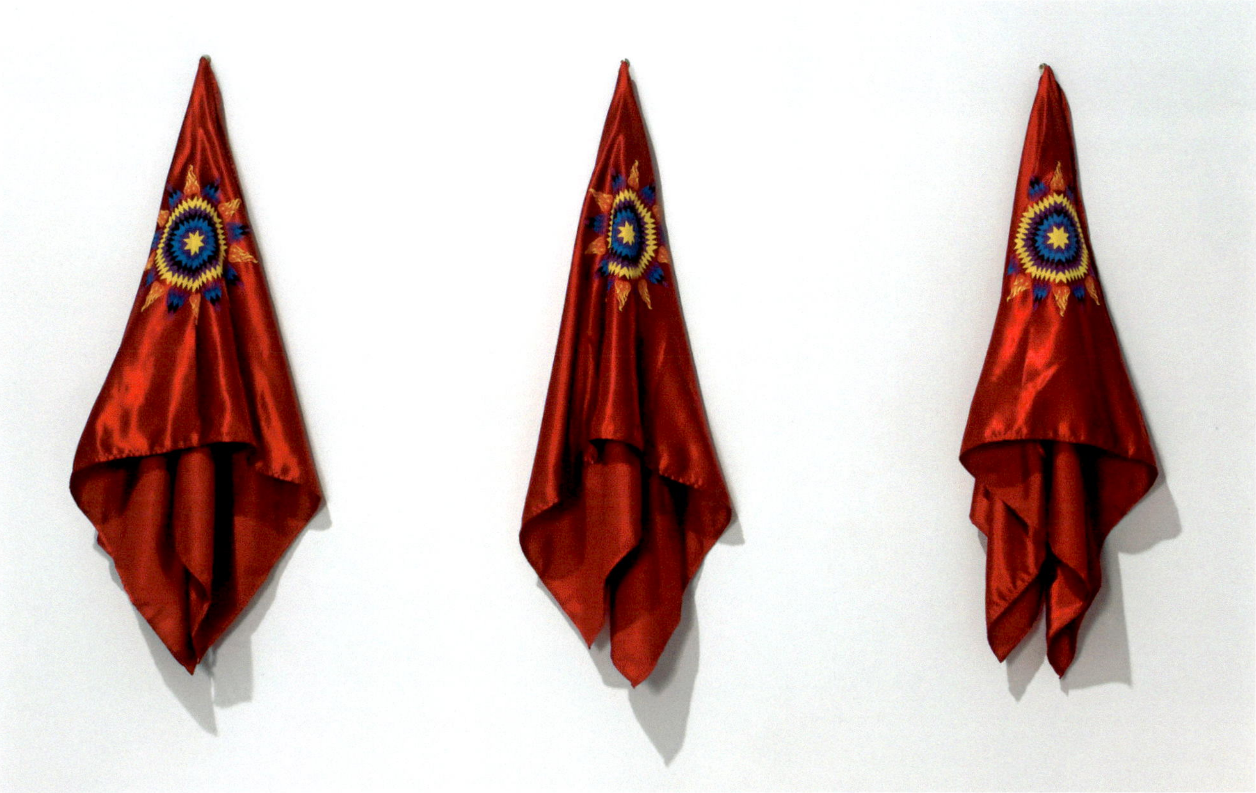

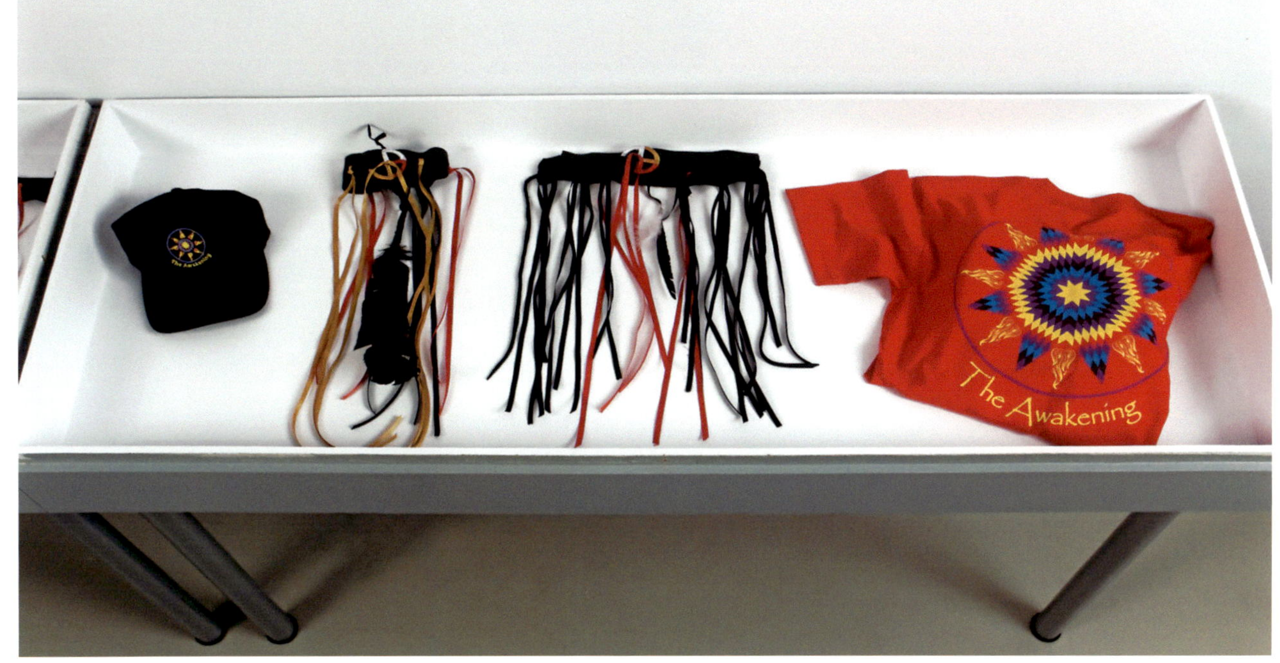
The Awakening

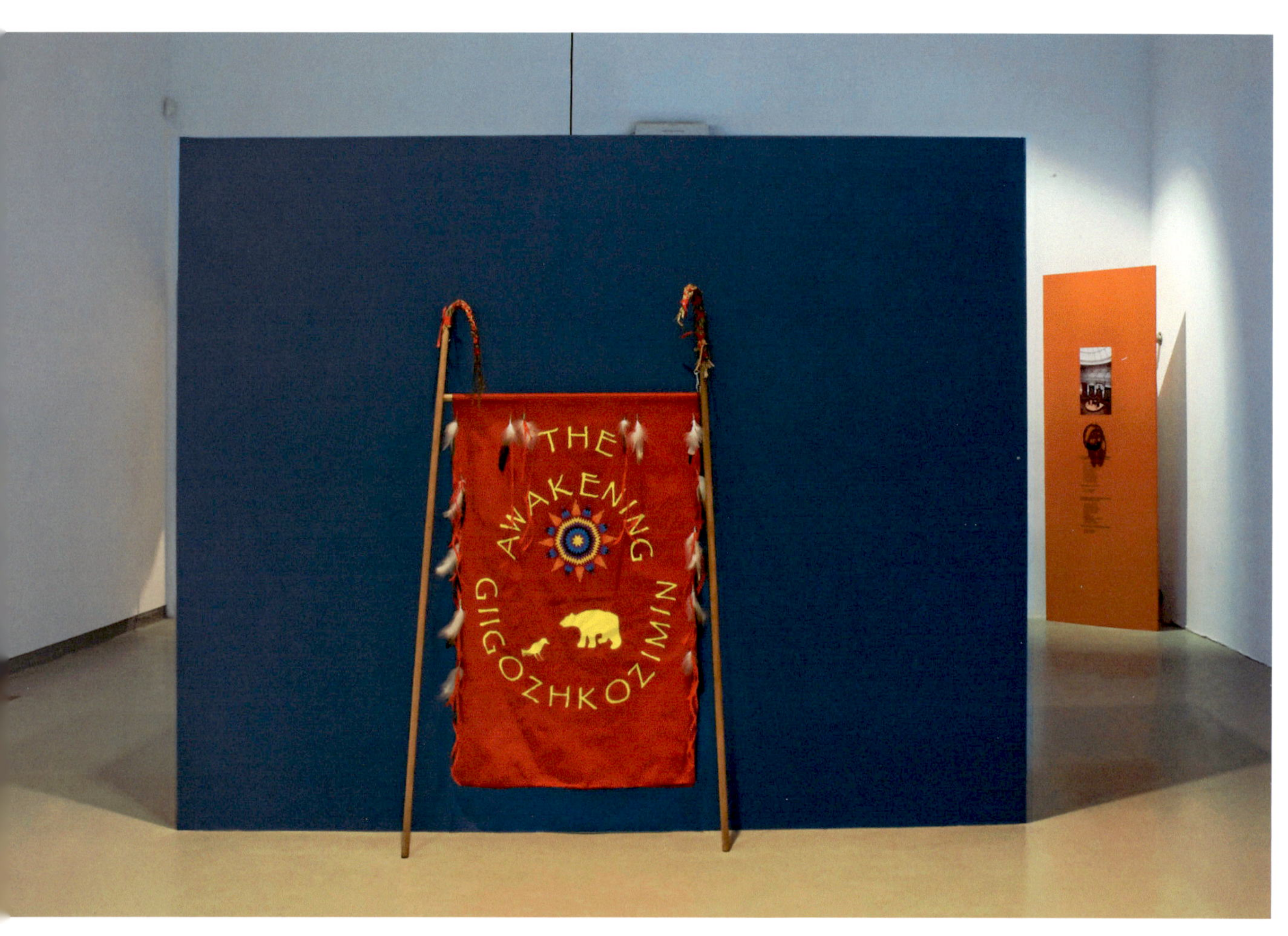
THE
AWAKENING
GIIGOZHKOZIMIN

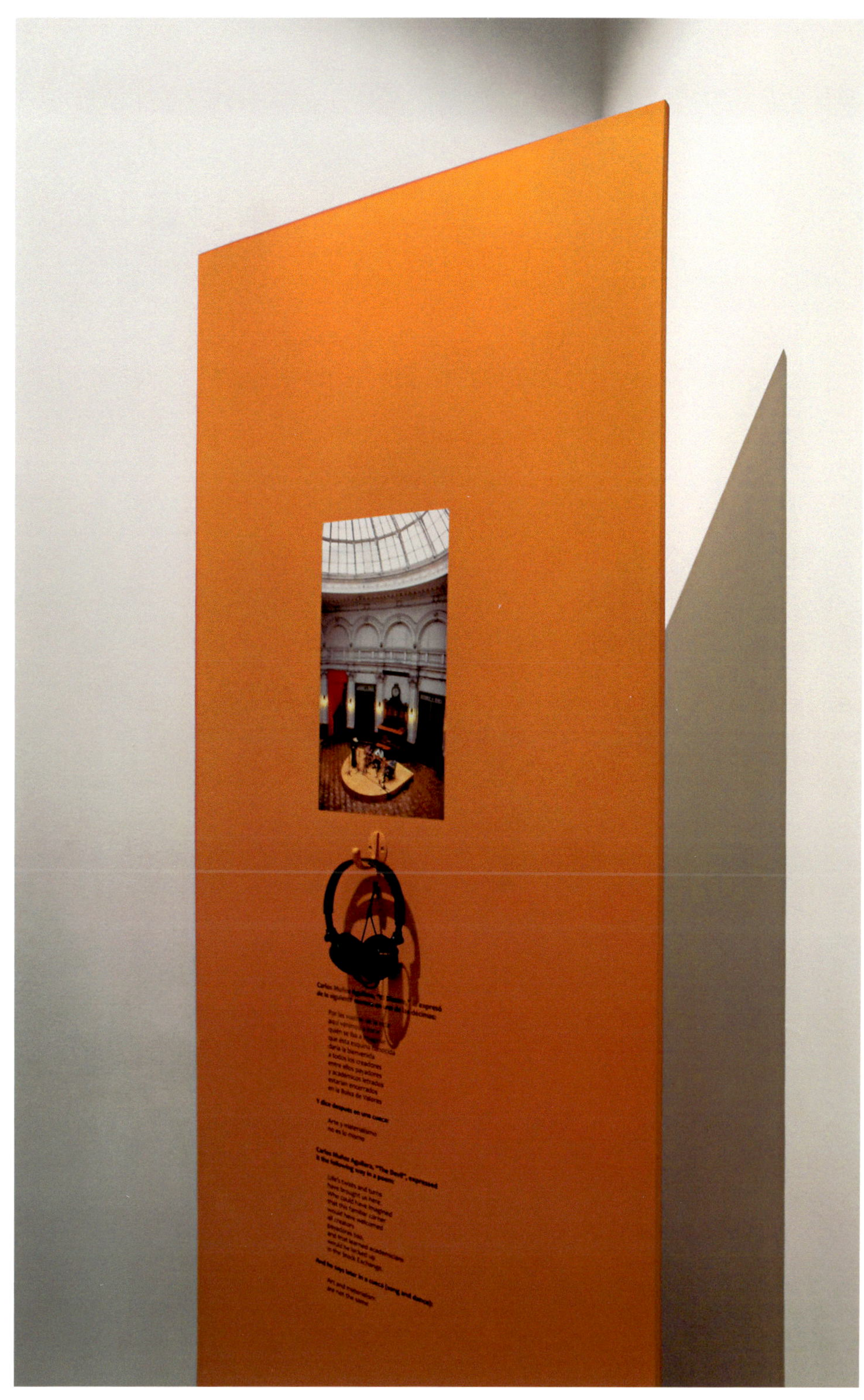

Y dice después en una canción:
Arte y matematismo
no es lo mismo
Life's twists and turns
have brought us here.
Who could have imagined
that this familiar curve
would have welcomed
all creators,
And he says later in a canción living and dancing
Art and mathematism
are not the same.

Works Exhibited

La carrera (Clásico VII Bienal de Panamá)
[The Horse Race (7th Panama Biennial
Classic)], 2005, radio performance,
Panama City, Panama
Single channel audio installation 2:13
Edition of 5 (no. 1/5)
Daros Latinamerica Collection, Zürich

Le Plongeon [The Dive], 2010, performance,
Paris, France
Video 7:14

La controversia del arte [The Controversy
of Art], 2004, radio performance,
Panama City, Panama
Audio on iPod 23:03

The Caretaker / El guachimán, 2002, video,
Manchester, England
Video 5:00

Un son para la bienal (Porque el Amor no existe)
[A Song for the Biennial (Because Love Does
Not Exist], 2003, performance, Havana, Cuba
Video 9:34

La Banda de mi Hogar [The Band of my Home],
2003, performance, Panama City, Panama
Audio 8:54, banner, photographs
Photographs: Fernando Bocanegra

Body Dream (Mr. Regenta), 2008, performance,
Las Palmas de Gran Canaria, Spain
Video slide show 3:42
Photographs: Len Grant

The Last Builder, 2008, super 8 transferred
to video, Panama City, Panama
Video projection 5:29
Soundtrack: Nikolas Wodjabasuta

The Fight, 2007, performance, London, England
Video projection 8:01, ephemera, banner
Photographs: David Williams

The Welcoming, 2006, performance,
Liverpool, England
Video projection 6:51, banner

Artists United, 2005, performance,
Sheffield, England
Video 18:30, banner

Mancunian Way, 2004, performance,
Manchester, England
Video slide show 6:09, banner
Photographs: Len Grant

Regata cantata, 2005, performance,
Venice, Italy
Photographs: Artway of Thinking

El contrapunto (del arte) [The Counterpoint
(of Art)], 2010, performance, Valparaíso, Chile
Audio installation 37:10, photograph, vinyl text
Photographs: César Pincheira

La más bella [The Most Beautiful], 2009,
performance, Cuenca, Ecuador
Video projection 5:08
Photographs: Byron Leiva

The Awakening / Giigozhkozimin, 2011,
performance, Toronto, Canada
Video slide show on projection, ephemera,
banner
Photographs: Len Grant, Michael Maranda,
Diana Morales, and Faaiza Mansoor

Obras expuestas

La carrera (Clásico VII Bienal de Panamá),
2005, performance por radio, ciudad de
Panamá, Panamá
Instalación de audio de un solo canal 2:13
Edición de 5 (no. 1/5)
Colección Daros Latinamerica, Zürich

Le plongeon [El clavado], 2010, performance,
París, Francia
Video 7:14

La controversia del arte, 2004, performance por
radio, ciudad de Panamá, Panamá
Audio en Ipod 23:03

The Caretaker / El guachimán, 2002, video,
Manchester, Inglaterra
Video 5:00

Un son para la bienal (Porque el Amor no existe),
2003, performance, La Habana, Cuba
Video 9:34

La Banda de mi Hogar, 2003, performance,
ciudad de Panamá, Panamá
Audio 8:54, estandarte, fotografías
Fotografías: Fernando Bocanegra

Body Dream (Mr. Regenta) [El cuerpo soñado
(Mister Regenta)], 2008, performance,
Las Palmas de Gran Canaria, España
Video con diapositivas 3:42
Fotografías: Len Grant

The Last Builder [El ultimo constructor], 2008,
súper 8 transferido a video, Panama City, Panama
Proyección de video 5:29
Son: Nikolas Wodjabasuta

The Fight [La pelea], 2007, performance,
Londres, Inglaterra
Proyección de video 8:01, efímera, estandarte
Fotografías: David Williams

The Welcoming [La bienvenida], 2006,
performance, Liverpool, Inglaterra
Proyección de video 6:51, estandarte

Artists United [Artistas Unidos], 2005,
performance, Sheffield, Inglaterra
Video 18:30, estandarte

Mancunian Way [A lo mancuniano], 2004,
performance, Manchester, Inglaterra
Video con diapositivas 6:09, estandarte
Fotografías: Len Grant

Regata cantata, 2005, performance,
Venecia, Italia
Fotografías: Artway of Thinking

El contrapunto (del arte), 2010, performance,
Valparaíso, Chile
Instalación de audio 37:10, fotografía,
texto en vinilo
Fotografías: César Pincheira

La más bella, 2009, performance,
Cuenca, Ecuador
Proyección de video 5:08
Fotografías: Byron Leiva

The Awakening / Giigozhkozimin [El despertar],
2011, performance, Toronto, Canadá
Proyección de video con diapositivas,
estandarte, artefactos
Fotografías: Len Grant, Michael Maranda,
Diana Morales y Faaiza Mansoor

Esta idea de un arte prefabricado
que no respeta a la gente es
lo que combato y en lo que difiero
de instituciones que ya tienen una idea
fija de lo que quieren que yo haga.
Ello va en contra del arte mismo.
Es un problema muy contemporáneo
que tenemos que enfrentar:
el vínculo entre ética y arte.

Humberto Vélez (diciembre del 2009)

This idea of prefabricated art that has no respect for people is what I'm fighting against and where I disagree with institutions that already have an idea of what they want me to make. This is against art itself. It's a very contemporary problem that we have to face: it's about ethics and art.

Humberto Vélez (December 2009)

The Really Good-Citizen Artist

Luis Camnitzer

Humberto Vélez was born in Panama in 1965, where he studied Law and Political Sciences. In a surprising shift, after he was installed in a barrister's office, he decided to study filmmaking in the prestigious *Escuela Internacional de Cine y TV de San Antonio de los Baños*, Cuba. From then on he focused on what could be called "constructed documentaries": films that pertain to the cultural expression of particular communities or, more accurately, to the cultural borderlines that separate them. Filmmaking-as-documentation remains important to his work, but what has consistently taken prominence of late are the events—the situations—he creates.

The focus of Vélez's aesthetic is the crossing of borders, the undermining of separations. Geography and nationality influence his sensibility, and show up in works such as the spectacle he orchestrated in Liverpool where a boatload of Afghan asylum seekers are welcomed at the dock by indigenous Whites and African, Caribbean, Irish, and Asian immigrants.[1]

Vélez's work, however, moves well beyond issues related to national identities. Isolations and cultural disenfranchisement based on class and race are consistently addressed. He punctures class divisions when he brings boxing clubs from Southwark in London into the atrium of the Tate Modern and then has the administrators of the institution climb through the ropes into the ring to give the awards.[2] He breaches class lines in Cuenca, Ecuador, when Indian families display their llamas in a beauty contest he organized in the Museum of Modern Art,[3] or in Las Palmas, in the Canary Islands, when he arranges a bodybuilding contest at the Centro de Arte La Regenta.[4] He crosses ethnic borderlines in the prologue to the boxing match at the Tate when he crosshatches Ghanaian drummers and Scottish bagpipers under and over the Millennium Bridge. And segregations in social memory are crossed in *The Awakening / Giigozhkozimin* at the Art Gallery of Ontario, a ceremony of music, dance, and gymnastics on the occasion of the concurrent exhibition of his work at the Art Gallery of York University (AGYU).

These unexpected and surprising mixtures of imagery and venue challenge segregation and social prejudice. They don't do so didactically, but by exuberant indirection. The process leads to carefully crafted films, but the essence of his work is neither in the content nor in the final viewable product shown in a gallery. The essence is embedded and effective in the area in-between.

Deeply conscious of political realities, Vélez uses his medium not to illustrate or denounce injustice, but rather to orchestrate the potential communities have to express themselves in the most creative and persuasive manner. He painstakingly sets up conditions that facilitate the expression of others and, save for his facilitation, allows the groups he includes to develop their own aesthetics. These events are not about Vélez-as-producer, his presence in the events are rare, and when he does appear it is as one of many participants.

Vélez reaffirms one of the primordial but neglected functions of the artist, that of mediator. An artist who shies away from the traditional branding of artworks, he ensures that the outcomes of his projects are as unpredictable as the wishes of the individuals or groups he engages. In this context one might be tempted to use the term "relational aesthetics." However, "relational aesthetics" still invokes authorship in the traditional sense, a notion that contradicts the whole intention of his work. Vélez himself carefully avoids that connection and describes his work as "collaboration aesthetics." As he states, "… I invented for myself the term 'aesthetics of collaboration' to establish a different kind and quality of relation with people in art and with artists, and new and differentiated strategies of formalization. For me the concept of ethics in relational aesthetics is easy, simplistic and accommodating. It is also one of the principal problems and dangers of so called 'engagement art'."[5]

To undertake these projects, Vélez inevitably has to learn the "language" of the groups he works with, in order to merge with them, and slowly earn their trust in his role of minimized and quasi-invisible leadership. The first person he approached with the idea for his boxing piece at the Tate was Mark, a semi-retired boxer. The first thing Mark said was: "I don't know anything about art, but I know I could be an artist. Do you know how to box?" The following week Vélez started taking classes. Similarly, he temporarily engaged in bodybuilding for his piece in Las Palmas, an exercise that had less to do with muscle building than with what really interested him: "the physical construction of a fictional image." These are the exact words he uses to describe the essence of that particular work. It is in this construction where the transition into art took place and, accordingly, the bodybuilding competition was performed not for a group of fans but in front of an art audience.

Vélez proposes a refinement of the definition of the role of the artist though the production of his work. Increasingly today, the role of the artist has been associated and confused with that of a producer who belongs to the manufacturing sector of society. The locus of art has been confined to the object and the artist has shifted from being a critical outsider—a jester in the court—to being one more worker, albeit an elite one. Interestingly enough, this absorption was not (only) the product of commercial cooption: It also addressed demands expressed by artists. Progressive ideologies asked that the artist be seen as a normal member of society, one who operates in its inside as a "cultural worker." And hopefully, this new image was not to be that of the artist working in a state of relatively benign derangement.

Neither the definition of the artist as a manufacturer nor the conception of the artist as a capricious outsider is socially constructive (or real). Both imply that the importance of a work of art is embedded in the act of creation rather than built up over time by a collective process of encounter and reception. The real "newness" of a work, the originality that ultimately will allow for the establishment in the commercial market, does not come from competitiveness. As far as that market also reflects and interacts with a cultural reality, it comes from its contribution to a body of knowledge, the way it enlivens something hitherto stultified. This doesn't happen with the pristine clarity and immediacy one would wish but over time. And even then the collective process that determines the placement of the work of art may not be definitive.

Thus, if the value of a work of art relates to its social contribution, it becomes more important and fairly clear that the artist should be a "good citizen." The "good" here implies a value judgment and is contingent upon who is applying the label. For this purpose, probably, the evaluator can only be the rigorous and self-critical artist that then measures him or herself against collective feedback. The parameters for evaluation then become personal ethics and self-criticism, a constructive critical view of society, the proper placement of the role of authorship and the application of its power, and the analysis of what the destination and function the work of art is to have in this context. The awareness of these parameters requires that the artist not be an insider in the traditional sense. The quality of outsider, a critical outsider, has to be kept. Vélez seems to have developed the perfect touch for these things and epitomizes this description of the good-citizen artist.

The exercise of outsider criticism is not an easy task. It runs the risk of deteriorating into paternalism and self-righteousness and thus achieving the opposite of what is intended. The danger is even greater when dealing with localities other than ones own. Vélez, remarkably, is a good-citizen artist wherever he goes. His work starts from a high-risk unpredictability and a nearly naïve confidence in collective dynamics. One of the rewards of his strategy, for Vélez as well as for the viewer/participant is that this confidence has never been betrayed. He merges into the project (in this case, a quasi-synonym for community) as catalyst, without leaving a personal trace beyond human relations.

Unlike many if not most artists with an ideological bent, Vélez avoids typical tourist judgments directed to cultural situations to which he is foreign. He approaches any situation equipped with a basic set of ethical concepts: opposition to xenophobia, racism, oppression, and repression on one hand and sympathy and endorsement for popular expression and culture on the other. With this very basic ethos he negotiates the terrain and seeks compromises between the parties, allowing himself the role of being merely a facilitator. His hand as author remains largely hidden, even in his tangible objects. The banners used in processions and parades are designed lightly. Vélez suggests some ideas representative and evocative of the event. Those who are directly involved in manufacturing the banners make the final formal decisions.

Most of Vélez's pieces comprise of parades as prologue to the culminating performance. One is tempted to put his pieces in a category with another worker with people: Trinidadian Mas artist Peter Minshall. Both Vélez and Minshall feed their work from the collective energy of masses of people who enthusiastically participate in their artistic "schemes," and both excel in what one might see as constructive crowd manipulation.

In normal usage, thanks to political and religious history and agendas, the concept of manipulation of crowds has acquired very negative connotations. The crowd acts like a new entity with its own dynamics, like a new individual whose aims and movements are at odds with the decisions of the individual units that comprise it. In a society where individualist competitiveness is seen as a primordial value, the awareness of this collective persona doesn't sit well, even if the experience of the crowd continues to be pervasive in quotidian life.

Minshall uses crowd dynamics by carefully designing grand spectacles for Carnival. The crowd is his material and as a whole his productions become totally interdisciplinary and comprehensive *Gesamtkunstwerk*. They affirm and continue the Carnival tradition but, instead of the older and expected Las Vegas aesthetics, function within a contemporary artistic formal language. Minshall makes a point to conserve the critical and subversive aspects that, since its origins, defined Carnival in Trinidad. In that sense he plays within the margins that define a collective culture, but he also aims for the "perfect work of art" in terms of what constitutes traditional authorship.

Vélez, on the other hand, uses a very different kind of manipulation, which this comparison with Minshall makes very clear. He moves back one step in order to avoid control, or at least the appearance of control. His manipulation is that of a dramaturge in an open play. The goals are still clear, but the formal result is relatively unpredictable because, unlike the traditional artist, Vélez yields obvious control into the hands of the participating crowds. In fact that is precisely one of the aims, and one of the difficulties, in most of his pieces. Relinquishing control is risky and can lead to a dead end with the emergence of a single individual who wants to take over. Vélez therefore must also break down the boundaries of egos. Unlike Minshall, the crowd is not his malleable material but a repository of potential expressions.

In creating situations with collaboration acting as the glue that makes his work possible, Vélez forces the examination and questioning of divisions and conflict. Participants that in daily life operate at odds and in tension are brought together to create what can be termed "new rituals." The "new ritual" is inclusionary and allows both museum-alienated performers and audiences to enter the space while keeping their own independent dignity. In an act of restitution, they come as the unjustly excluded—not as specimens for observation.

Confronting the success of these situations, institutional reaction shifts from initial fear and skepticism to "why didn't we think of this." While education and outreach departments often are the initiators of the organization of Vélez's pieces, as was the case in his Tate and Pompidou performances, the curatorial areas claim credit after the fact.

What the works by Vélez represent and how they place him as an artist may be considered a call to awakening on many levels, including his own. It is therefore not surprising that Louis Riel's 1885 statement caught Vélez's attention: "My people will sleep for one hundred years, but when they awake, it will be the artists who give them their spirit back." Fittingly, the piece designed in conjunction with his exhibition at the AGYU became *The Awakening*. A leader of the Métis (the Canadian *mestizos*), Riel was executed the same year of the quote for treason against the Canadian Government yet he carried (and seems to continue carrying) the voice of a marginalized segment of the population. Riel tried to break down the racist and political barriers that prevented this voice of resistance and the wish to maintain a distinct unity and language rights from being heard. *Mestizaje* is a huge component of Latin American tradition and culture, and therefore an issue very close to Vélez. In the broadest metaphorical sense of the word, this is the unification aim that probably best describes his mission as artist. He tries to achieve more than just a meeting and integration of the minds; his goal is the awakening to an understanding of commonality.

The Awakening took three years of preparations. Over the course of several residencies, Vélez identified the groups he wanted to involve in the project: the Mississaugas of the New Credit First Nation, the original inhabitants of the Toronto area, and the Monkey Vault Parkour Artists, a group of youth interested in street gymnastics. He persuaded them to work together to develop a new ritual for this occasion. The challenge was to not remain in the past but instead and without breaking with tradition, to "update" a ritual to encompass a new situation. It included a new and open interest, and a new group that to some extent could be seen as a contemporary form of tribe. Both groups were hitherto considered as lacking mutual interest and incompatible for cultural and ethnic reasons. Given the format, the piece could also have been called *The Welcome*, but as that the very important reference to Riel would have been lost.

Three years of work resolved into a one-hour event. If one were to consider the work in traditional terms, as an object or as spectacle-oriented art, one would be puzzled by this disproportion. No matter how well documented—and photographers and cameramen seemed seamlessly integrated in the ritual—there is no way to have the document substitute for the experience. But Vélez's work—no matter how moving and engaging—is not really about what one sees; it is about what remains in the imagination of the participants (which includes the observing public) and the paths of understanding it opens. Everybody here became Métis.

Riel's vision of the artists as those best equipped to return the spirit to his people—rather than, as one might presume, soldiers or enlightened politicians—was prescient. Prophetically, his quote seems to describe Vélez as one of these artists in terms of his mission. But it also seems to announce and proclaim his work in terms of its effect. Vélez addressed his concerns in a statement of 2009: "This idea of prefabricated art that has no respect for people is what I'm fighting against and where I disagree with institutions that already have an idea of what they want me to make. This is against art itself. It's a very contemporary problem that we have to face: it's about ethics and art." [6]

NOTES

1. *The Welcoming*, 2006, Liverpool Biennial, Liverpool
2. *The Fight*, 2007, Tate Modern, London
3. *La más bella* [The Most Beautiful], Municipal Museum of Modern Art in Cuenca, Ecuador
4. *Body Dream (Mr. Regenta)*, 2008, Centro de Arte La Regenta, Las Palmas de Gran Canaria
5. Communication with the author, 19 June 2011.
6. *Out There*, newsletter of the AGYU with announcement of Vélez's exhibition.

El artista ciudadano

Luis Camnitzer

Hace muchos años Humberto Vélez solía ser abogado. Sin embargo, poco después de abrir su oficina decidió convertirse en cineasta y fue a estudiar a la Escuela Internacional de Cine y TV de San Antonio de los Baños, en Cuba. Desde entonces ha organizado eventos en lugares diseminados por todo el mundo, entre ellos la Tate Modern en Londres y el Centro Pompidou en París. En la actualidad, la *Art Gallery of York University* (AGYU) en Toronto exhibe una muestra retrospectiva de su obra.[1] Normalmente, haber empezado su carrera profesional como abogado no tendría relevancia dentro de la biografía de un artista. Pero en el caso de Vélez resulta ser un dato de importancia. Su arte refiere íntegramente a los problemas de las relaciones humanas y de la justicia, para lo cual los estudios legales y de ciencias políticas proveen un contexto mucho más útil de lo que pueden dar las especulaciones formalistas que resultan del estudio más tradicional del arte.

Nacido y educado en Panamá, Vélez hoy vive en Inglaterra, aunque sus obras abarcan el mundo y exploran la discriminación y las relaciones entre diversos grupos étnicos y clases sociales de cualquier nacionalidad. Esta retrospectiva en Toronto presenta una colección de filmes documentales, fotografías y accesorios icónicos. Como "arte relacional" ¿una clasificación frecuentemente aplicada a su obra?, esta retrospectiva puede considerarse un ejemplo insigne del género. Pero esta clasificación apenas rinde justicia a la complejidad y sofisticación de su obra. De hecho, la consideración de su trabajo bajo esta etiqueta conduce a malentendidos. El propio Vélez evita las asociaciones con la estética relacional y denomina sus actividades como una "estética de la colaboración". El arte relacional, según él, incluye la noción de autoría individual, algo que contradice los planteos centrales de su propia obra.[2]

La obra de Vélez, por lo tanto, no se concentra en las películas documentales que produce. A pesar de su alta calidad cinematográfica, estos filmes no pueden aspirar a ser más que souvenirs de eventos que son mucho más complejos de lo que puede captarse en una película. Los eventos mismos, que normalmente transcurren en una o dos horas, en realidad son sólo eflorescencias de un proceso abierto que se desarrolla a través de varias etapas de colaboración y que puede llevar varios meses, incluso años. El trabajo de Vélez no es del tipo que cabe en el formato de una galería o que pueda reconstruirse desde una documentación.

Uno de los motivos para ello, y también uno de sus aspectos fuertes en la obra de Vélez, es su propio papel de facilitador, por encima del de autor. Profundamente consciente de la realidad política, Vélez no utiliza el medio para ilustrar o denunciar la injusticia. En su lugar, orquesta el potencial que tienen las comunidades para expresarse con respecto a estos temas, de la forma más creativa y convincente. Vélez no encara los problemas para expresar sus opiniones o para afirmarse como artista. De hecho, si acaso aparece en sus propios eventos, se limita a una labor funcional. En cambio, organiza cuidadosamente las condiciones que promueven la expresión de los demás y, excepto por la edición del documental, permite que los grupos elaboren su propia estética. Ello hace que su obra empiece desde un nivel impredecible de alto riesgo, con una confianza casi ingenua en las dinámicas colectivas. Una de las recompensas del proceso, tanto para él como para el espectador, es que esta confianza nunca ha sido traicionada.

Consciente de la naturaleza del trabajo de Vélez, la AGYU lo invitó a armar un proyecto durante una residencia que duró tres años. El resultado fue *The Awakening / Giigozhkozimin* [El despertar], mezcla de ceremonia y espectáculo comunal que tuvo lugar en la *Art Gallery of Ontario,* un espacio más céntrico que la AGYU. La ceremonia fungió como la pieza central de su presencia en Toronto y como un ancla para su muestra retrospectiva paralela.

Durante varias visitas, Vélez terminó identificando los grupos que más le interesaron: los *Mississaugas of the New Credit First Nation* (habitantes originales de la zona en donde luego se formó la ciudad de Toronto) y los *Monkey Vault Parkour Artists,* un grupo de jóvenes avezados en actividades gimnásticas y danzas callejeras. Una "tribu original" y un grupo contemporáneo que antropológicamente se podrían identificar como poseedores de una especie de estructura tribal. Pero en esencia son dos grupos que normalmente no considerarían la existencia de intereses en común o la necesidad de interacciones mutuas. Vélez los convenció de que trabajaran juntos y desarrollaran un nuevo ritual compartido para esta ocasión. El desafío consistió en no permanecer dentro de un pasado nostálgico y pintoresco, sino de "poner al día" un rito que no rompiera con la tradición. El nuevo grupo, encarando una nueva situación, necesitaba un rito nuevo e híbrido que lo representara.

La inspiración de Vélez vino de una cita de Louis Riel, dirigente militante de los métis, los canadienses que descienden del mestizaje de los amerindios nativos y los blancos. En 1885 Riel declaró: "Mi pueblo dormirá durante cien años, pero cuando despierte serán los artistas quienes les devolverán su espíritu."

Riel fue ejecutado ese mismo año por traición al Gobierno de Canadá. Sin embargo, parece seguir llevando la voz de un segmento marginado de la población para tratar de romper las barreras racistas y políticas que impedían, e impiden, que esa voz se escuche. Considerando que Riel era un líder político, resulta asombroso que, con tanta claridad, designara a los artistas como los guardianes del espíritu de su movimiento. Lo que no sorprende es que Vélez se sintiera atraído por la cita de Riel. Y en cierto modo pareciera como si la atracción fuese mutua. Si hiciéramos una proyección antropomórfica sobre la cita de Riel, podríamos imaginar que ese párrafo elegiría a Vélez como el albacea de su testamento.

En este cruce entre política y arte se podría afirmar que Vélez usa la manipulación para poner sus obras en escena. Pero lo hace de una manera muy particular. Contrario al artista o al director autoritario, Vélez da un paso atrás para evitar controlar, o por lo menos dar la apariencia de control. Su manipulación es la misma que se utiliza en el servicio social. Las metas están claramente establecidas, pero el resultado formal queda fuera de sus manos porque, a diferencia del artista tradicional, Vélez deja esas decisiones en manos de las masas de gentes que participan en el proyecto. Ésta es una de las metas y también una de las dificultades de su obra. Renunciar al control es peligroso y puede llevar a un callejón sin salida o al vacío. En ese momento cabe la posibilidad de que surja otro individuo que tome las riendas, y el proyecto puede descarrilarse. Vélez, por lo tanto, no solamente rompe las fronteras entre los grupos con los que trabaja sino que también apunta a la desaparición de los egos.

Al crear situaciones en las cuales la colaboración actúa como el pegamento que hace posible su obra, Vélez obliga al examen y al cuestionamiento de divisiones y conflictos. Participantes que normalmente operan en desacuerdo, y con tensiones, terminan aunados en lo que podemos llamar "nuevos ritos". El "nuevo rito" es incluyente y permite que tanto actores como públicos ajenos al museo accedan a sus espacios, manteniendo su dignidad. En un acto de restitución, llegan al museo como víctimas de una exclusión injusta, y no como especímenes listos para ser observados. La reacción institucional pasa de un miedo y escepticismo inicial a un "¿por qué no se nos ocurrió a nosotros?". Luego, cuando se considera que la operación tuvo éxito, los departamentos curatoriales se adjudican el mérito.

La noción de "nuevo rito" es particularmente apropiada para *The Awakening*, pero también se aplica a la mayoría de los eventos que Vélez diseña. En *The Fight* [La pelea], varias escuelas de boxeo de Southwark (un barrio obrero londinense en la vecindad de la Tate Modern) fueron invitadas al atrio de la Tate para un campeonato público. Los grupos llegaron en barcas siguiendo el río Támesis para luego comenzar una procesión hacia el espacio de la galería. Iban acompañados de gaiteros escoceses y tamborileros de Ghana.[3] En *La más bella*, un conjunto de llamas fue llevado al Museo Municipal de Arte Moderno de Cuenca, Ecuador, para participar en un concurso de belleza. En el Centro de Arte La Regenta, en Las Palmas, de las Islas Canarias, Vélez organizó una competencia de culturistas. Con ello, simultáneamente, cambió significado, contexto y público, logrando un espectáculo completamente nuevo.[4]

En forma atípica para artistas interesados en problemas ideológicos, Vélez evita los juicios turísticos superficiales dirigidos a situaciones culturales a las que es ajeno. Más bien, se acerca a cualquier situación equipado con una serie básica de posiciones éticas: por un lado, opuesto a la xenofobia, al racismo, a la opresión y a la represión; y por otro, con simpatía y apoyo a la expresión y cultura del "otro". Con esa plataforma muy simple negocia el terreno y busca los acuerdos entre las partes. Eso le permite ubicarse como facilitador. Incluso en el caso de los elementos tangibles y exhibibles, como las pancartas utilizadas en desfiles y procesiones, su influencia en el diseño es mínima. Vélez sugiere algunas ideas representativas y evocadoras para el evento. Quienes luego fabrican los objetos toman las decisiones formales finales y se quedan con los resultados. De hecho, esto dificulta las exposiciones posteriores, ya que nunca se sabe bien en qué manos terminan las cosas.

Vélez describe en un escrito lo que probablemente sea el obstáculo mayor para sus obras. Mientras trabajaba para un proyecto de la Bienal de Liverpool, le tocó hablar de su proyecto a un exiliado político congolés. La conversación, no amigable, terminó con algo así como: "Gracias por las buenas intenciones. Avíseme cuando tenga algo real para ayudarme". Vélez luego explica: "Siempre aclaro que el proyecto no paga dinero a los participantes; sólo a los artistas profesionales que ayudan. Los grupos sociales que colaboran lo hacen porque reconocen que hay una conexión genuina entre ellos y yo: una posición o un interés emocional o social que tenemos en común. Su deseo de expresarse es igual o mayor que el mío. Yo lo identifico, me relaciono con él y lo proyecto con su ayuda, como un grupo."[5]

De cierto modo, la muestra en la AGYU es heterodoxa. Un espacio de la galería quedará vacío hasta cuando la documentación de *The Awakening* esté completa. Entretanto, el público puede ver otros trabajos y entender cómo se mueven más allá de los temas de identidades nacionales, aislamientos y privación de derechos basados en clases sociales y razas, para buscar los elementos comunes y las comprensiones mutuas. Al cruzar fronteras étnicas en el prólogo al torneo de boxeo en la Tate Modern y desmontar divisiones culturales cuando los administradores de la institución se treparon a través de las sogas al cuadrilátero ubicado en el atrio para dar los premios; o al desafiar las verdaderas líneas clasistas, cuando familias aborígenes mostraron con orgullo sus llamas en el museo de Cuenca; o al entrecruzar a los tamborileros de Ghana con los gaiteros escoceses debajo y por encima del Millenium Bridge… todos los proyectos de Vélez reconocen las divisiones para luego tratar de borrar la idea de que hay fronteras que las separan.

Para *The Awakening*, la estratificación social fue rota una vez más. La escalera escultural de Frank Gehry, una especie de megamueble que por lo general compite agresivamente con las exposiciones en la *Art Gallery of Ontario*, esta vez fue utilizada con acierto para las acrobacias de los artistas del *Monkey Vault Parkour*. La danza ritual de los Mississaugas integró, sin quiebre alguno, a los camarógrafos y a la burocracia del museo. La tradicional rigidez de las exposiciones fue transmutada en una fiesta de celebración en donde todo el mundo tuvo conciencia de que la experiencia tenía que interiorizarse, ya que nada tangible de la verdadera realidad del momento permanecería para aquellos que no la vieron y sintieron.

La exposición en la AGYU también incluyó dos obras que corresponden a una visión más conocida en las artes contemporáneas.

Una es *La carrera* (2005), pieza sonora en la que se escucha a un locutor deportivo profesional que describe una carrera de caballos. Todo suena muy bien, salvo que los nombres de los caballos no son totalmente creíbles: *Miss Panamá, Negro de Mierda, Visa Americana, Sida, Papá Rico, Extranjera, One Dollar, Oligarca* y *I Have a Dream* (que cita el famoso discurso antirracista de Martin Luther King). *La carrera* se convierte en una de sueños locales y valores en toda la gama colonialista. Creada para la Bienal de Panamá, Vélez tuvo que dictar y dirigir la obra por teléfono, ya que no se le concedió la visa para cambiar de avión en Estados Unidos en su viaje de Inglaterra a Panamá.

La otra pieza, *The Last Builder* [El último constructor], muestra a un culturista envejecido que solitariamente hace sus gimnasias en la playa. Filmada en blanco y negro, en súper 8 y con una asombrosa banda de sonido compuesta por Nikola Kodjabashia, la pieza sumerge al espectador en cinco minutos de intensa melancolía. El cuerpo asume el rol de una mente que nostálgicamente recuerda su pasado físico con todas sus connotaciones.

A fin de cuentas, los temas que la obra de Vélez plantea apuntan a la ética y a la forma artística. Su preocupación fue formulada en un texto de 2009: "Esta idea de un arte prefabricado que no respeta a la gente es lo que combato y en lo que difiero de instituciones que ya tienen una idea fija de lo que quieren que yo haga. Ello va en contra del arte mismo. Es un problema muy contemporáneo que tenemos que enfrentar: el vínculo entre ética y arte".[6]

¿Es posible darle una forma artística a la ética sin recurrir a simples declaraciones narrativas? La obra de Vélez propone que sí. Nos lleva a imaginar un tiempo en el que ya no se necesitará la "y" en la frase "ética y arte".

NOTAS

1. 13 de abril a 26 de junio de 2011.
2. "Me inventé el término de 'estética de la colaboración' para establecer una clase y calidad distinta de relación con la gente en el arte y con los artistas, y estrategias nuevas y de formalización diferentes. Para mí el concepto de ética en las estéticas relacionales es fácil, simplista y acomodaticio. Es también uno de los problemas y peligros principales del llamado 'arte comprometido'." (Vélez, en conversación con el autor, el 19 de junio de 2011).
3. *The Fight*, 2007, Tate Modern, Londres.
4. *Body Dream (Mr. Regenta)* [El cuerpo soñado (Mister Regenta)], 2008, Centro de Arte La Regenta, Las Palmas de Gran Canaria.
5. Mencionado en Humberto Vélez, "La educación emocional," ponencia presentada en el Encuentro Internacional de Educación, Arte y Analfabetismo, Casa Daros, Río de Janeiro, Brasil, 2008.
6. *Out There*, boletín de la AGYU con el aviso de la exposición de Vélez.

El arte empodera. En algunas ocasiones sirve
para algo. Tiene el poder de hacernos sentir
mejor con nosotros mismos—¿acaso no es este
su significado? A veces olvidamos que significa,
no su significado académico, sino lo que significa
para la gente. El arte nos hace sentir mejor,
quizás más inteligentes, tal vez nos ayuda a
entender algo, o nos brinda la posibilidad de tomar
una posición frente a la vida. Mi trabajo es
una manera de comunicar estas cosas,
es conectar el arte con lo real, y hacer que
el arte signifique algo para la gente;
no sólo dentro de las artes, sino también
para las personas ajenas al mundo del arte.

Humberto Vélez (diciembre del 2009)

Art empowers. Sometimes it has a real use.
It can make you feel better about yourself—
and isn't that the meaning of art, really?
Sometimes we forget what the meaning of art is.
It's not the academic meaning, it's what it
means to people, no? It's to make you
feel better, or more intelligent, or understand
things, or give you a position in life, all that.
My work is a way for me to communicate this,
to connect art to the real, that is, having
it mean something to other people,
not only to the arts but to the people
outside the art world.

Humberto Vélez (December 2009)

The Caretaker / El guachimán

Manchester, England / Manchester, Inglaterra 2002 Video

Harkening back to his film and television training at the famous *Escuela Internacional de Cine y TV de San Antonio de los Baños* in Cuba, *The Caretaker / El guachimán* precedes the collaborative performance work for which Vélez is primarily known today.

The Caretaker / El guachimán utilizes a mirrored or split screen as a metaphor for the identities of migrant and immigrant members of society, especially as the artist personally observed and experienced it in Manchester. Set in the once decadent Victoria Baths, an immigrant caretaker plays out his role minding this now empty, once public, space. Living in Manchester, Vélez was struck by the psychological and physical presence of these immigrants, mainly from South Asia (though Humberto has chosen an actor who is mixed race, like himself), who now watch over and care for these historic buildings with their lingering, haunting histories of the imperial glory of the British Empire.

The video was first presented at the 6th Panama Biennial in 2002 and later that year won an honourable mention at the *Bienal de Artes Visuales del Istmo Centroamericano*. In 2003, it was a finalist for best experimental film in the *Festival Ícaro de Cine Centroaméricano*.

En el corto *The Caretaker / El guachimán*, Vélez muestra sus habilidades como cineasta graduado en la famosa Escuela Internacional de Cine y TV de San Antonio de los Baños, Cuba, y anunciado con los temas y personajes que presentará en sus futuras obras participativas por las cuales es conocido hoy en día.

En este corto utiliza el recurso técnico y expresivo de dividir la pantalla en dos, como un reflejo en el espejo, en este caso una metáfora de las múltiples identidades de los inmigrantes en Manchester, donde el artista se afincó en la segunda mitad de la década de los noventa. La obra se filmó en los *Victoria Baths*, un complejo público de piscinas y baños turcos de estilo eduardiano, que en ese momento estaba clausurado, y que antaño fuese el más lujoso del norte de Inglaterra.

El personaje del film es un joven conserje, un hijo de inmigrantes que cumple con el rol de cuidar permanentemente este abandonado y majestuoso edificio histórico, símbolo del *glorioso* pasado imperial Británico. Los conserjes del *Victoria Baths* que Humberto conoció cuando escribía el guión eran de origen paquistaní aunque para el film eligió un actor de herencia caribeña como él.

El corto fue presentado por primera vez en la Sexta Bienal de Arte de Panamá de 2002 y posteriormente obtuvo una mención de honor en la Bienal de Artes Visuales del Istmo Centroamericano en Managua en ese mismo año. También fue finalista en la sección experimental del Festival Ícaro de Cine Centroaméricano en 2003.

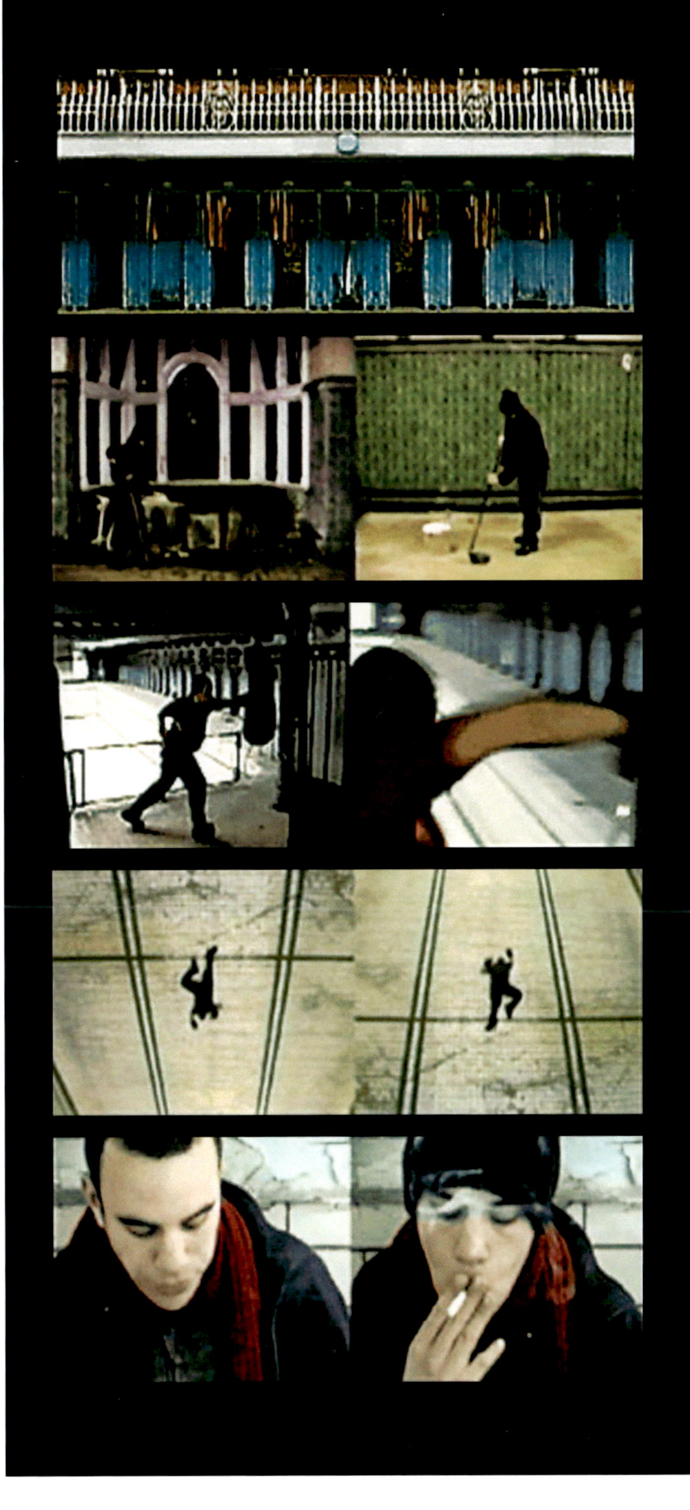

Un son para la bienal (Porque el Amor no existe)
A Song for the Biennial (Because Love does not Exist)

Havana, Cuba / La Habana, Cuba 2003 Performance

Collaborating with the Havana-based all-female music group, Krystal, *Un son para la bienal (Porque el Amor no existe)* was performed as a concert at the Wifredo Lam Centre in 2003, opening the 8th Havana Biennial. The performance was repeated as an unofficial event at the Fortaleza de San Carlos de la Cabaña. The song, combining elements of Cuban music and Panamanian reggaeton, is based on a poem found in an old diary from the Panama Canal Zone by archeologist Carlos Fitzgerald (a friend of Vélez's).

The song details the story of a Latin American student in Havana who is abandoned by his Cuban girlfriend for a more mature, and wealthy, American tourist. The performance was curated by José Manuel Noceda and realized with the support of *Escuela Internacional de Cine y TV de San Antonio de los Baños* and the British Council.

Un son para la bienal (Porque el Amor no existe) fue una performance en forma de concierto en colaboración con el grupo musical femenino Krystal que se presentó durante la ceremonia de apertura de VIII Bienal de La Habana del año 2003 en el Centro Wilfredo Lam. La obra se repitió pocos días después, a petición de la organización de la Bienal, en la apertura de la exhibición de la Fortaleza de San Carlos de la Cabaña.

Para la performance, Vélez creó una canción (un *son* cubano) que combinaba elementos de la música cubana y el reggaetón panameño, con letra inspirada en un poema de un diario perdido que encontró un arqueólogo amigo, Carlos Fitzgerald, en el edificio de la antigua sede del canal francés (posteriormente también sería la del estadounidense) en el casco viejo de Panamá.

En el *son* se canta la historia de un estudiante de La Habana a quien su novia abandona por un acomodado turista estadounidense, y comenta sobre el cambio de valores en aquella sociedad socialista en medio de una grave crisis económica. La performance tuvo como curador a José Manuel Noceda y el apoyo de la Escuela Internacional de Cine y TV de San Antonio de los Baños y del British Council.

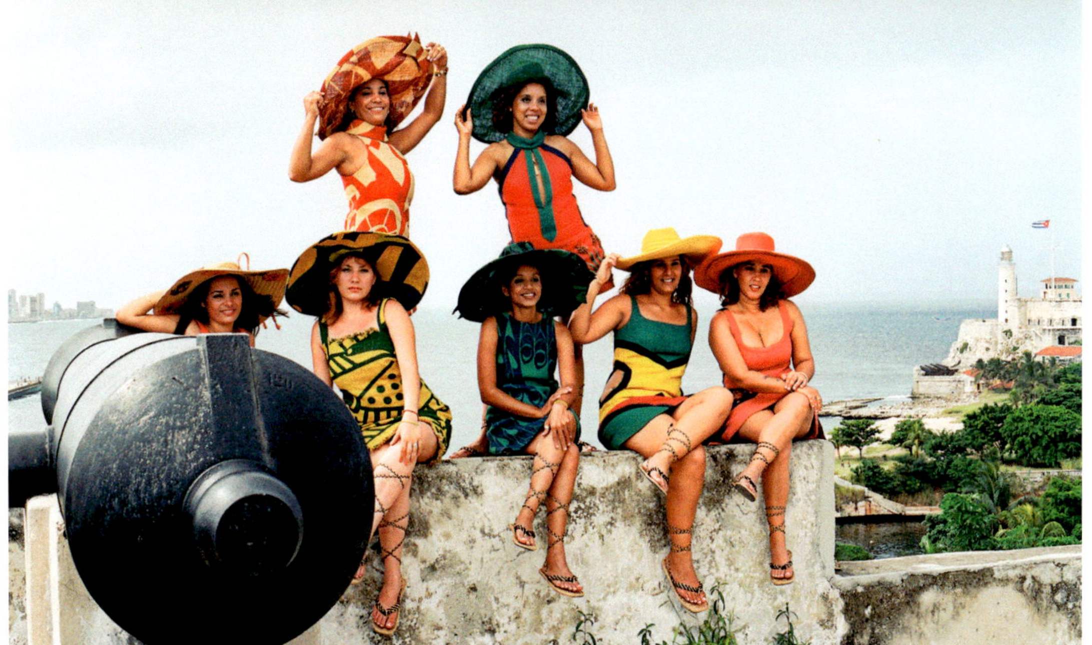

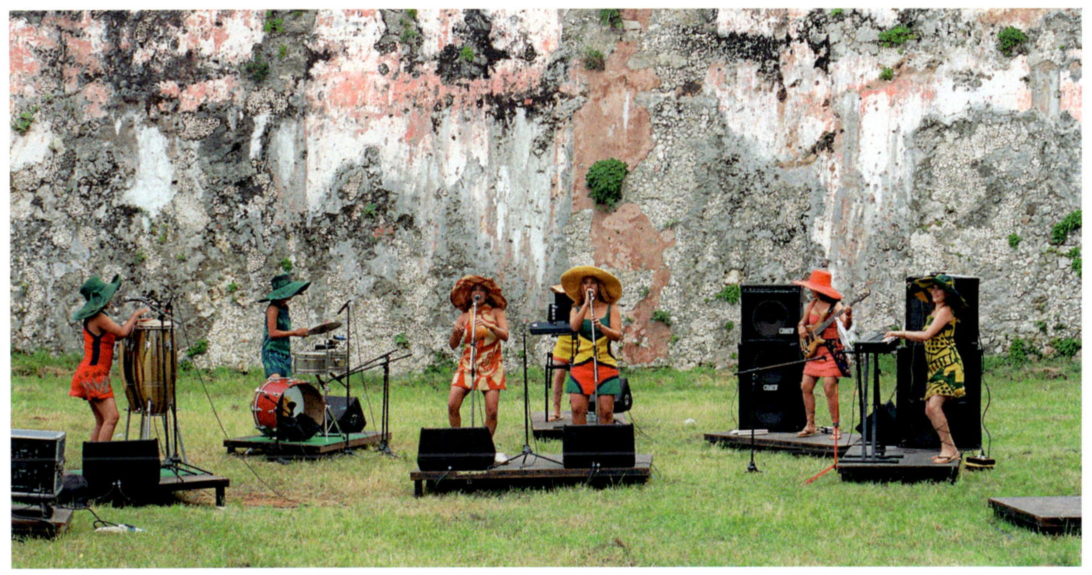

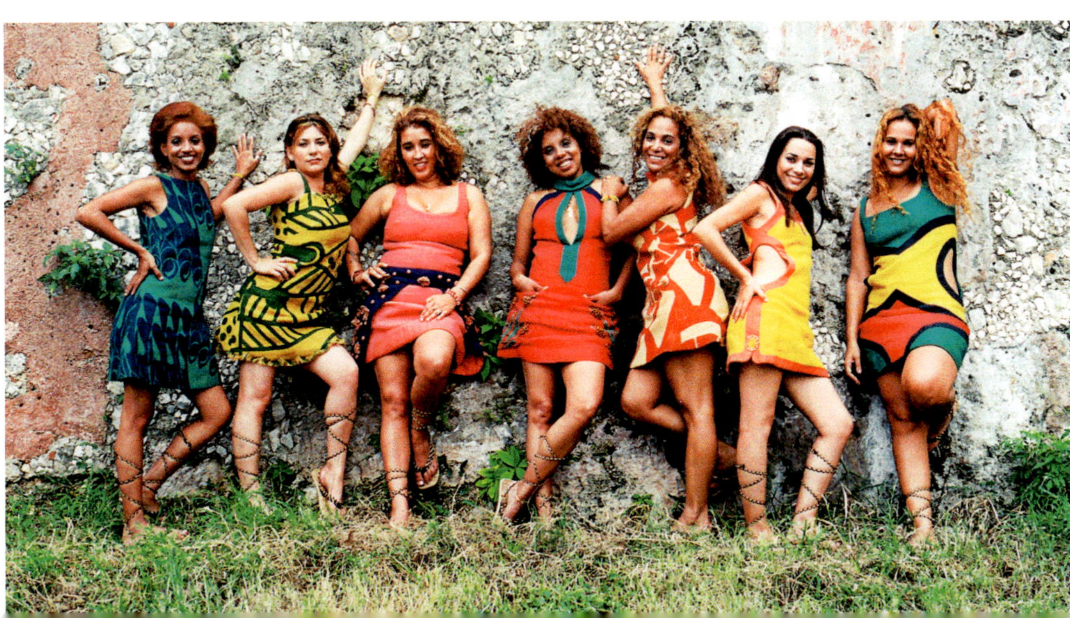

La Banda de mi Hogar The Band of my Home

Panama City, Panama / Ciudad de Panamá, Panamá 2003 Performance

La Banda de mi Hogar was a series of surprise parades produced in collaboration with *La Banda de la Escuela Vocacional El Hogar* and commissioned as part of the *ciudadMULTIPLEcity*, a celebration of the Republic of Panama Centennial co-curated by Gerardo Mosquera and Adrienne Samos.

La Banda del Hogar is a brass and percussion marching band composed of mainly mestizo musicians and majorettes, of all ages, affiliated with the vocational school El Hogar. Though wildly popular, *La Banda del Hogar* was only permitted to parade publically on Independence Day.

Breaking with this tradition, Vélez and the band marched numerous times on non-holidays, modeling their homemade uniforms and banners in public squares and along the Panama bridge (given back to the Panamanians by the USA) as well as other politically charged locations throughout the city, making this performance a symbolic act of repatriation.

La Banda de mi Hogar es una performance que consistió en una serie de desfiles sorpresivos en distintos espacios simbólicos de la ciudad de Panamá con la colaboración de *La Banda de la Escuela Vocacional El Hogar*. La obra fue parte de *ciudadMULTIPLEcity*, un evento de arte público internacional con motivo del Centenario de la República de Panamá cuyos comisarios fueron Gerardo Mosquera y Adrienne Samos.

La Banda del Hogar es una banda de viento y percusión compuesta mayormente por músicos mestizos de todas las edades afiliados a la escuela vocacional *El Hogar* que imparte clases de sastrería, modistería y belleza. Aunque de corte popular, en ese entonces a *La Banda del Hogar* sólo se le permitía desfilar públicamente durante las festividades patrias en noviembre.

Rompiendo esta tradición, Vélez y la banda marcharon en numerosas ocasiones fuera de dicho calendario en momentos y lugares inesperados de la ciudad con emblemas y uniformes confeccionados especialmente para el evento. Por ejemplo marcharon durante la celebración semanal de la lotería nacional; en Punta Paitilla, el barrio de la clase acomodada capitalina; en la entonces nueva terminal de autobuses construida en la antigua Zona del Canal; y también en el Causeway, lugar de recreación a las orillas del canal que estaba bajo la jurisdicción del gobierno estadounidense en el que las nuevas autoridades panameñas del canal les prohibieron marchar en un acto que recordó la antigua política segregacionista del gobierno colonial estadounidense. Sin duda el desfile más simbólico de la serie fue cuando la banda se tomó el Puente de Las Américas que cruza el Canal de Panamá, como símbolo de la recuperación del territorio nacional por y para todos los panameños.

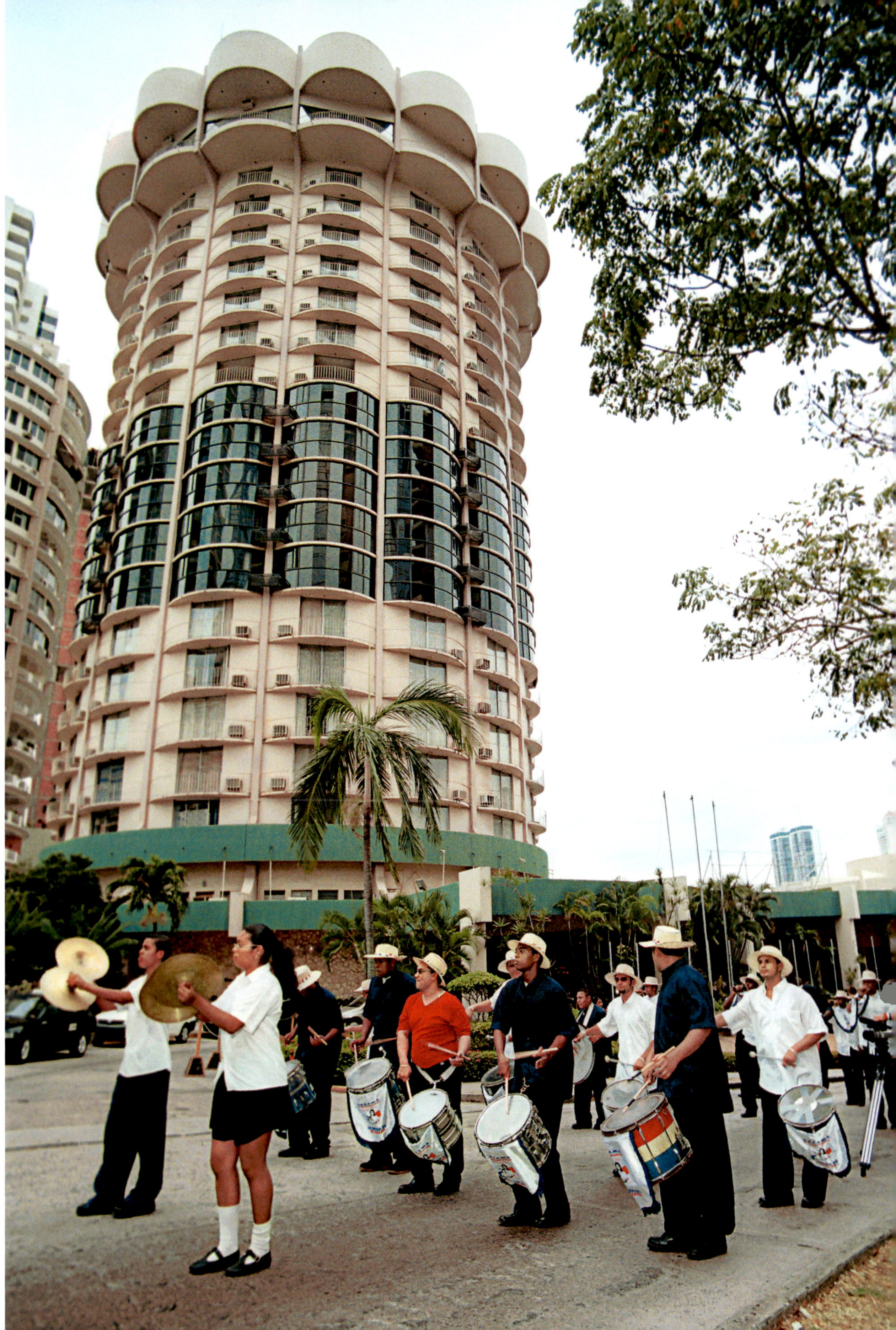

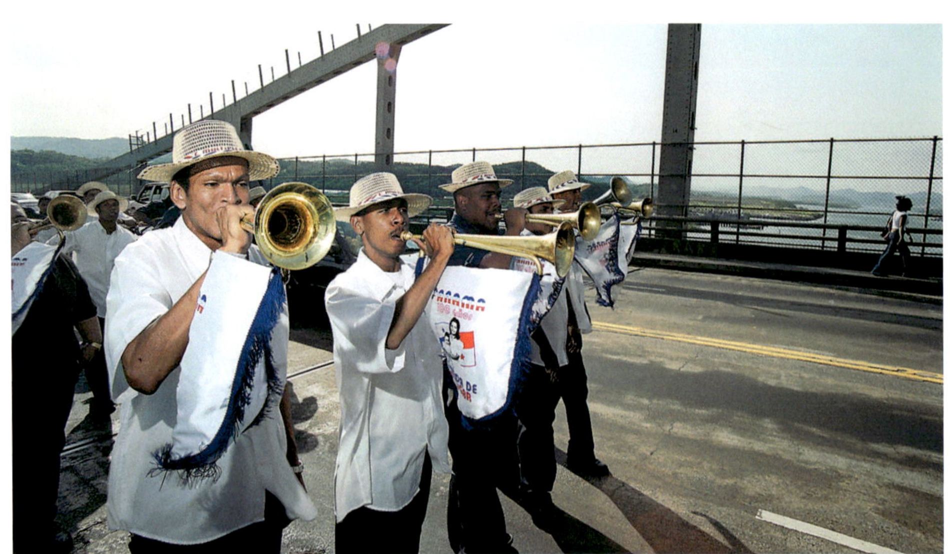

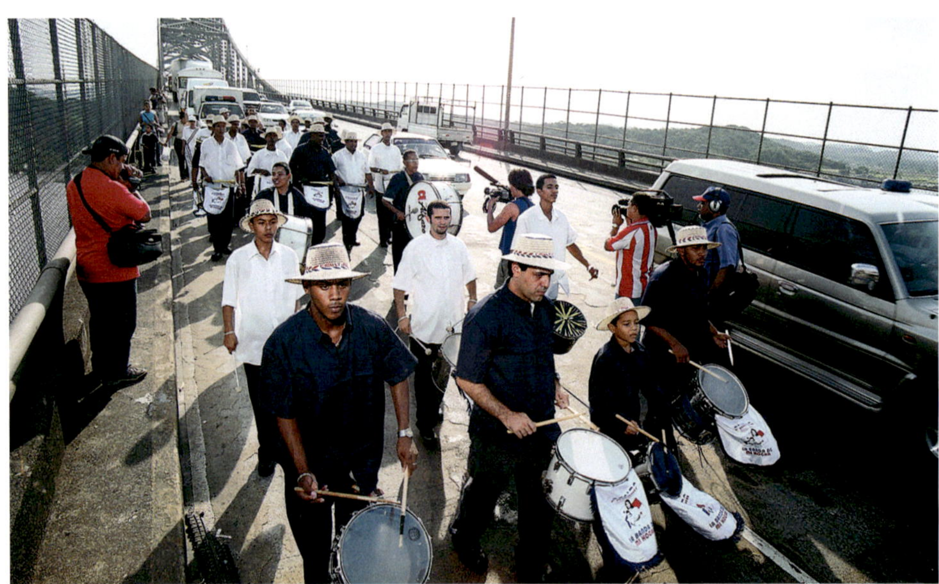

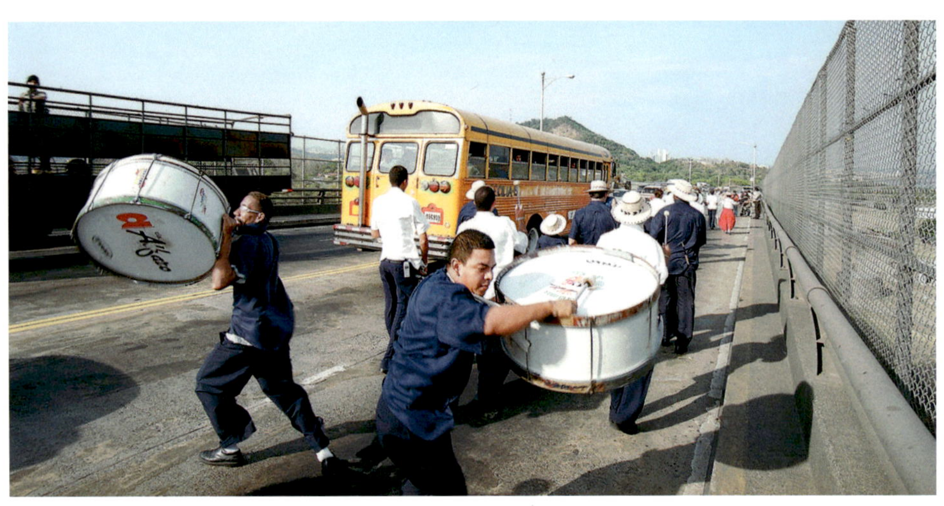

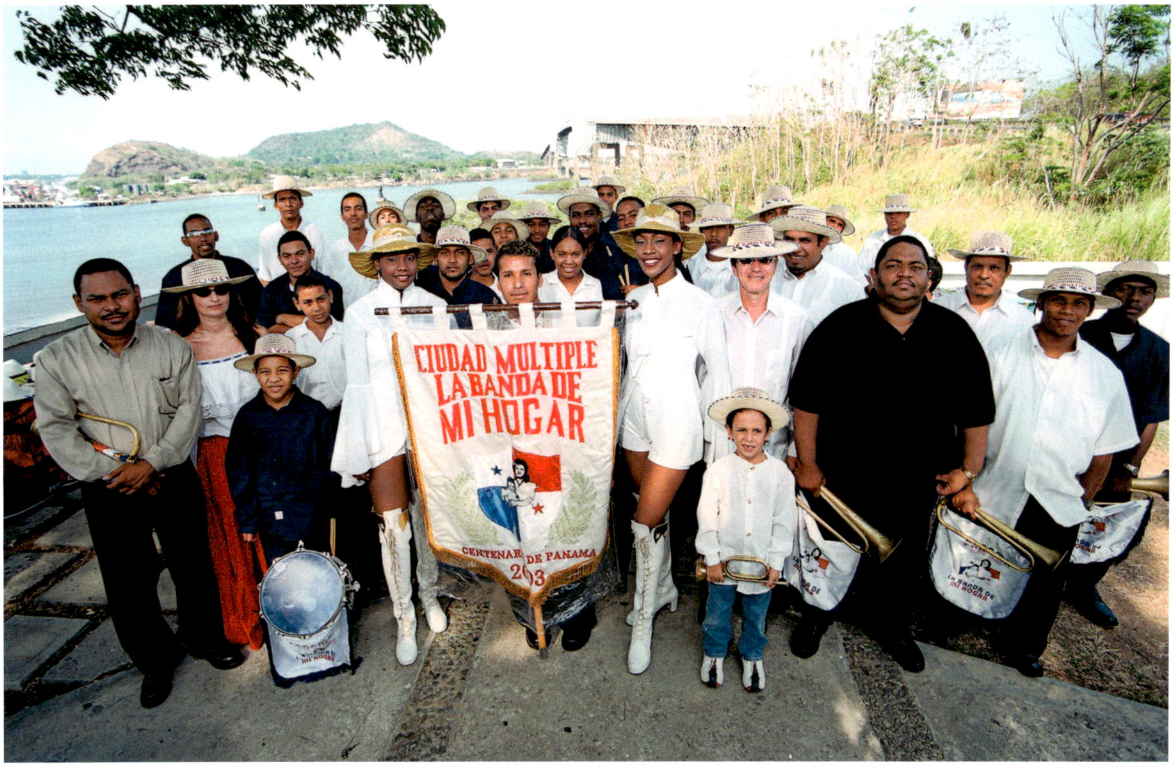

CIUDAD MULTIPLE
LA BANDA DE
MI HOGAR
CENTENARIO DE PANAMA
203

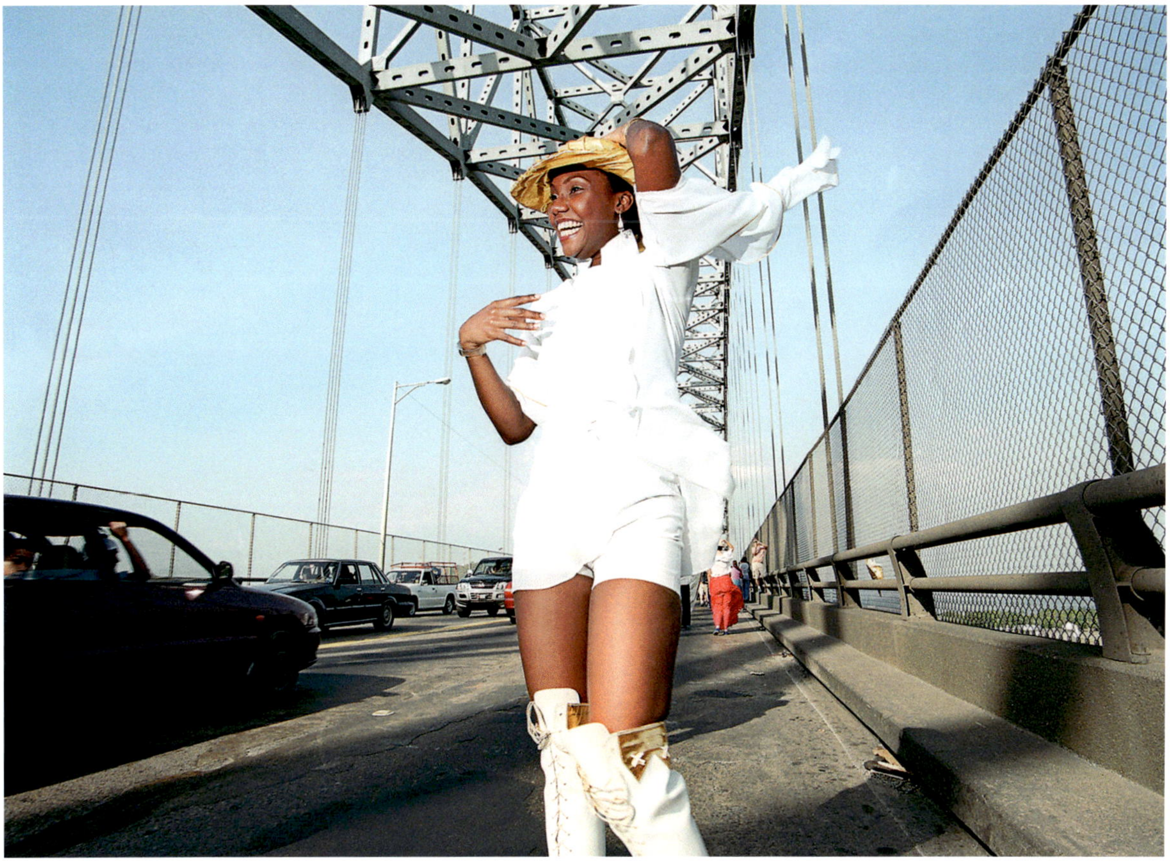

Mancunian Way A lo mancuniano

Manchester, England / Manchester, Inglaterra 2004 Performance

While the Victoria Baths, located in Manchester, was under-going a restoration to take it "back to its former Edwardian Glory," the Victoria Baths Trust commissioned a group of artists to make public projects thematically exploring the past and future of this historic building. The resulting project, curated by Alison Kershaw, was called *For the Time Being, A Promise of Progress.*

For his project, Vélez chose to talk about the "Mancunian Way" using a different language—indeed a different "dialect"—than that used in association with the Victoria Baths' restoration. Situating his project firmly in the present, Vélez created a "returning local heroes" style parade with the youth of Longsight and Ardwick, the neighbourhoods surrounding the Baths. Commissioning a new song based on garage and hip hop, they toured the streets on a double-decker bus only to arrive at the Baths where the mobile street party stopped and a "storming" of the space and dance recital by local residents took place inside the Baths during the August 1st open day.

Durante la restauración de los *Victoria Baths*, un complejo de piscinas y baños turcos de estilo eduardiano en Manchester, un grupo de artistas fue comisionado por el proyecto de arte público *For The Time Being, A Promise of Progress*, curado por Alison Kershaw, para realizar obras sobre el pasado y el futuro de este edificio histórico.

Vélez optó por hablar sobre los *Victoria Baths* de una manera distinta a la usual en esta línea de proyectos de arte, utilizando una especie de "dialecto artístico" si lo comparamos con la forma de hablar de los habitantes de Manchester. Afincando su proyecto firmemente en el presente, Vélez creó un desfile en que celebraba el "regreso de los héroes locales" para lo cual trabajó en conjunto con jóvenes de los barrios vecinos de Longsight y Ardwick.

Para esto organizó una serie de talleres de creación musical y de baile en los que se compuso una canción original al estilo garaje y hip hop, y crearon distintas coreografías. El día de la performance, los participantes recorrieron en un característico autobús inglés de dos pisos las calles de los barrios del distrito hasta llegar a los *Victoria Baths*, donde se tomaron el edificio con un concierto y una serie de bailes contemporáneos, ante la sorpresa de los visitantes que acudieron a ver el monumento en uno de los pocos días de apertura que anunciaba *The National Trust*, la institución británica inglesa que cuida y protege el patrimonio histórico del pais.

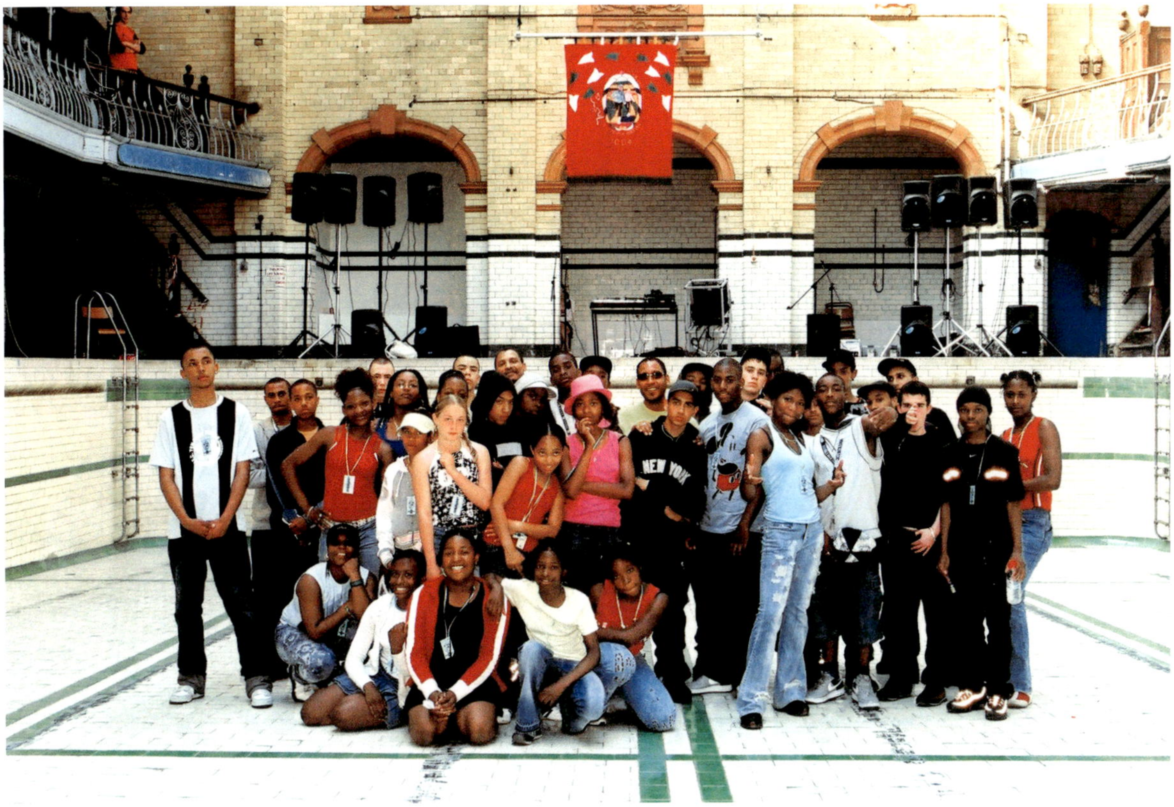

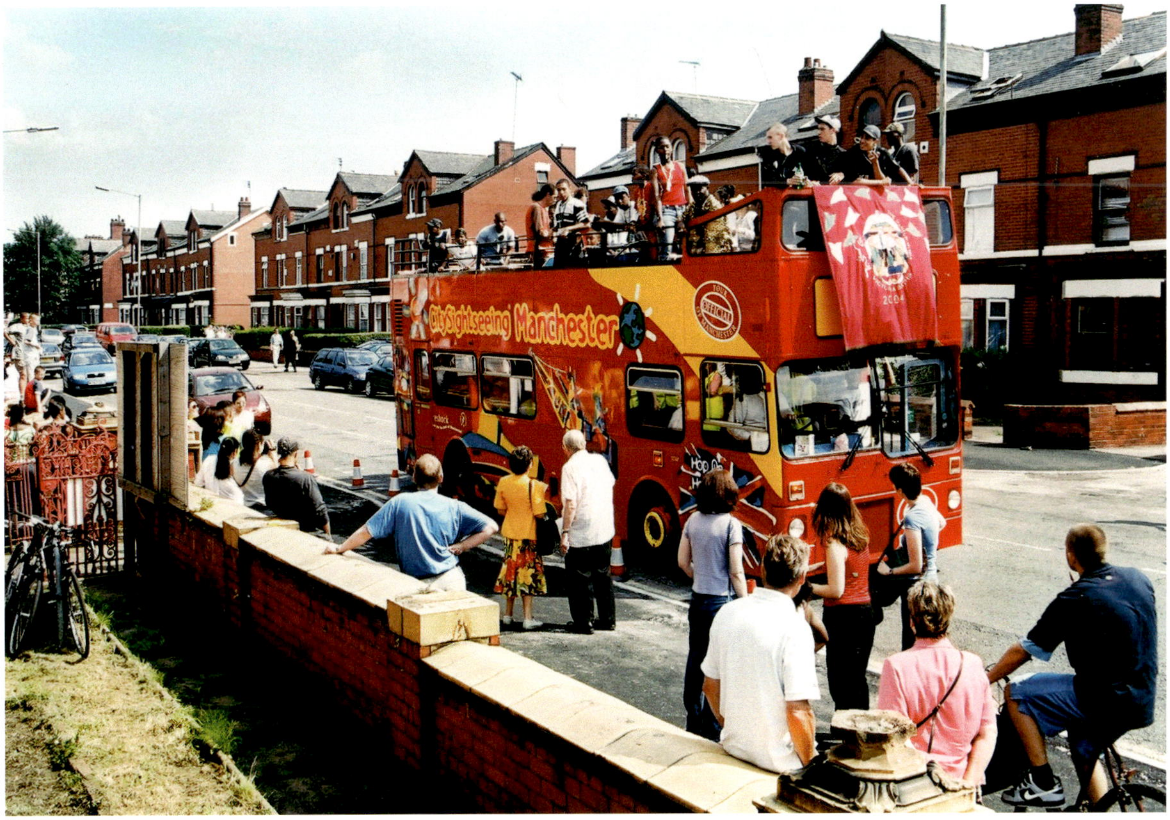

CitySightseeing Manchester
OFFICIAL
TOUR
of Manchester
2004
Hop

La controversia del arte
The Controversy of Art

Panama City, Panama / Ciudad de Panamá, Panamá 2004
Radio Performance / Performance por radio

La controversio del arte was staged at the Plaza de la Catedral in Panama City and transmitted live nationwide by radio for the 2004 *Bienal de Artes Visuales del Istmo Centroaméricano*. It is the only concept that Vélez has tried out twice in two different places, as it was followed by the 2010 work *El contrapunto (del arte)* in Valparaíso, Chile. Both works discuss the role of art in society today.

For *La controversia del arte*, Vélez collaborated with two young singers, Dayra Moreno and Richard Rodriguez, the poet Luis "Cholo" Bernal, and a band that included Colaquito Cortez on violin and Manolito Corrales on guitar. In addition to the main "characters" in this radio drama about art, *La Banda de la Escuela Vocacional El Hogar* participated as special guests during the intermission when, drawing upon the local music traditions and political history of Panama City, they performed a military-style music performance. *La controversia del arte* was produced by Pitu Jaén and Carlos Fitzgerald.

La controversia del arte es una performance en forma de concierto de décimas, una tradición iberoamericana en que un grupo de cantantes mantiene un duelo de versos en base en a un tema establecido. La obra se presentó en la Plaza de la Catedral en la ciudad de Panamá como parte de la Bienal de Artes Visuales del Istmo Centroaméricano de 2004 y fue transmitida por radio y en directo a todo el país. Pitu Jaén y Carlos Fitzgerald estuvieron a cargo de la producción del evento. Este es el único concepto de un performance que Vélez ha repetido, siendo la segunda ocasión en Valparaíso en 2010 y con el título de *El contrapunto (del arte)*. Ambas obras dialogan sobre el papel del arte en la sociedad actual.

Para *La controversia del arte*, Vélez trabajó con los jóvenes cantantes de décimas, Dayra Moreno y Richard Rodríguez, con el poeta Luis "Cholo" Bernal, con los conocidos músicos panameños Colaquito Cortez en el violín y Manolito Corrales en la guitarra. Además participó como invitado especial en esta performance *La Banda de la Escuela Vocacional El Hogar*, que en el intermedio del programa, ejecutó un espectáculo musical con elementos militares que extrañamente mezcló formas de expresión popular con signos de identidad nacional relacionadas con la historia política del país.

La carrera (Clásico VII Bienal de Panamá)
The Horse Race (7th Panama Biennial Classic)

Panama City, Panama / Ciudad de Panamá, Panamá 2005
Radio Performance / Performance por radio

Originally conceived as a performance for the 7th Panama Biennial in 2005, this audio work is the commentary of an imaginary horse race, developed in collaboration with his family (brothers Eric Vélez and Carlos Alberto Fernández)—now the "artists"—and performed by sports broadcaster Arquímedes Fernández, Vélez's stepfather.

Coming out of Vélez's own personal history with equestrian racing, *La carrera* pays homage to Panamanian culture while also poking fun at the seriousness with which Panamanians regard equestrian races. Using humour, Vélez turns this local tradition into an allegory: set in the context of the biennial, the horse race also functions as a parody of the international art world. The horses are ironically named with terms that categorize and polarize social classes in Panama: *Miss Panamá, Negro de Mierda, Visa Americana, AIDS, Papi Rico, Extranjera, One Dollar, Oligarca*, and *I Have a Dream*. It's a close race between the economic, social, and racial conditions/perceptions deeply embedded within Panamanian society, and that also permeate the international art world.

La carrera fue concebida originalmente como una performance para la VII Bienal de Arte de Panamá en 2005 y posteriormente tomó la forma de una instalación sonora. La obra es la narración imaginaria de una carrera de caballos realizada en colaboración con la Familia de Vélez—en este caso entre "los artistas colaboradores" están sus hermanos Eric Vélez y Carlos Alberto Fernández—y está narrada por el conocido periodista y locutor deportivo Arquímedes Fernández, el padrastro de Vélez.

La obra está inspirada en las frecuentes visitas dominicales de Vélez con su familia al hipódromo local durante su infancia y adolescencia. *La carrera* es un homenaje a la cultura panameña y a su obsesión por los deportes, y a la vez una parodia al mundo del arte. Los nombres de los caballos que compiten en el Clásico VII Bienal de Arte de Panamá son un comentario irónico y humorístico de la sociedad panameña: *Miss Panamá, Negro de Mierda, Visa Americana, SIDA, Papi Rico, Extranjera, One Dollar, Oligarca* y *I Have a Dream* (Tengo un sueño).

Regata cantata

Venice, Italy / Venecia, Italia 2005 Performance

Realized in collaboration with the Venetian collective *Artway of Thinking* (Stefania Mantovani and Federica Thiene), *Regata cantata* (also named *Uomo in mare! Terra in vista!*) was a parade and regatta that took over the streets and canals of the historic city of Venice.

Produced on the occasion of "International Maritime Day" and in contrast to the international function of the Venice Biennial, *Regata cantata* was designed for the locals, celebrating the diverse people of Venice and the different identities that make up this "Italian City," mixing traditions, movements, and sounds. *Banda Musicale di Sant'Erasmo*, a traditional-style band from the local island San Erasmo, and *Lost and Found* (Mezen + Ledo + Kave), an Italian rap band from the city of Mestre, played together as hundreds of Venetians—invited artists, art students, immigrants, and mariners—paraded over every canal in the city, ending at the Academia Bridge on the Grand Canal where the crowds were met by a series of barges and gondolas carrying *remeros* (rowers) singing traditional Venetian songs.

Vélez fue invitado por el dúo artístico veneciano conocido como *Artway of Thinking* (Stefania Mantovani y Federica Thiene) a crear en colaboración un evento artístico en la "ciudad de los canales" para el Día Marítimo Internacional de 2005. Vélez propuso una performance bajo el título de *Regata cantata* (que fue también conocida como *Uomo in mare! Terra in vista!*) en forma de desfile y regata que cruzó las calles peatonales, puentes y canales de Venecia. En contraste con la función internacional de la Bienal de Venecia, la idea de Vélez fue crear una obra que fuese un homenaje a los residentes de la ciudad, los inmigrantes y los marineros del puerto que cuestionase el concepto de identidad de esta *isla-ciudad* mezclando tradiciones e invadiendo los espacios terrestres y marinos.

Para esto el proyecto *fusionó* dos bandas: la *Banda Musicale di Sant'Erasmo*, de corte tradicional, casi *fellinesco*, que pertenece a la vecina Isla de San Erasmo, y el grupo de rap *Lost and Found* (Mezen + Ledo + Kave) de la colindante ciudad obrera de Mestre.

La performance comenzó en la Piazzale Roma con un cortejo musical integrado por las bandas, artistas invitados, agrupaciones marinas, colectivos de inmigrantes y estudiantes de arte, que cruzó el centro histórico de Venecia hasta llegar al Puente de la Academia. Allí cerca, en el muelle de la comisaría, la procesión abordó un grupo de góndolas, barcas y una gigantesca barcaza con dieciocho remeros que navegó el Gran Canal cantando viejas melodías venecianas.

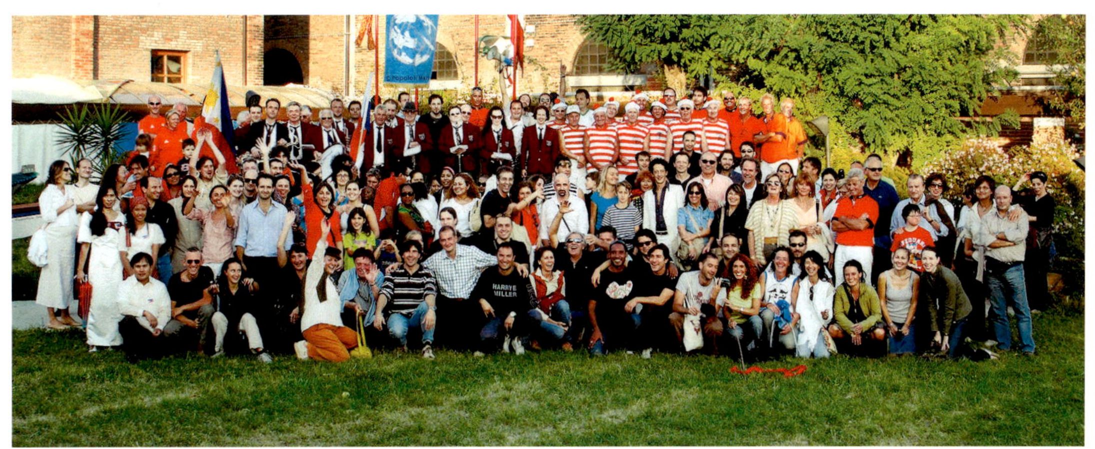

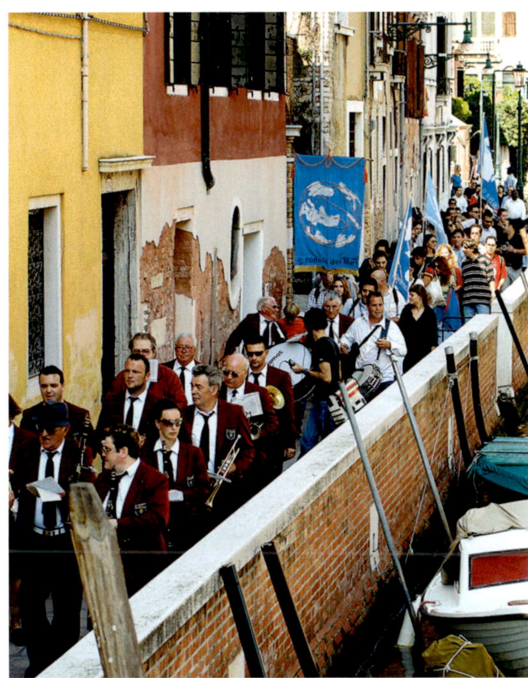

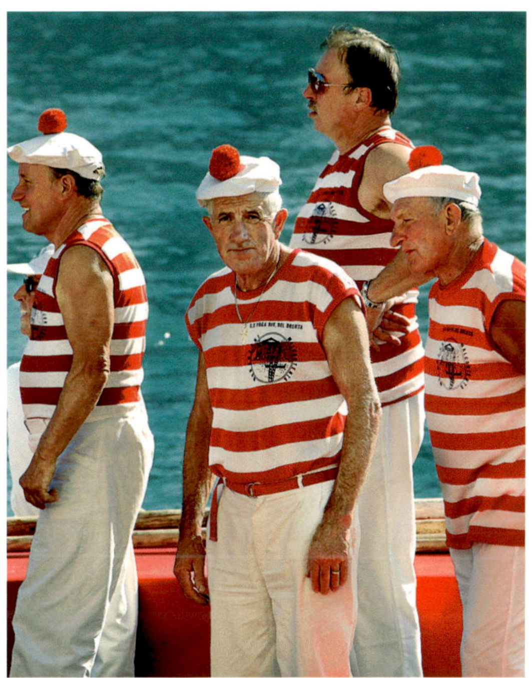

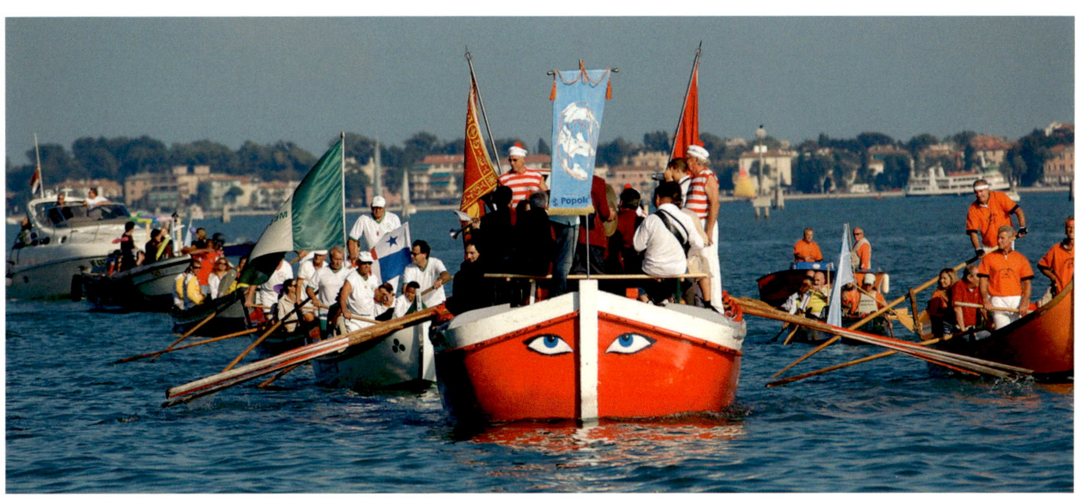

Artists United Artistas Unidos

Sheffield, England / Sheffield, Inglaterra 2005 Performance

Commissioned by Yorkshire Artspace and curated by Rachael Dodd, *Artists United* was a collaborative community project that took place at the Sharrow Festival in July 2005. This hip hop football derby brought together local talent in the visual arts, music, and dance. Football teams were created specifically for this occasion and involved players from different generations and backgrounds, especially refugees and asylum seekers. Local young musicians *The Collaboration Crew* developed and performed a special song and and a group of young women performed a choreographed dance that incorporated football moves.

Artists United fue una performance creada para el *Sharrow Festival* en Sheffield en julio de 2005 producida por *Yorkshire Artspace* y bajo la curaduría de Rachael Dodd. Esta performance fue una combinación de fútbol, hip hop y bailes que reunió a jóvenes artistas contemporáneos con jugadores aficionados de fútbol de Sheffield.

Para el proyecto se crearon equipos en los que participaron jugadores de distintas generaciones y procedencias, especialmente refugiados y asilados políticos. Durante el evento, mientras los futbolistas jugaban, *The Collaboration Crew*, un grupo de jóvenes músicos locales, interpretaba un concierto especial para el evento al mismo tiempo que un grupo femenino de adolescentes bailaba una coreografía inspirada en el fútbol.

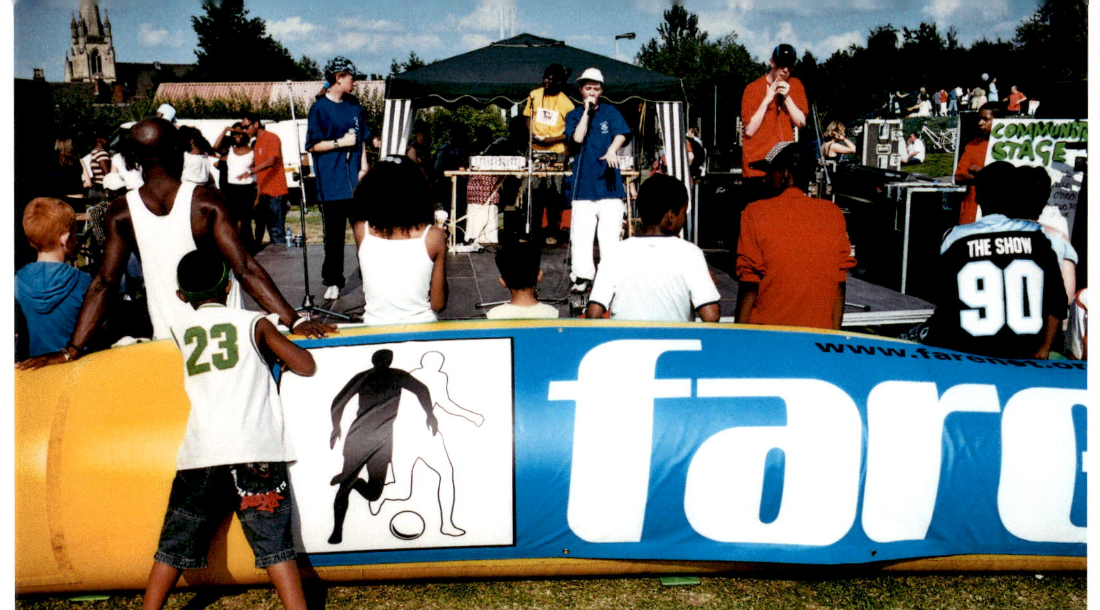

COMMUNITY
STAGE
THE SHOW
90
23
www.farenet.o
fare

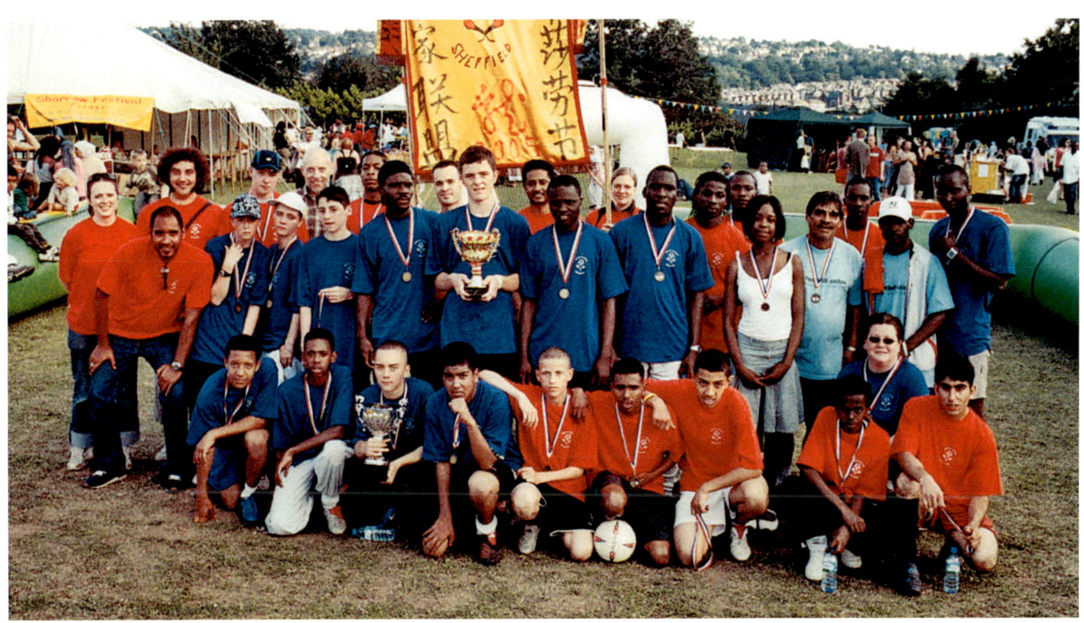

Sharrow Festival
SHEFFIELD

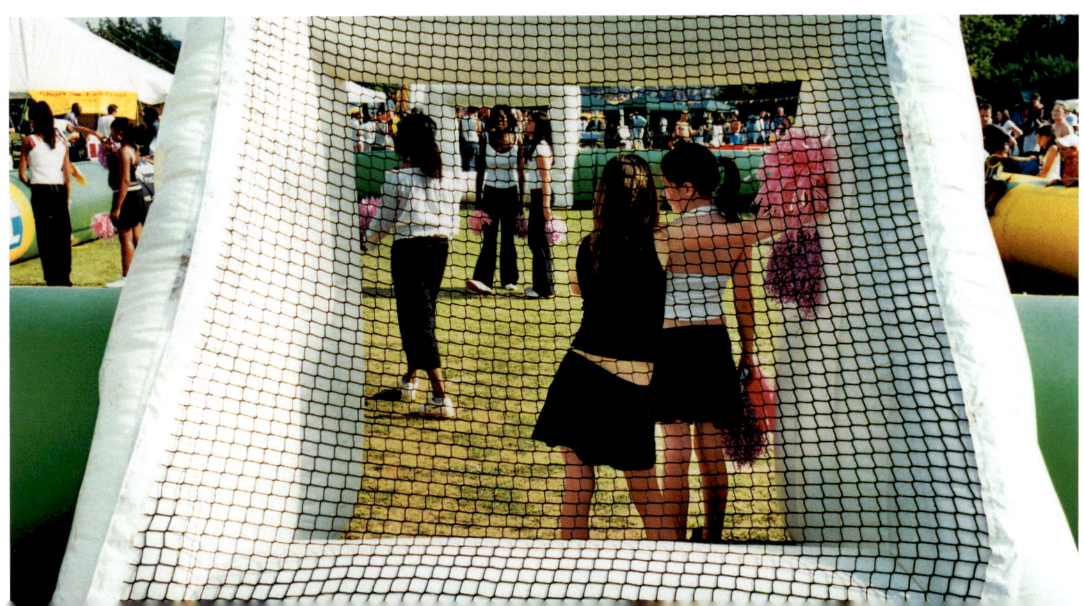

The Welcoming La bienvenida

Liverpool, England / Liverpool, Inglaterra 2006 Performance

For the 4th Liverpool Biennial in 2006, Vélez worked with a group of 16–21 year old Afghan refugees and asylum seekers in collaboration with Liverpool's Chinese, African, Caribbean, and Irish communities to create a symbolic welcome for new arrivals to Liverpool.

Vélez used the historical role of the city's docks—the point of departure for thousands of migrants hoping for a new life in the "new world"—to pose the question: what kind of welcome do we give those who now arrive in "our" country, our city, seeking refuge and a new life?—a poignant question to ask given the increasing hostility toward migrant groups in England following the terrorist attacks in London earlier that year.

The performance started with a street demonstration by asylum seekers—including a group of asylum seeker artists—who walked through the former slave trade district to the Albert Docks where a boat with the young asylum seekers from Afghanistan was waiting to dock. With everyone gathered together outside Tate Liverpool, audience members listened to the viewpoints of many of the participants, who gave speeches about the current situation of their respective communities in both English and their native languages, and danced traditional dances. This project was initiated by Gerardo Mosquera, one of the curators of that edition of the Liverpool Biennial and co-curated by Bec Jones from Bluecoat Arts Centre, Liverpool.

Vélez fue invitado a participar en la IV Bienal de Liverpool de 2006 por el curador Gerardo Mosquera, quien fue parte del comité seleccionador, y desarrolló su propuesta con la curadora Bec Jones del Bluecoat Arts Centre. En su proyecto, titulado *The Welcoming*, el artista trabajó en colaboración con un grupo de jóvenes refugiados y asilados políticos afganos con edades entre los 16 y los 21 años, y con las comunidades china, africana, caribeña e irlandesa de Liverpool. La idea era crear una bienvenida simbólica a los recién llegados afganos para hablar sobre la delicada situación de los inmigrantes en el Reino Unido, especialmente después de los atentados terroristas en Londres.

Vélez utilizó los espacios públicos de Liverpool para comentar sobre la historia de la inmigración en la ciudad, desde el tráfico de esclavos hacia las Américas hasta el presente, a través de las comunidades de inmigrantes ya firmemente establecidas en la ciudad a quienes les preguntó durante el proceso de creación de la obra: ¿Qué clase de bienvenida le damos a quienes llegan ahora a "nuestro" país?

La performance comenzó con una manifestación de grupos de refugiados y asilados políticos (incluyendo un grupo de artistas que también eran refugiados políticos), que caminaron desde la plaza donde antiguamente se vendían los esclavos hasta los muelles históricos de Liverpool (*Albert Docks*) donde un velero con los jóvenes refugiados afganos les esperaba para desembarcar.

Después de la entusiasta ceremonia de bienvenida con distintos bailes y cantos que las comunidades y los grupos de asilados le ofrecieron a los jóvenes afganos, los participantes se reunieron al lado de la Tate Liverpool donde se realizó un cabildo integrado por representantes de cada comunidad en que hablaron sobre la historia y la situación de sus comunidades.

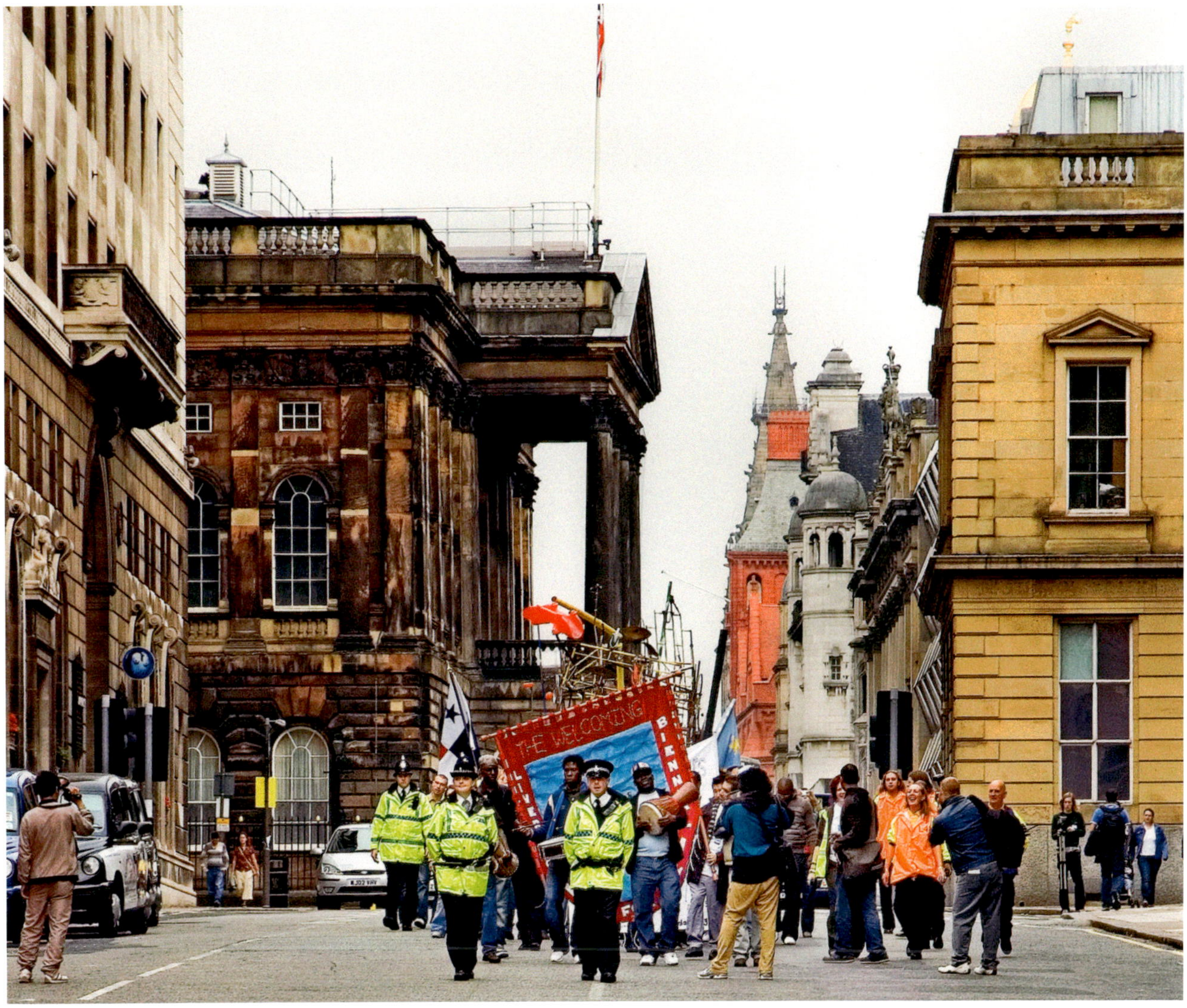

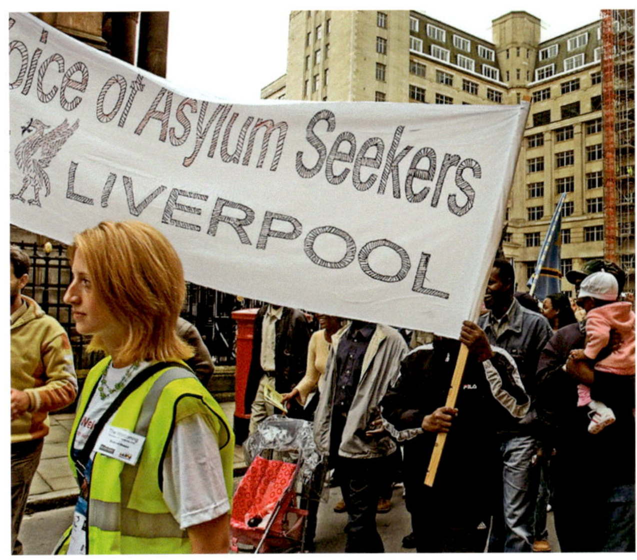

Voice of Asylum Seekers
LIVERPOOL

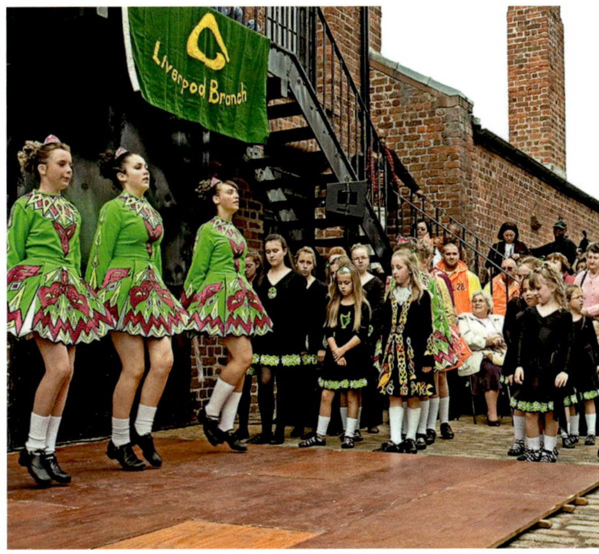

Liverpool Branch

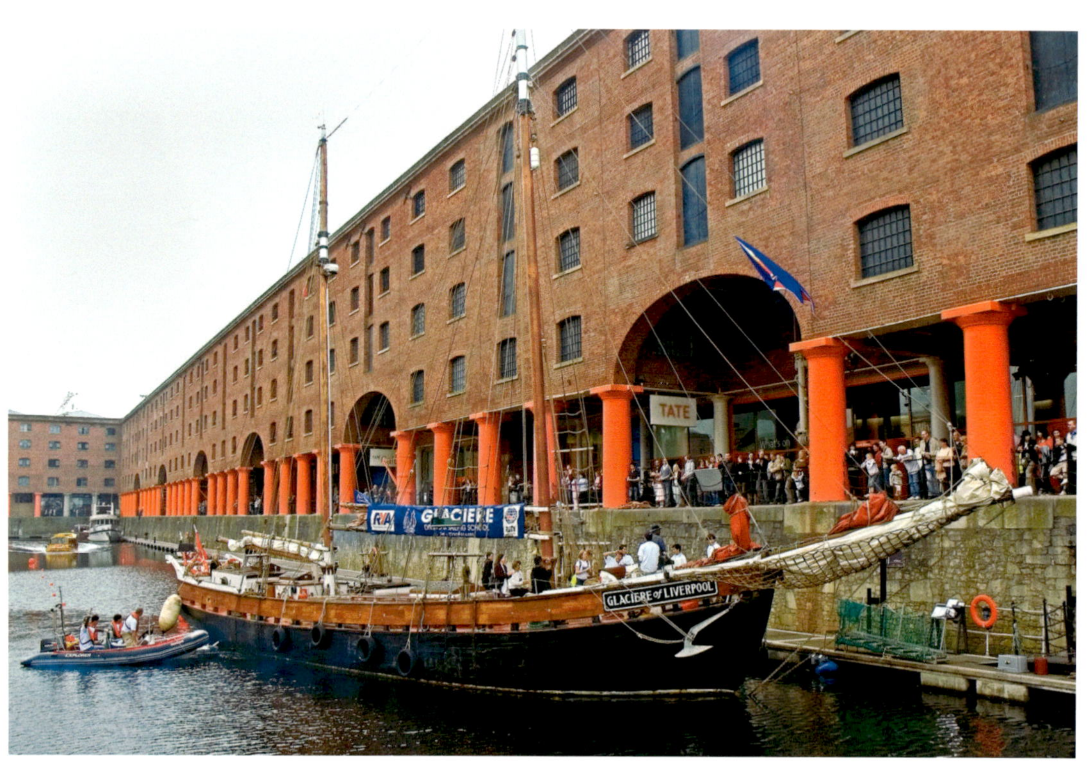

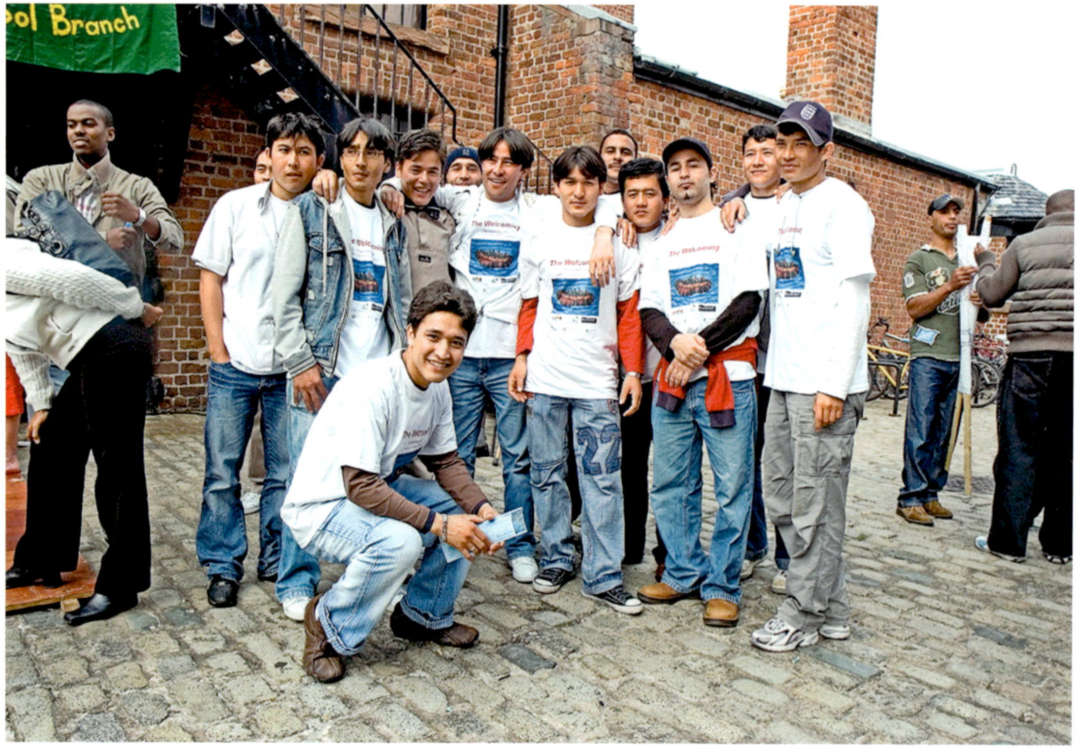
ool Branch
The Welcoming

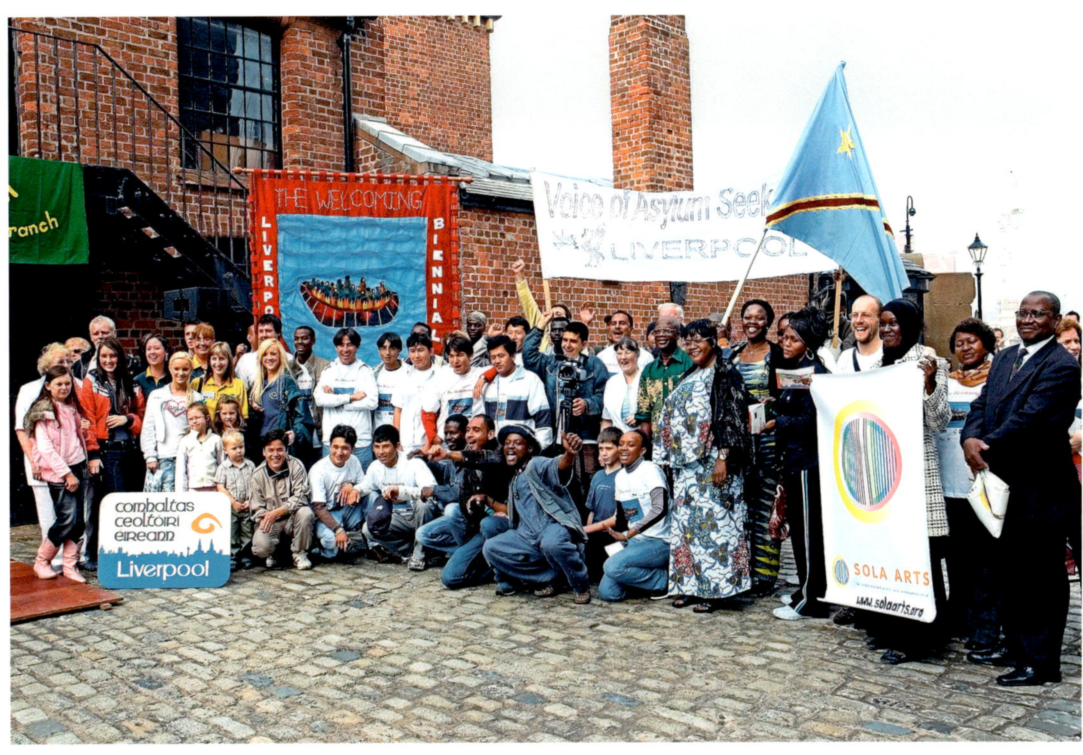
ranch
THE WELCOMING
LIVERPOOL BIENNIAL
Voice of Asylum Seek
LIVERPOOL
combaltas
ceoltóiri
éireann
Liverpool
SOLA ARTS
www.solaarts.org

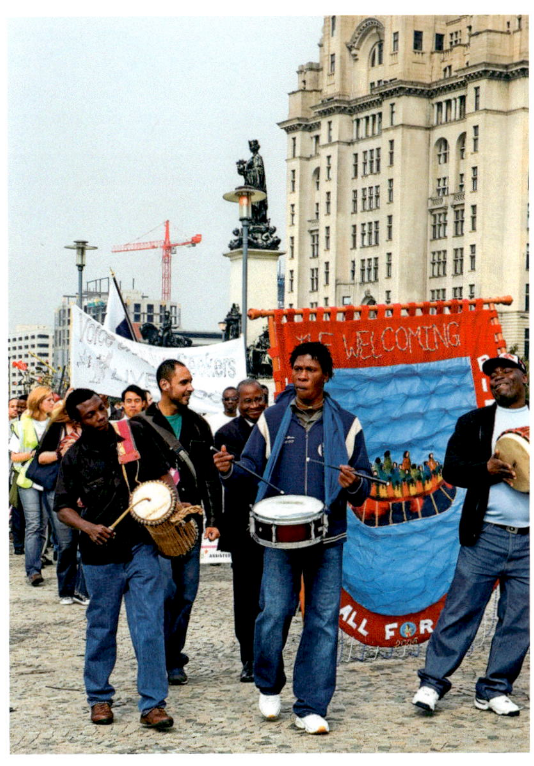
Voice
LIVERPOOL Seekers
THE WELCOMING
ALL FOR

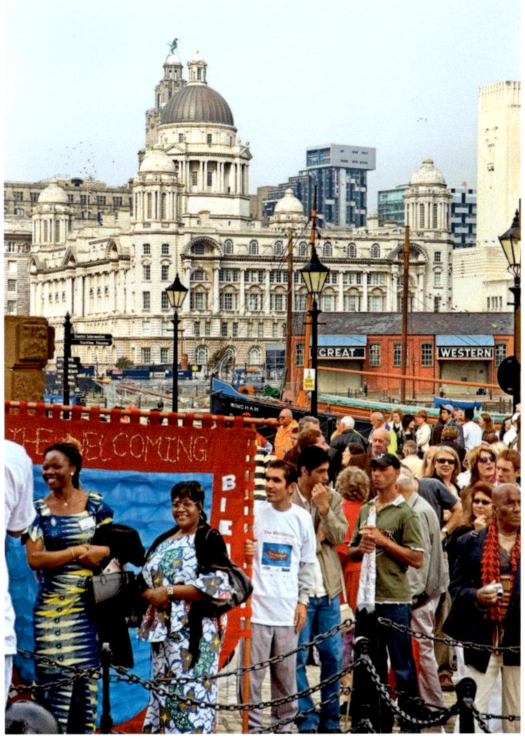
GREAT WESTERN
THE WELCOMING
BIE

The Fight La pelea

London, England / Londres, Inglaterra 2007 Performance

Commissioned by the Tate Modern and curated by Gabriela Salgado, *The Fight* was created by Vélez in collaboration with three boxing clubs from South-wark: Fitzroy Lodge ABC, Fisher Downside ABC and Lynn ABC. Members of the boxing clubs arrived from the Millennium Bridge and the River Thames in two simultaneous processions, one led by a Scottish bag-piper and the other by African drummers. The participants gathered outside the Tate Modern before entering the building to perform in the Turbine Hall. The performance included five amateur boxing fights, specifically composed music by *MC Mic Assassin*, and choreography created by the street dance company *Flawless*. The performance linked the Tate Modern with the neighbourhoods that surrounds the museum but rarely enter its doors.

Vélez fue invitado por la curadora Gabriela Salgado a crear una performance en la Tate Modern, con el propósito de vincular a la institución con un público londinense que habitualmente no asiste al museo, especialmente el de las comunidades que se encuentran cerca del mismo. El resultado fue *The Fight*, una performance boxística realizada en colaboración con los clubes de boxeo aficionado *Fitzroy Lodge ABC, Fisher Downside ABC* y *Lynn ABC* del distrito londinense de Southwark, al que pertenece la Tate.

En la performance, los boxeadores se tomaron el museo con dos procesiones simultáneas: una dirigida por un gaitero escocés que cruzó el Puente del Milenio; y la otra en un barco, encabezada por un grupo de percusionistas africanos que junto con los pugilistas cruzaron el Támesis y desembarcaron en un muelle cercano, como homenaje a los trabajadores del puerto que practicaron este deporte.

Mientras los cortejos se acercaban al museo, en su interior un grupo de jóvenes boxeadores ejercitaban un calentamiento coreografiado saltando la soga y simulando peleas. Ambas procesiones se unieron y llegaron a un tinglado montado sobre el puente del *Turbine Hall*. El evento incluyó peleas amateur de boxeo, música compuesta para la ocasión por *MC Mic Assassin* y una coreografía inspirada en este deporte creada por la compañía de danza urbana *Flawless* que incorporó a luchadores de los clubes.

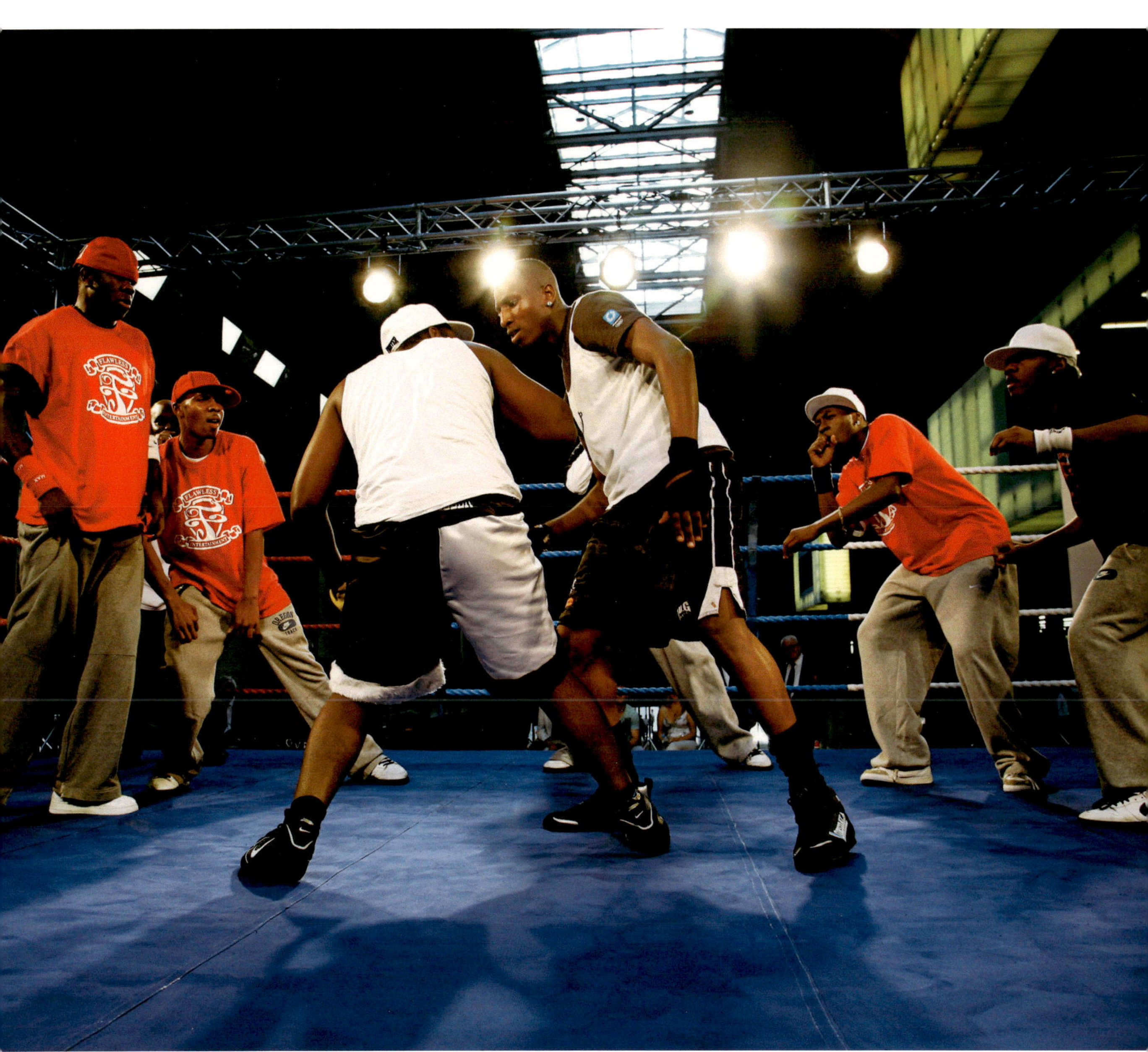

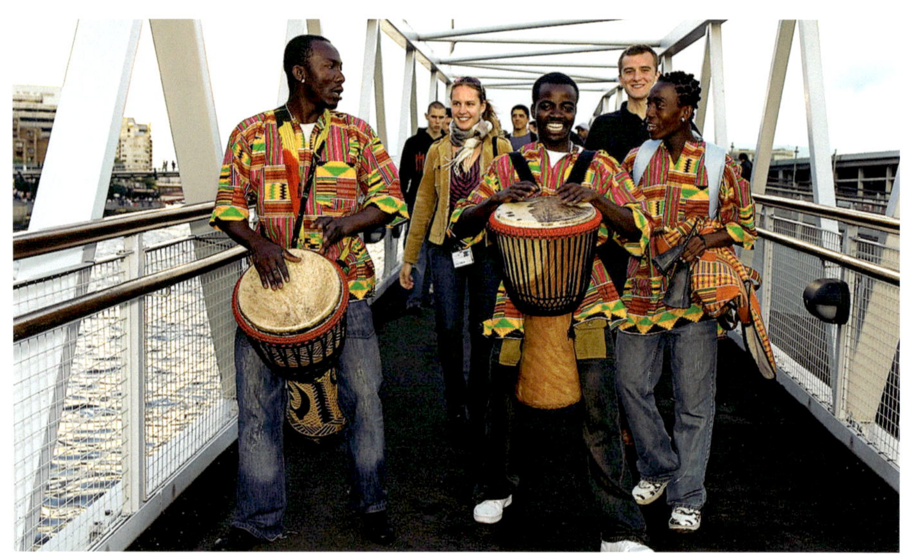

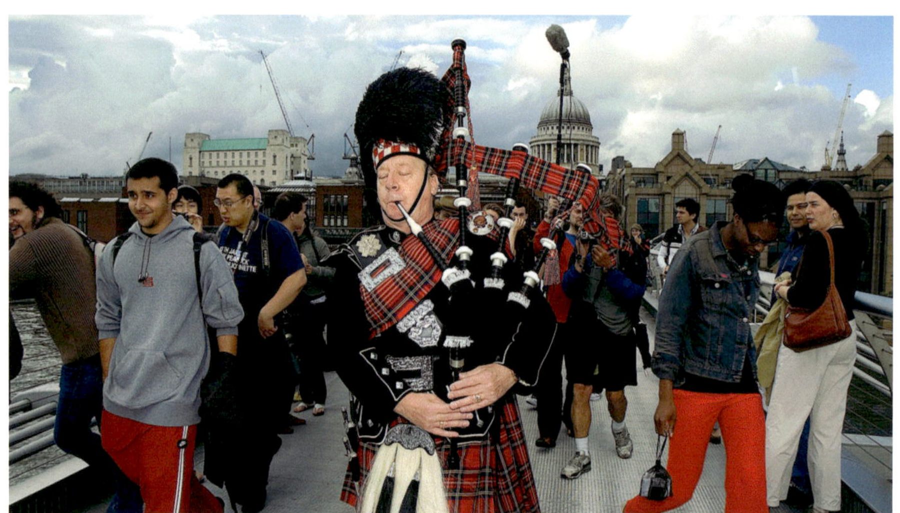

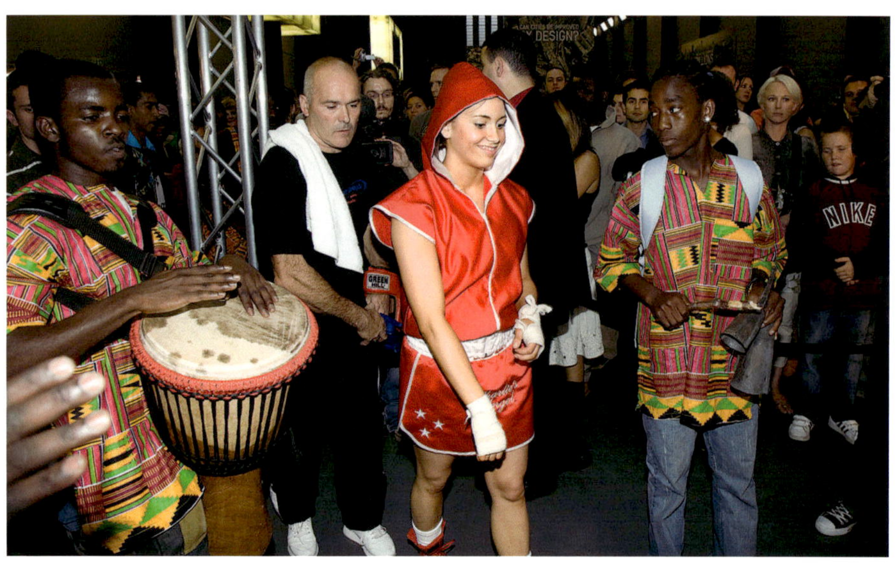

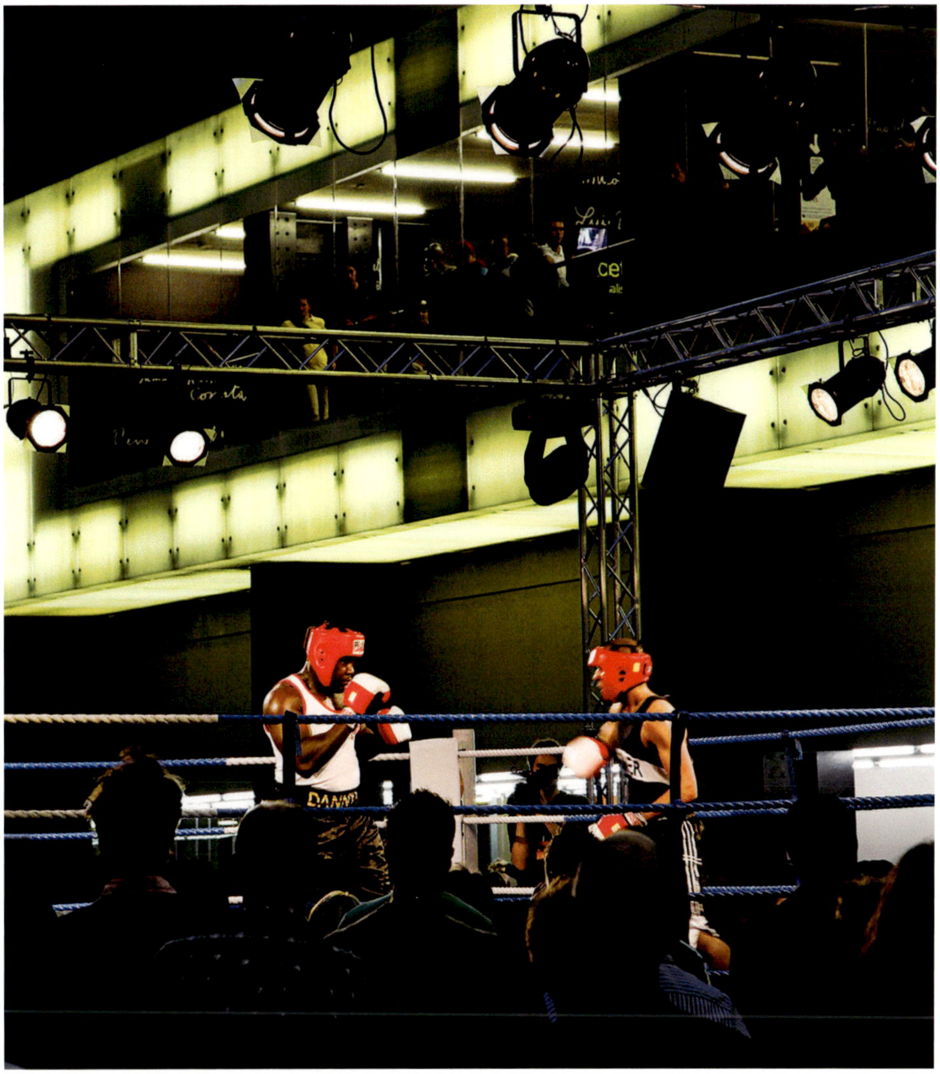

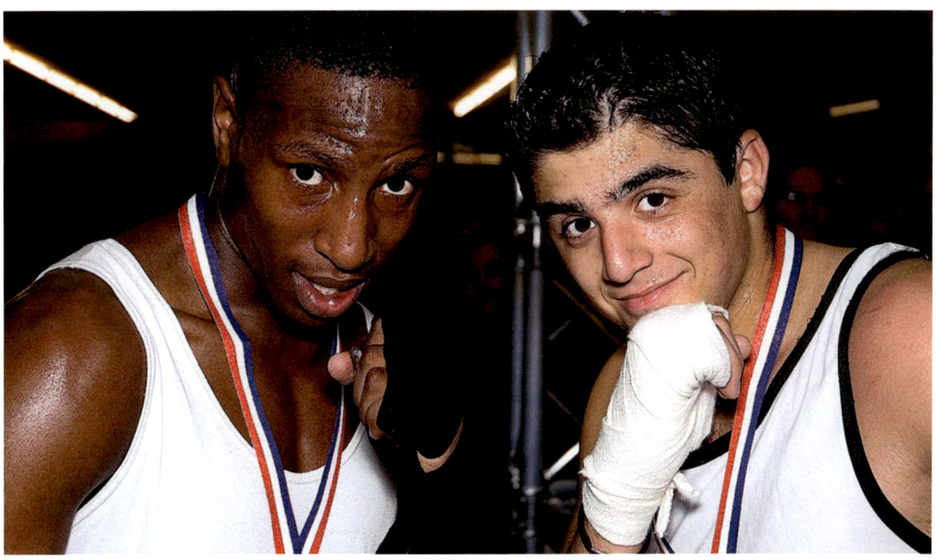

Body Dream (Mr. Regenta) El cuerpo soñado (Mr. Regenta)

Las Palmas de Gran Canaria, Spain / Las Palmas de Gran Canaria, España 2008 Performance

This work was developed for *Distrito Regenta*, an art project curated by Orlando Britto Jinorio that took place at the Centro de Arte La Regenta in Las Palmas de Gran Canaria, Spain. Vélez travelled on several occasions to Las Palmas where he took part in the everyday life of the body building gyms located there. Adopting the format of a body-building and fitness competition with male and female bodybuilders, a performance was created for the opening of the event. The extraordinary physiques of the body-builders, hairless and oiled, were paraded before an art audience more used to the sanguine poses of classical nudes rather than the hardened, striated classed and racialized bodies of the athletes.

This work expresses a concern that Vélez returns to in a number of his works: that athletic beauty is a matter of selecting codes, and that some of these codes have meanings that are already beginning to slip—as in other areas of aesthetics, such as the visual arts.

Esta performance fue creada para la apertura de la exhibición *Distrito Regenta*, bajo la comisaria de Orlando Britto Jinorio y se realizó en el Centro de Arte La Regenta en Las Palmas de Gran Canaria, España. La obra consistió en un concurso de fisicoculturismo aficionado en que participaron hombres y mujeres de distintas edades, en que también un grupo de gimnasia de mujeres de mediana edad presentó una coreografía con ritmos caribeños. Un jurado compuesto por un artista, un curador y un experto en fisicoculturismo escogió al "cuerpo soñado" que recibió el título de "Míster Regenta".

Para este proyecto, el artista viajó en varias ocasiones a Las Palmas en donde visitó los gimnasios de la isla y convivió con los fisicoculturistas. En este trabajo, Vélez toca uno de los temas recurrentes en su obra: la idea de la belleza en el arte como un asunto de selección de códigos de valores personales y formales relacionados con la cultura y el poder, idea que se debate cada vez más en el arte contemporáneo.

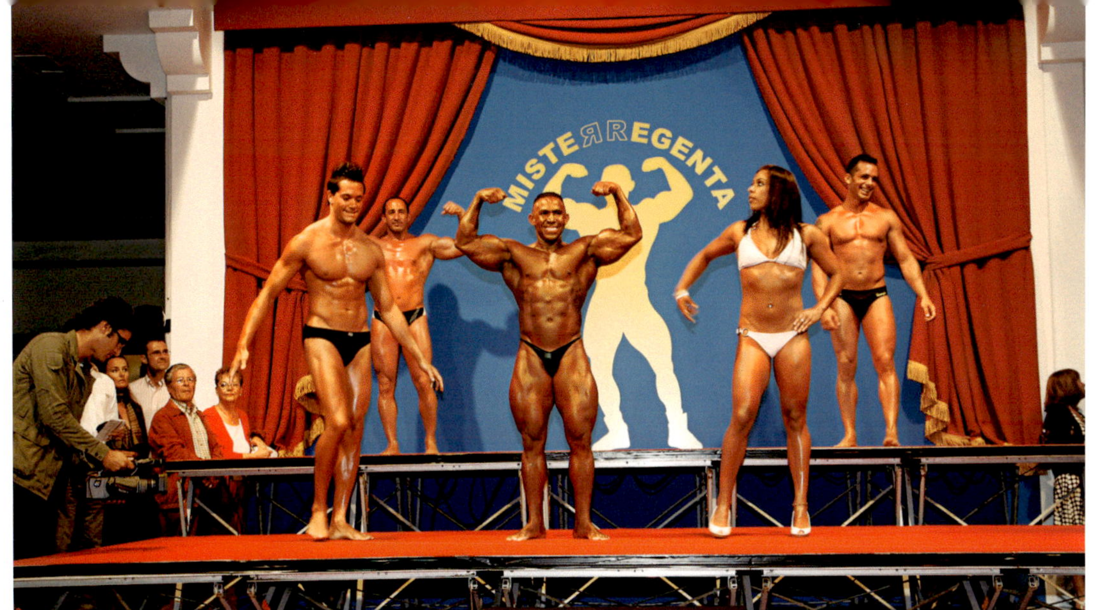

MISTERREGENTA

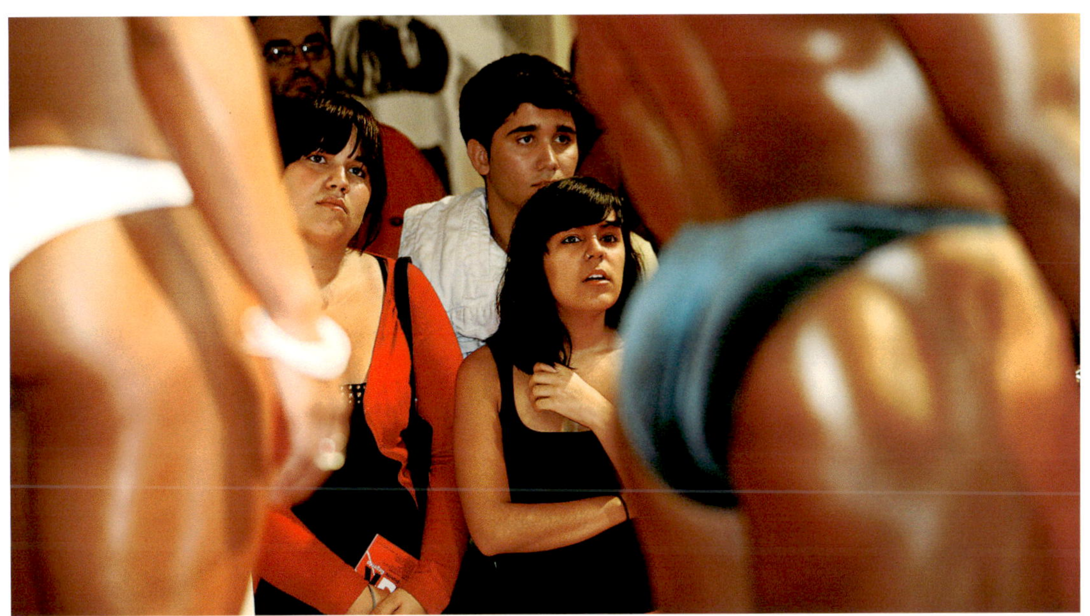

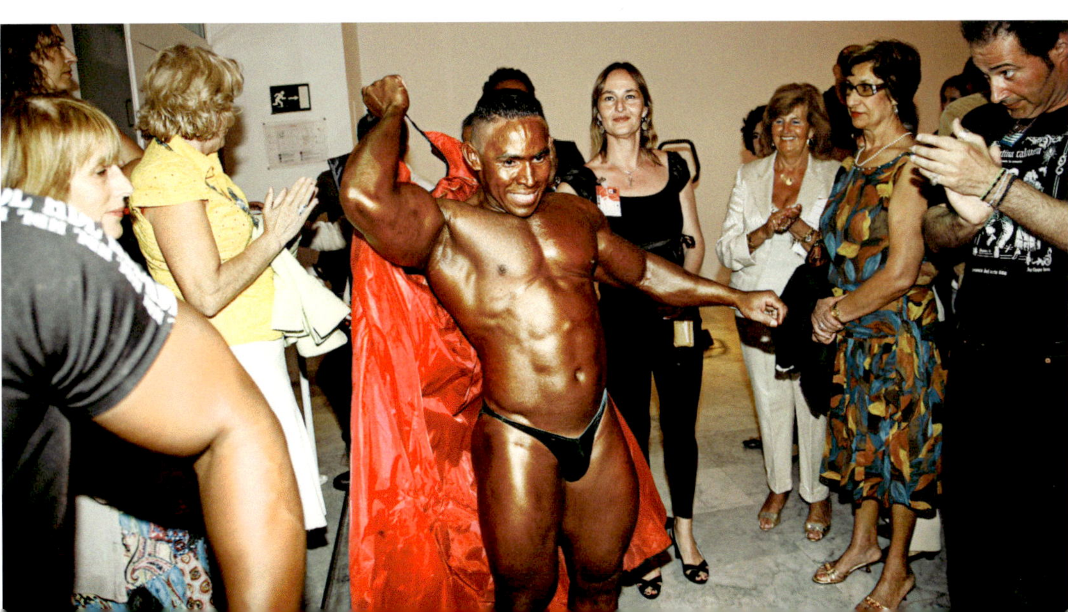

The Last Builder El último constructor

Panama City, Panama / Ciudad de Panamá, Panamá 2008
Super 8 transferred to video / Súper 8 transferido a video

The Last Builder is a black and white film by Humberto Vélez shot on super 8. It features Dionisio Herrera González, also known as José, a seventy year old bodybuilder from Cuba whom Vélez had developed a relationship with during the making of *Body Dream (Mr. Regenta)*. Here, Vélez was interested in getting back to the power and simplicity of the "pure" image, as in silent films, allowing the presence of the body's form and movement guide the emotional impact of the work and tell the story of this individual. Presented with a sense of romantic nostalgia, *The Last Builder* is an ode to the art of bodybuilding and to the history of cinema. Vélez collaborated with José on the choreography and developed the music with Nikola Kodjabashia. The film was edited by William Aldersley and was first presented at the 8th Panama Biennial.

The Last Builder es un corto en blanco y negro filmado en súper 8 con la participación de Dionisio Herrera González, también conocido como José, un fisicoculturista de setenta años al momento de la filmación, y fue presentado por primera vez en el VIII Bienal de Arte de Panamá que tenía como tema el Canal de Panamá. *The Last Builder* es una oda nostálgica al cine mudo y a los signos del paso del tiempo sobre el cuerpo. La música es del compositor macedonio Nikola Kodjabashia y la edición del mancuniano William Aldersley.

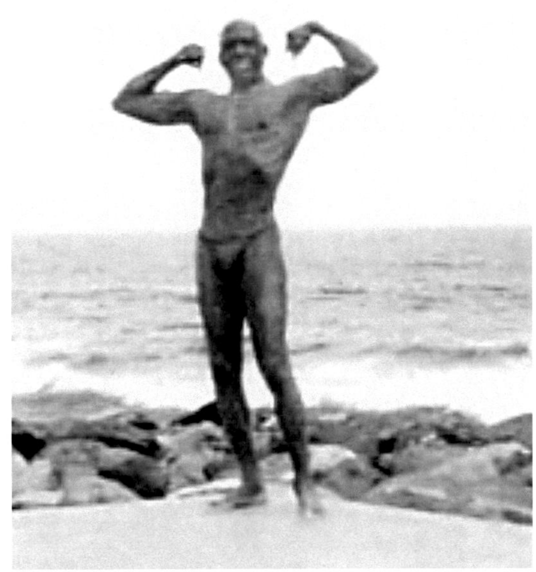
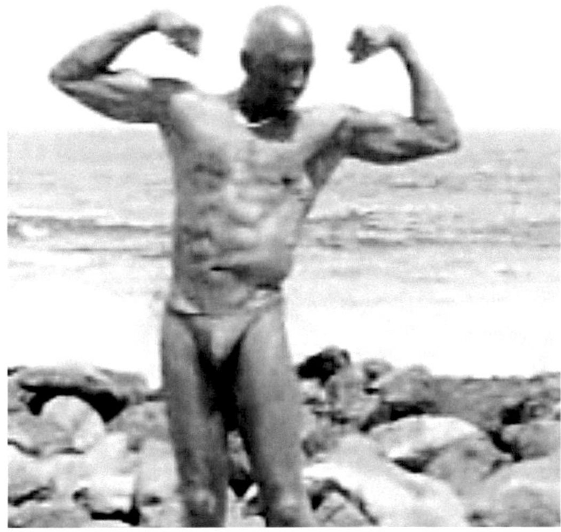
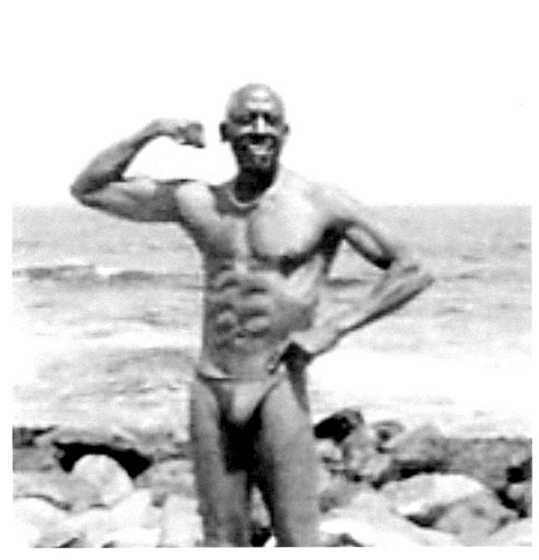
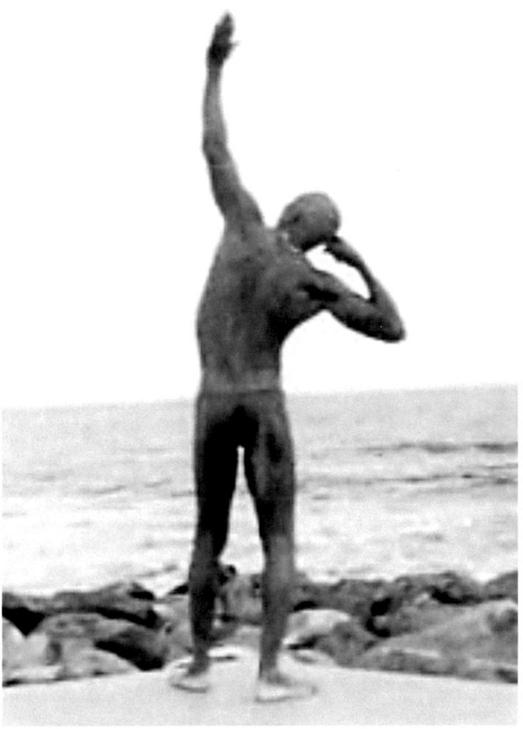

La más bella The Most Beautiful

Cuenca, Ecuador 2009 Performance

La más bella is a participatory artwork conceived for the X Cuenca Biennial together with two communities, one urban (Cristo del Consuelo, in Cuenca's periphery) and one indigenous (Ingapirca, an ancient Incan settlement). Set to the music of two live bands (a popular urban percussion band and an indigenous group playing wind instruments), a parade of llamas and alpacas, adorned in costumes and make-up, alongside women, children, and men from both communities, was to begin at the entrance of the Modern Art Museum, travel through the historic district, and continue on to the Inca ruins of Pumapungo. However, due to rain, the project became instead an improvised public act inside the museum.

When the rain settled, a parade took place around the museum and finished again inside where there was a "beauty" contest. A jury chose the "most beautiful" llama on the basis of the participants' aesthetic and cultural tastes. *La más bella* was curated by Adrienne Samos.

La más bella fue una performance creada para la X Bienal Internacional de Cuenca en colaboración con dos comunidades, una urbana, la del Cristo del Consuelo, en la periferia de Cuenca, y la otra indígena, de Ingapirca, un antiguo asentamiento inca.

La performance se había planeado como un desfile de llamas y alpacas a través del distrito histórico de la ciudad con las comunidades participantes, una banda urbana de viento y percusión, y otra indígena, con instrumentos tradicionales de viento, que terminaría en las ruinas incas de Pumapungo.

Sin embargo, debido a una intensa lluvia, el desfile se acortó y los participantes volvieron al Museo Municipal de Arte Moderno, donde comenzó el cortejo. Allí se realizó un "concurso de belleza" en que un jurado compuesto por artistas y curadores eligió a la llama "más bella" de acuerdo a los patrones estéticos y culturales de los participantes. *La más bella* estuvo bajo la comisaría de Adrienne Samos.

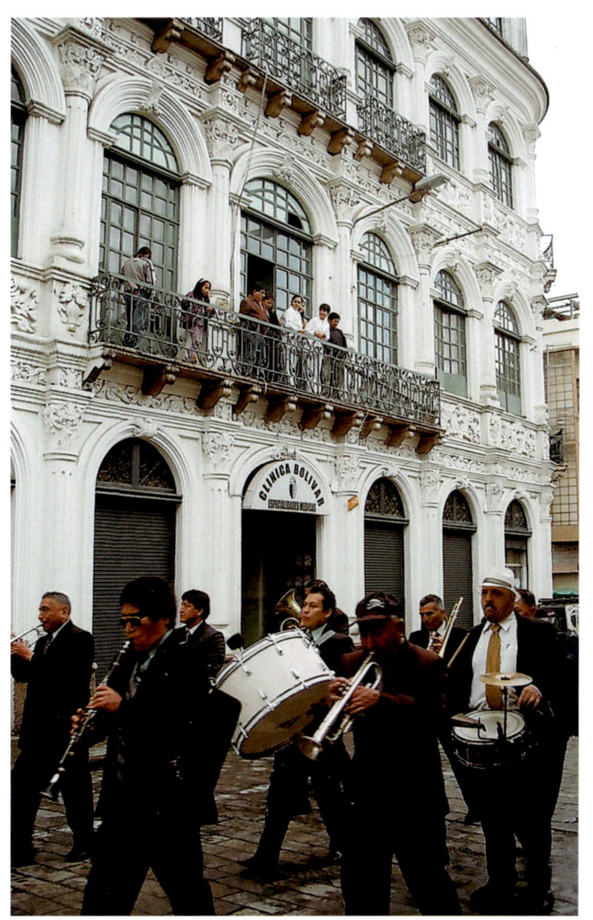

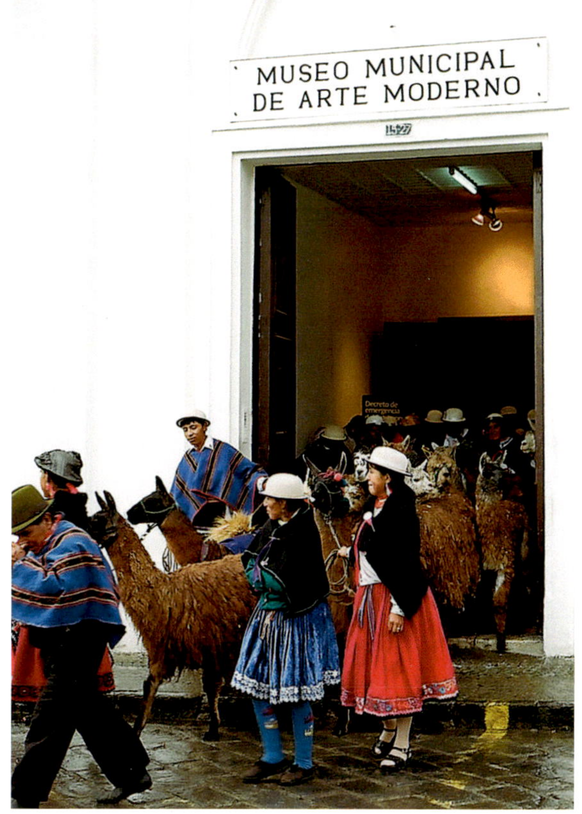

MUSEO MUNICIPAL
DE ARTE MODERNO

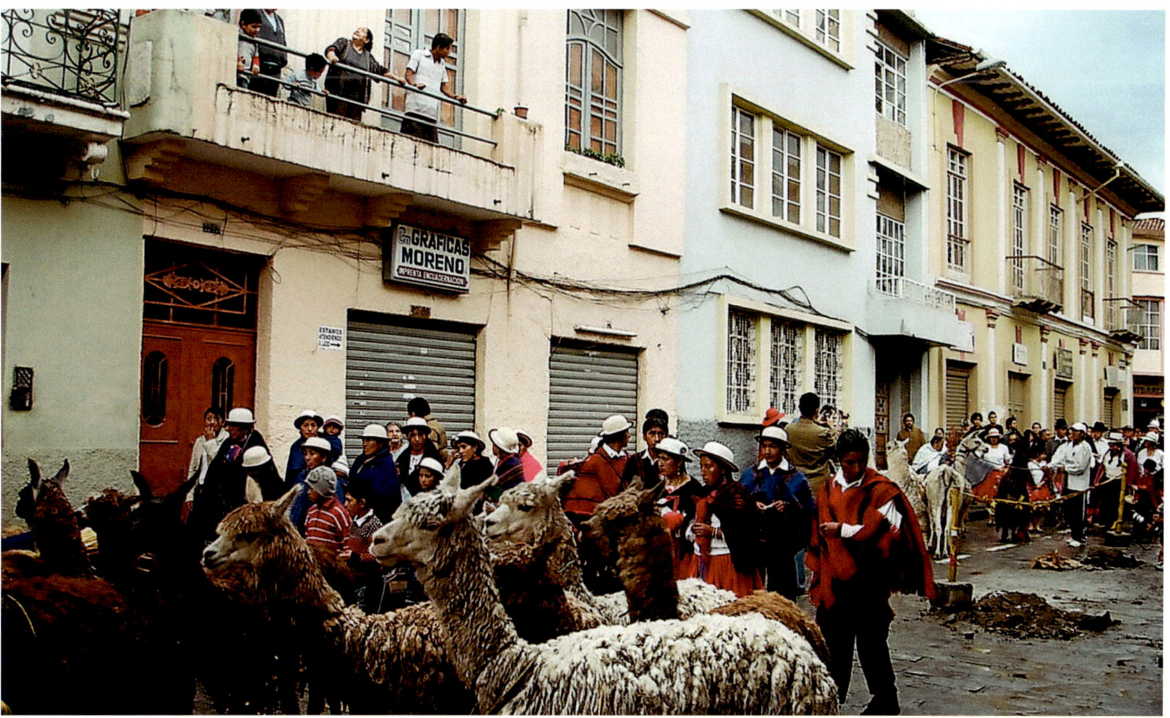

GRAFICAS
MORENO

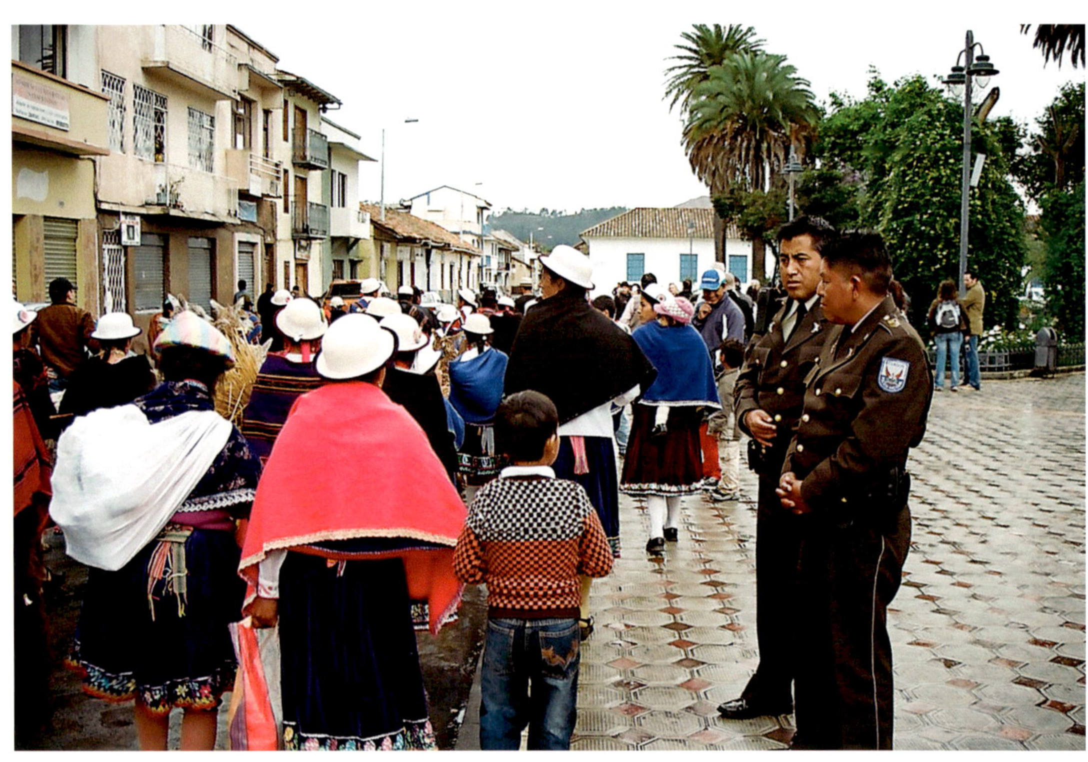

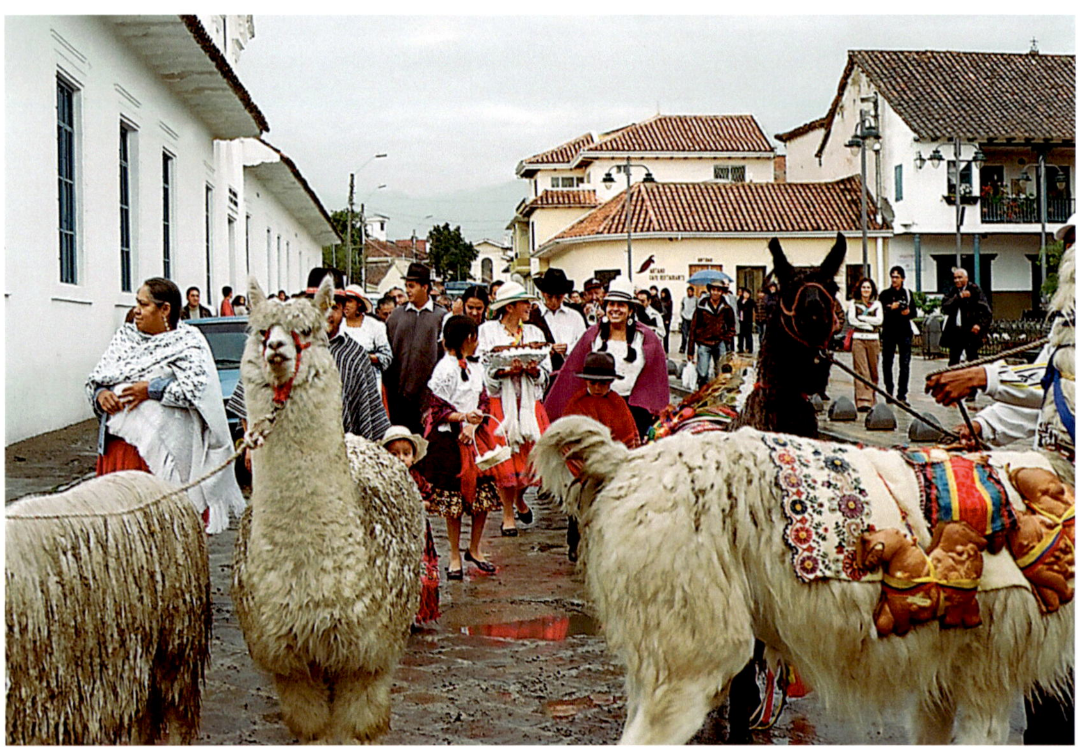

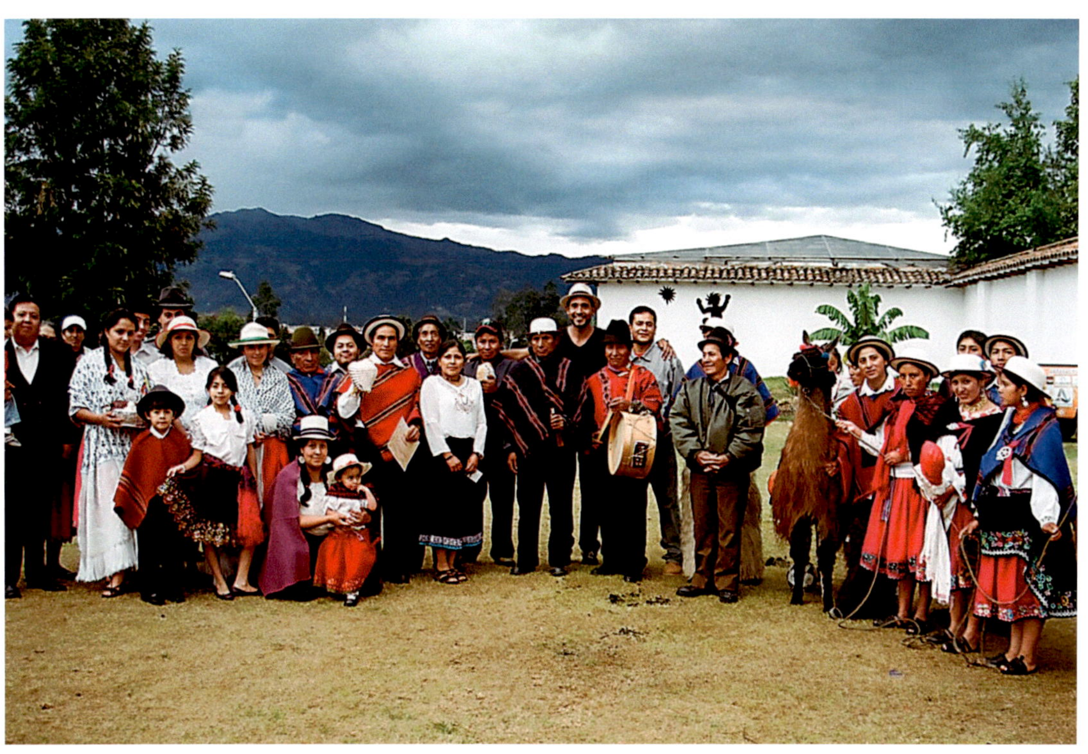

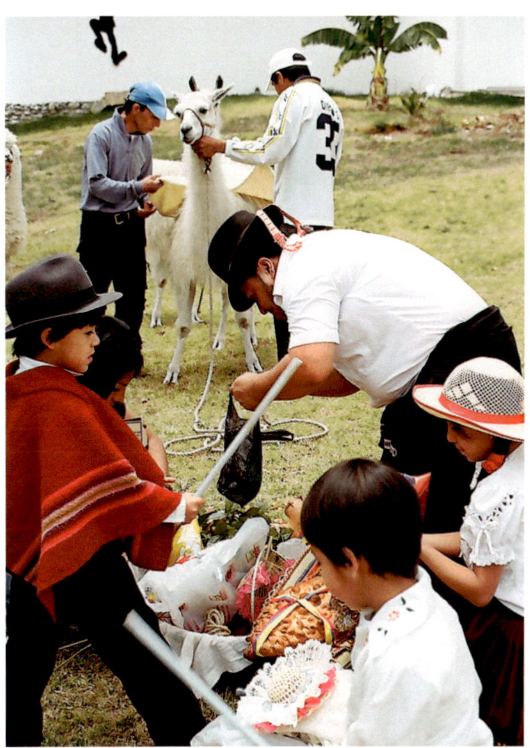

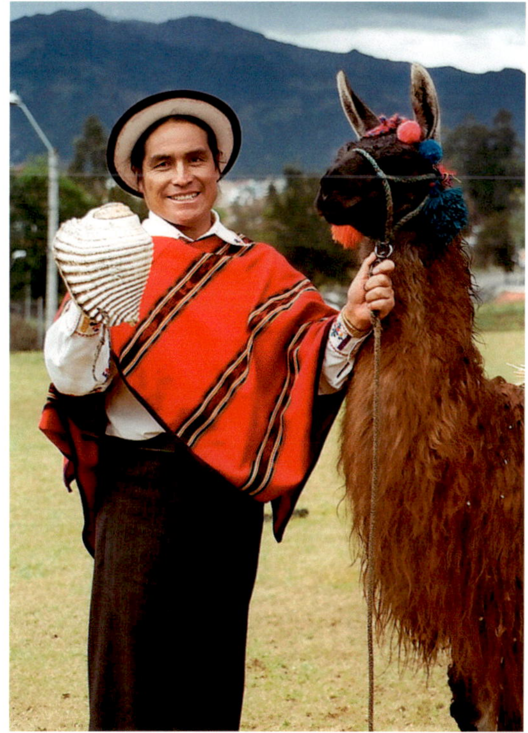

El Contrapunto (del arte) The Counterpoint (of Art)

Valparaíso, Chile 2010 Performance

Organized by curators José Roca, Jorge Díez, and Paulina Varas, *Välparaíso: in(ter)venciones* brought artists from Spain and Latin America to the Chilean port of Valparaíso as part of the *Congress of the Spanish Language* to produce works related to language, to words, and to meaning. Vélez had initially proposed *El contrapunto (del arte)*, a concert with popular poets and "payadores," a folkloric Latin American genre of improvisational songs often performed as a contrapuntal duet/duel of questions and answers.

The concert, planned for February 28 at the Old Stock Exchange of Valparaíso, was postponed due to the February 27 Chilean earthquake. The organizers, artists, and curators of *Välparaíso* decided to continue with their projects "as a way of integrating the arts to the recovery process after the tragedy." Thus, one week later, *El contrapunto (del arte)* was performed at the same location, but with no live audience. The concert was broadcast by Radio Valentín Letelier from Valparaíso on April 15, 2010, at 10 pm so that everyone in Chile could hear the concert.

Välparaíso: in(ter)venciones reunió a artistas de España y América Latina en el puerto chileno de Valparaíso para realizar obras relacionadas con el idioma castellano dentro del contexto de la ciudad. El evento era parte del V Congreso de la Lengua Española y contaba con la curaduría de José Roca, Jorge Díez y Paulina Varas.

Vélez propuso *El contrapunto (del arte)*, una performance en forma de concierto de *payas* (que es como se llama en Chile al género folclórico iberoamericano que es un duelo cantado de décimas improvisadas en base a un tema establecido) en la que trabajó con poetas populares y *payadores*. El concierto, previsto para el 28 de febrero en la antigua Bolsa de Valores de Valparaíso como parte de los eventos de apertura del congreso, se pospuso debido al terremoto del 27 de febrero.

Vélez y los artistas populares decidieron continuar con el proyecto "como una forma de integrar las artes al proceso de recuperación después de la tragedia." Una semana más tarde, *El contrapunto (del arte)* se realizó en el mismo lugar pensado pero sin público debido a las restricciones reinantes. El artista propuso utilizar la radio para compartir la obra con los habitantes de Valparaíso, todavía inmersos en la tragedia. El concierto fue transmitido por Radio Valentín Letelier el 15 de abril de 2010 a las 10 pm.

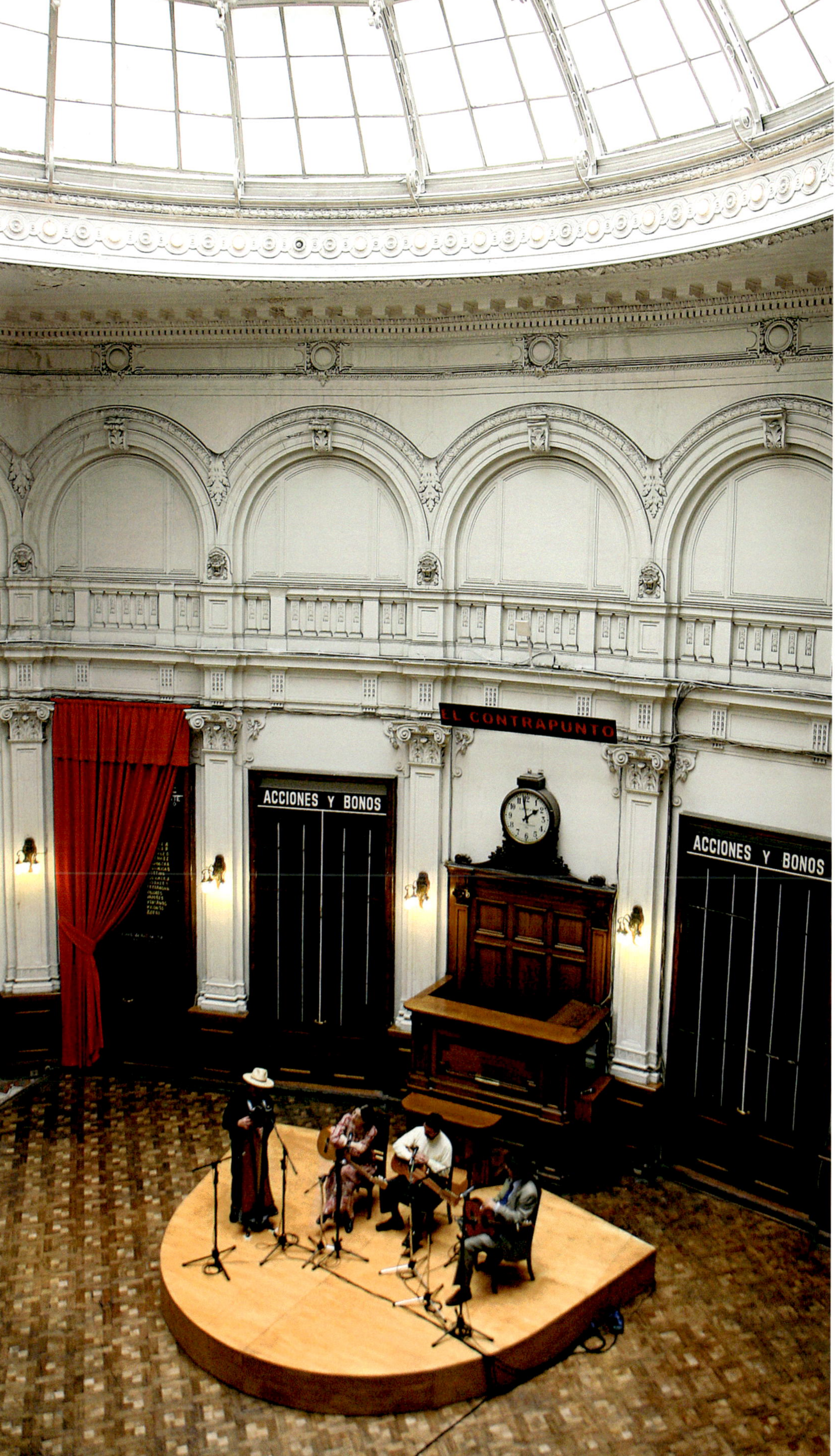
EL CONTRAPUNTO
ACCIONES Y BONOS
ACCIONES Y BONOS

Le plongeon The Dive, El clavado

Exploring the idea that art can leave the museum to be a part of the daily activities of youth, Vélez "plunged" the Centre Pompidou into the world of aquatics and hip hop, engaging with participants not generally part of the Pompidou's audience.

Curated by Mauricio Estrada-Muñoz, *Le plongeon* was an "aquatic cabaret" and musical performance at the *Piscine Joséphine Baker*, a swimming pool floating in the Seine. The pool was chosen purposefully by Vélez to make a historical connection with Baker's work in the defense of human rights, equality, and civic freedom through popular artistic forms such as the cabaret. A choreographic and narrative scenario that incorporated elements from contemporary dance, synchronized swimming, water polo, and free swimming was jointly written with the participants ensuring that the work expressed the position of the collaborators, not necessarily that of the museum. A specially commissioned soundtrack was produced by Mahdyar Aghajani that combined Iranian rhythms and hip hop, and included some of Baker's songs.

Le plongeon proposed a culture different than Parisian "high" culture and art world snobbery, one with roots in hip hop, poetry slams, and artistic movements that come from the body—swimming and urban dance—rather than the mind.

Con la idea de que el arte debe salir del museo y ser parte de la vida cotidiana de las personas, Vélez "sumergió" al Centro Pompidou en el mundo de la natación, la poesía urbana y el hip hop con una performance en la que participaron jóvenes deportistas y artistas de la escena *underground* de París, colectivos que tradicionalmente no visitan el Pompidou.

Le Plongeon fue una performance en forma de "cabaret acuático" con la curaduría de Mauricio Estrada-Muñoz y realizada en la *Piscine Joséphine Baker*, una piscina flotante en el Sena. La piscina funcionó como un inesperado escenario para las artes y como homenaje a la Baker, la artista negra de origen estadounidense, activista de los derechos civiles en los Estados Unidos, y una de las grandes representantes del canto popular en París.

Para *Le Plongeon* se diseñó una coreografía acuática con distintas modalidades como la natación sincronizada, el clavado, el nado libre y el wáter polo. Esta coreografía se combinó con declamaciones de artistas urbanos, bailes contemporáneos inspirados en la natación y música compuesta especialmente por Mahdyar Aghajani para el evento con ritmos iraníes y hip hop que incluían canciones de la Baker.

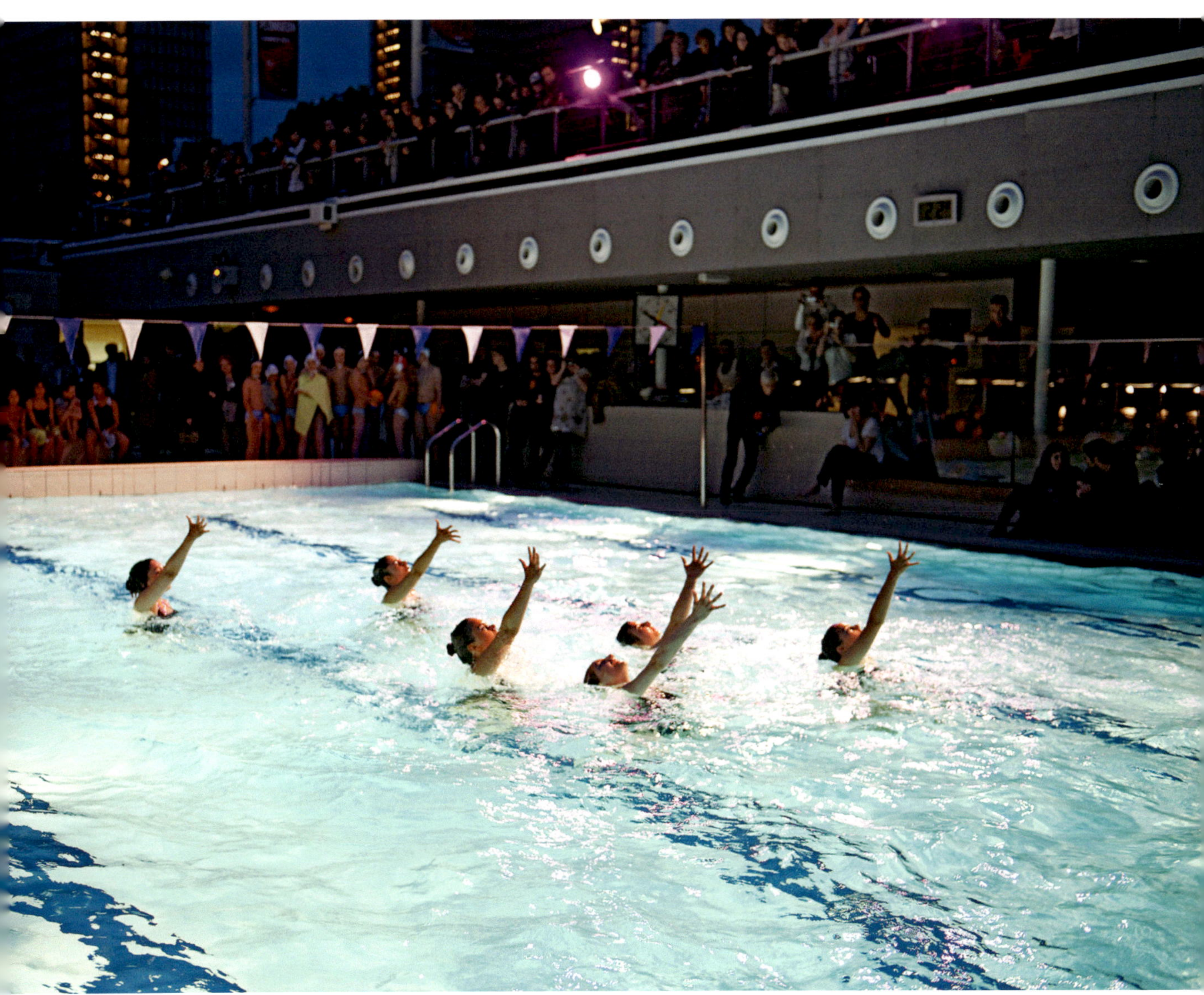

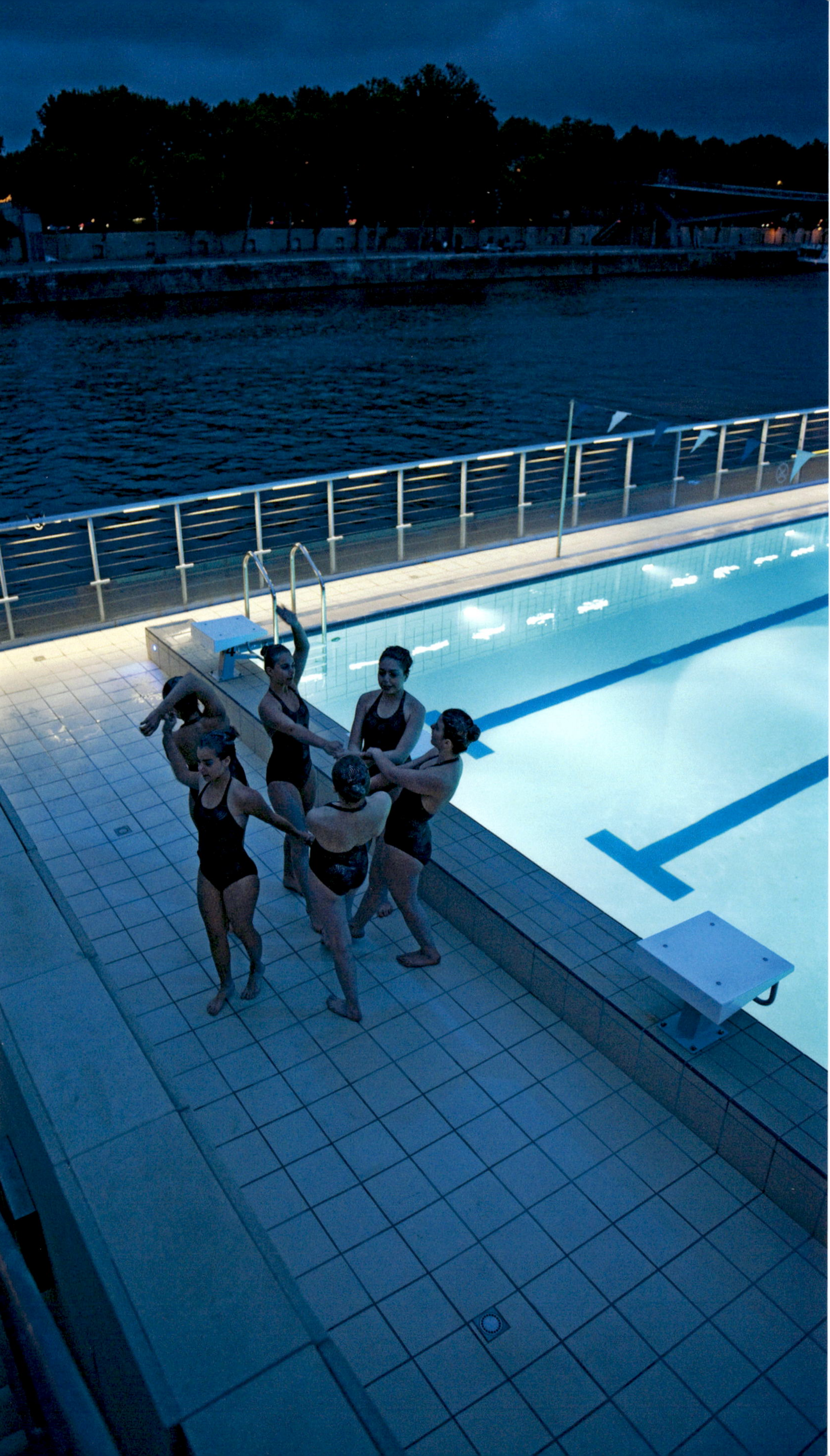

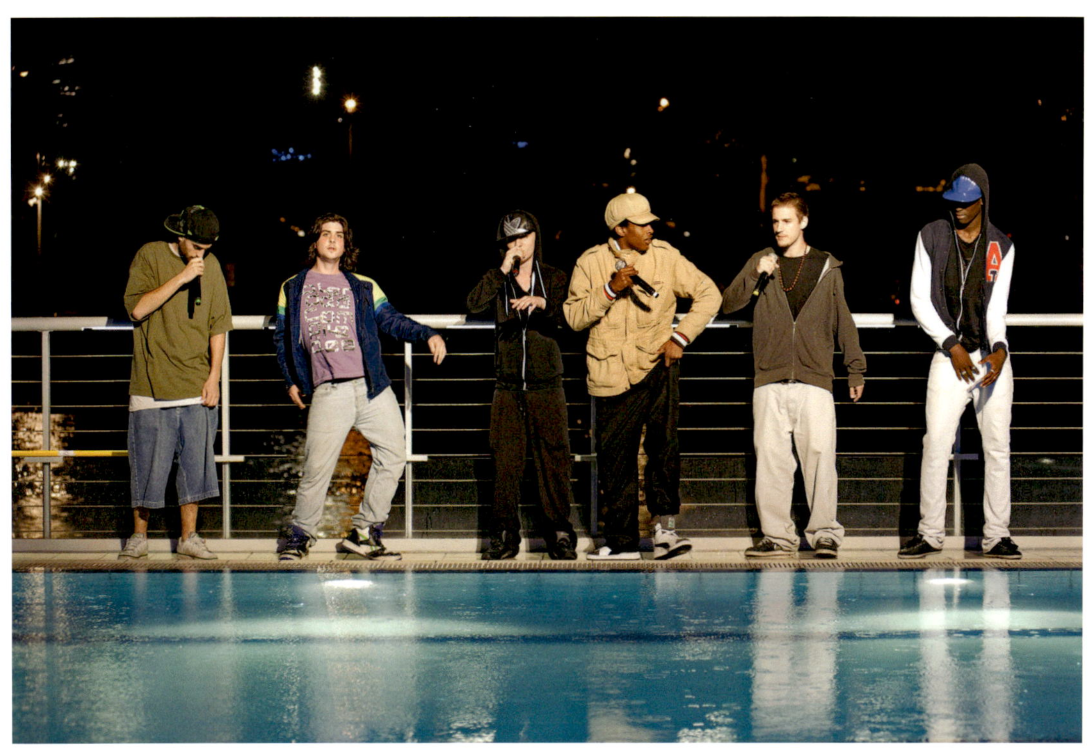

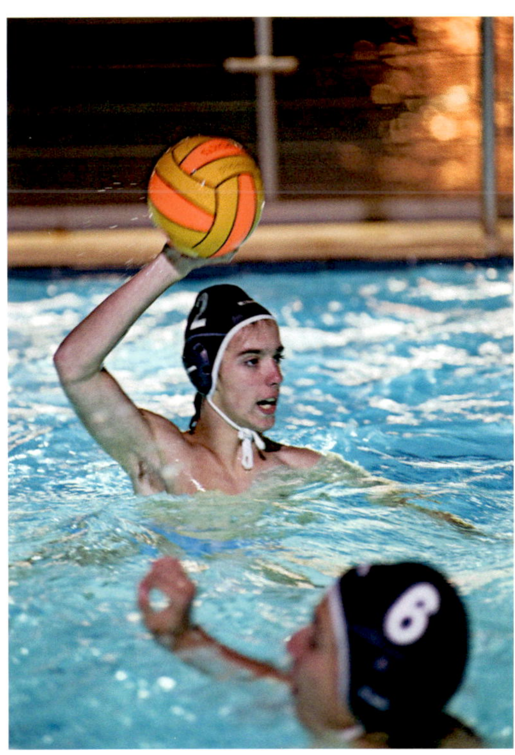

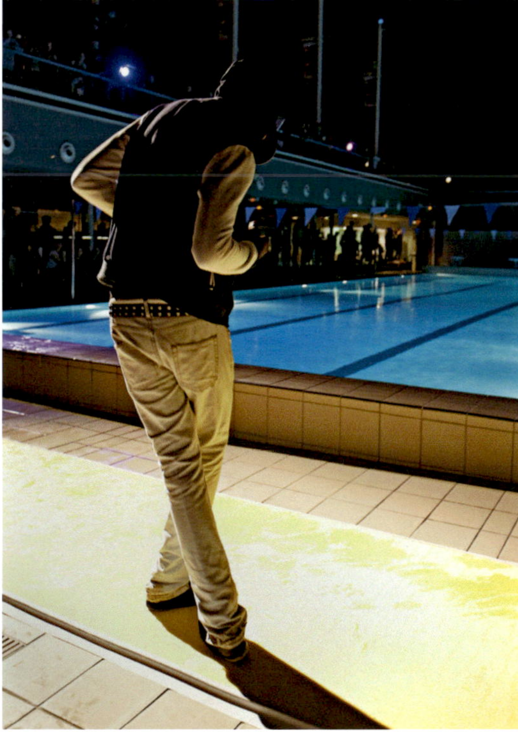

The Awakening / Giigozhkozimin El despertar

Toronto, Canada / Toronto, Canadá 2011 Performance

The Awakening /Giigozhkozimin took its cue from Métis leader Louis Riel's famous 1885 quotation, "My people will sleep for one hundred years, but when they awake, it will be the artists who give them their spirit back." Commissioned by the Art Gallery of York University (AGYU) and three years in the making through residencies in 2009, 2010, and 2011, *The Awakening* was the culmination of a sustained relationship between Humberto and the people of Toronto and surrounding area.

Curated by Emelie Chhangur, the performance brought together First Nations artists, musicians, and dancers (from the Greater Toronto Area and the Mississaugas of the New Credit First Nation), the Youth Councils from the Art Gallery of Ontario (AGO) and New Credit First Nation, the Tecumseh Collective First Nations Community Organization, and Toronto's Urban Runners (parkour) from the Monkey Vault Gym in a new "art ceremony" staged at the symbolic centre of Toronto's visual culture—the AGO's Walker Court.

The Awakening follows the strategies employed in Vélez's other New World performances by creating a cyclical return of the past into the present (i.e., Indigenous traditions), which are different from his "European/British" performances that often insert the "newcomer" (i.e., migrant, immigrant, asylum seeker) within the Old World's historical trajectory.

The Awakening fue una performance en forma de ceremonia artística inspirada en la famosa frase del líder métis Louis Riel de 1885: "Mi pueblo dormirá durante cien años, pero cuando despierte, serán los artistas quienes le devuelvan su espíritu."

Una producción de la *Art Gallery of York University* y bajo la curaduría de Emelie Chhangur, el proyecto tomó tres años para su realización a través de distintas residencias entre el 2009, 2010 y 2011, durante las cuales Vélez estableció y fortaleció una sólida relación de trabajo y entendimiento entre los colaboradores y la institución.

La performance reunió a distintos grupos y organizaciones de la provincia de Ontario, entre ellos los *Mississaugas of the New Credit First Nation*, el Consejo Juvenil de la *Art Gallery of Ontario*, el grupo artístico *Tecumseh Collective First Nations Community Organization*, y los acróbatas urbanos (parkour) del *Monkey Vault Gym.*

La "ceremonia" se realizó en el centro simbólico de la cultura (y el poder) artístico de Toronto, en el *Walker Court* de la *Art Gallery of Ontario*, como parte de la estrategia de Vélez de tomarse los espacios artísticos con grupos de personas que no son parte del mundo del arte.

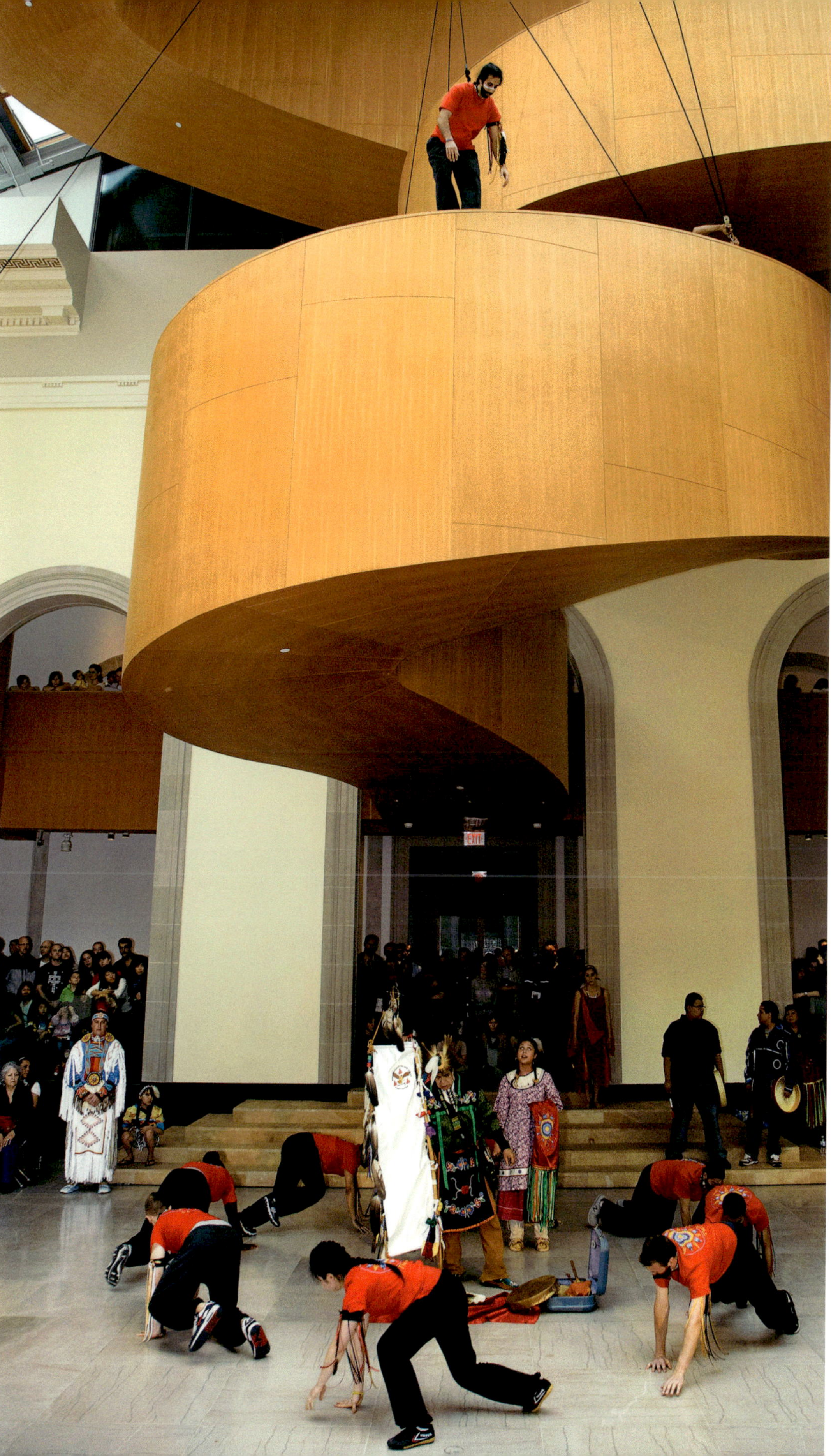

Me gusta creer que, quizás, este tipo de obra
le brindará nuevas posibilidades a los participantes,
que nos ayudará a todos a mejorar nuestra
presencia y nuestra capacidad de proyectarnos
en el mundo, porque está hecha especialmente
para las personas y los grupos con los que colaboro.
Eso es lo que ellos quieren, es lo que todos
queremos. Queremos visibilidad, queremos crear
entusiasmo y emoción alrededor de lo que
hacemos, y vernos a nosotros mismos más allá
de los límites que la sociedad nos impone.
Creemos que el trabajar juntos va a cambiar esta
actitud y forma de pensar. Es interesante para mí
como el arte puede realmente ayudar en esto.

Humberto Vélez (diciembre del 2009)

I think, maybe, the work is going to encourage people; it's going to improve our presence and our ability to project ourselves into the world, especially because of the individuals and groups with whom I've been working. That's what they want, what we all want. We want visibility, we want to create enthusiasm and excitement about what we do and to see ourselves beyond the limits society imposes on us. We think that's going to help attitudes change—working together. It's interesting to me how art can really help in this.

Humberto Vélez (December 2009)

El grano de arena

Humberto Vélez en conversación con Hans-Michael Herzog

El director de Daros Latinamerica conversó con Humberto Vélez en la Casa Daros de Río de Janeiro (que abrirá al público en 2013) sobre sus complejas performances colaborativas y la relación entre la educación y el cambio social en las artes. Río de Janeiro, 4 de julio de 2011.

Hans-Michael Herzog: ¿El arte tiene que servir para algo? Si es así, ¿para qué?

Humberto Vélez: El arte no sirve para nada. No tiene función directa, como en cambio sí la tienen la arquitectura o las leyes. Quizás esa falta de funcionalidad sea la condición más perturbadora para la sociedad, pues el arte se expresa libremente, sin el agobio de la utilidad ni la necesidad de certeza a la que están sujetas la academia y las ciencias. Sin embargo, esta libertad del arte está siendo socavada más y más por el mercado. Para el artista es casi siempre necesario vender para vivir o sobrevivir, pero la sumisión del mundo del arte al objeto diseñado y al precio del mercado está cambiando el concepto del arte. Cada vez se piensa menos en los valores estéticos y temáticos de la obra, y más en el circo mediático que puede producir. Si el arte sirve para algo, como tú preguntas, es para romper con la idea de lo establecido, de lo racional, para continuar esa eterna querella—como decía Apollinaire—entre el orden y la aventura.

Herzog: ¿Qué provecho sacan los colaboradores y los participantes de tus performances? ¿Estás seguro de que reciben algo a cambio de su participación? O quizás ocurre que, cuando nadie habla más del evento, ellos se sienten más solos y abandonados que antes, peor que nunca, porque por un momento y por poco tiempo estuvieron integrados al arte, pero ese vínculo termina con la obra.

Vélez: Para contestar esta pregunta es necesario que explique cómo desarrollo mis performances colaborativas. Después de recibir la propuesta de un museo, galería o la dirección de un evento, voy a investigar a la ciudad donde se realizará la obra. Por supuesto que tengo mis ideas, pero ello no significa que las llevo para imponerlas como un menú.

Una vez que llego al lugar, empiezo a conocer a su gente, pasear por los espacios más significativos y me reúno con los grupos o individuos que los organizadores quieren que conozca. De alguna u otra manera, trato de entender si tengo algo en común con este lugar y esas personas. Si no hay nada en común, pues no habrá proyecto, pero si encuentro un sentimiento e interés en común, existe la posibilidad de una obra. Hago una propuesta a los organizadores y fijamos una nueva vuelta para presentar la idea a los posibles colaboradores y participantes. Usualmente la idea que propongo se relaciona con un tema que a los participantes y a mí nos interesa; una idea o una acción personal, grupal, social, política, o todo a la vez. Un vínculo y una necesidad vital, social y expresiva que compartimos: ese es nuestro contrato de interés, nuestra alianza. Después de ponernos de acuerdo sobre la idea de la performance, empieza la etapa de desarrollo en que participan no sólo los grupos, sino también los que encargan y producen la obra. Yo escribo un guión inicial o "escaleta" (como se le llama en el cine), que estructura la base dramática y de acción, y que también servirá para la documentación. Durante el proceso, los colaboradores van agregando progresivamente su presencia y sus sellos personales y colectivos. Esta es una etapa muy difícil porque aparecen las enormes dificultades de lo que significa trabajar en grupo con instituciones y personas que no han realizado una obra de arte. Mi función no es sólo de mediador, sino de guía e instigador. Quizás aquí tenga que imponer algunas estrategias tomadas tanto de mi práctica como abogado, cuando trabajaba con grupos campesinos y sindicatos en Panamá, como de documentalista, que aprendí en la Escuela Internacional de Cine y TV de San Antonio de los Baños en Cuba. Algo que digo claramente a los participantes de la performance es que se trata de un proyecto único e irrepetible, y que yo, como artista, no puedo ofrecer continuidad. Juntos crearemos un momento, pero después cada uno deberá sacarle provecho a su manera.

Puedo pensar en mi obra como un proceso de aprendizaje, si entendemos el arte como la posibilidad de abrir la imaginación a nuevas formas de pensamiento y acción. En la obra todos aprendemos unos de otros. Yo advierto a las instituciones que después del proyecto los participantes volverán con nuevas ideas y propuestas. Este es un reto para las instituciones, acostumbradas como están a imponer sin escuchar al público. Por ejemplo, después de *The Fight* [La pelea], la performance que realicé en el Tate Modern con clubes de boxeo, y en la que nos tomamos el Turbine Hall, la Asociación Inglesa de Boxeo Aficionado, uno de los colaboradores del evento, solicitó presentar en el Tate eventos boxísticos.

Otro ejemplo del provecho que pueden sacar los participantes en estas obras es el de *La Banda de la Escuela Vocacional El Hogar* en Panamá, con quienes realicé mi primera performance. Esta es una banda multitudinaria de tambores, trompetas y fastuosas batuteras, integrada por gente de la clase trabajadora y mestizos, y famosa por sus desfiles en las fiestas de Independencia de Panamá. En una visita a Panamá (resido en el Reino Unido desde hace muchos años), me encontré por casualidad con el director de la banda y me dijo: "Aquí te dejo mi tarjeta. Ahora estamos en la televisión y en la radio, y hemos grabado varios CDs. También nos han invitado a tocar en Nueva York … todo esto desde que hicimos el proyecto. Hablemos para ver si volvemos a hacer algo juntos, *brother*, ¿okey?".

Herzog: Me disgusta la palabra educación y por eso creo que la podríamos sustituir por aprendizaje, o no usarla más. ¿Piensas que con todo lo que hiciste en tus performances alguien (los organizadores, los participantes, los grupos …) aprendió algo?

Para mí la educación significa transferir los valores de los viejos a los jóvenes; es un factor cultural. Los valores de la humanidad siguen siendo los mismos, pero el asunto es que la humanidad va a cambiar en los próximos cincuenta años, y también lo harán estos valores. Seguramente terminaremos como androides, o los verdaderos androides nos sustituirán en muchas de las actividades productivas e intelectuales. Los valores dejarán de ser lo que son ahora y en cien años nadie tendrá una discusión sobre la educación y el arte.

Vélez: Si entendemos por educación la oportunidad de tener nuevas perspectivas de pensamiento y de vida, entonces el arte es educación. "Instruir no es educar", decía César Quintero, uno de mis profesores más queridos de la Facultad de Derecho en Panamá. "Instruir es dar herramientas para sobrevivir. Educar, en cambio, es enseñar a pensar libremente". Creo importante que la obra de arte colaborativa ofrezca a los participantes algo a cambio. Por eso a veces desarrollo componentes "educativos" y ocupacionales en mis proyectos. Por ejemplo, en *The Welcoming* [La bienvenida], la performance que realicé para la Bienal de Liverpool del 2006, trabajé con adolescentes afganos que eran asilados políticos, y les ofrecimos talleres de video. De esta manera, ellos crearon un video que documentaba su versión de la performance y, al mismo tiempo, se acercaron a un nuevo oficio.

Herzog: ¿Dónde ves tu huella artística? ¿En los libros y publicaciones? ¿Por qué, para qué y para quién estás haciendo todo este enorme esfuerzo y trabajo que pones en tus performances?

Vélez: Durante mucho tiempo me dediqué exclusivamente a desarrollar mi idea de colaboración en el arte a través de la performance. Quizá fui ingenuo en dedicarme tanto a crear performances y no obras objetuales, pero estaba apasionado por el tema. Este año, la *Art Gallery of York University* (AGYU) en Toronto mostró una retrospectiva de mis performances con los filmes, fotos, estandartes y demás artefactos, lo que me dio la oportunidad de ver la unidad de la obra. Ahora que hablas de "la huella artística", me viene a la mente la metáfora de la montaña de arena que utiliza Luis Camnitzer cuando se refiere a la contribución cultural y al impacto del autor individual en la sociedad. Según Camnitzer, los artistas somos como "granitos de arena" y no influimos en la forma que toma la montaña. Lo máximo que podemos lograr, si hacemos un gran movimiento, es una pequeña avalancha en una pequeña zona, pero la montaña sigue igual; no cambiará mucho, a menos que todos los granitos se muevan simultáneamente. Mi huella artística es la documentación, la experiencia y la memoria de los participantes y del público que asisten a mis performances. Un granito efímero pero acompañado en esa gran montaña de arena.

Herzog: En lo que estuviste haciendo, ¿dónde ves la diferencia entre el arte y la obra social? En tu opinión, ¿cuál es el valor estético de tu obra?

Vélez: No me interesa hacer obra social. Ya hice trabajo social cuando era abogado en Panamá y cuando dirigía videos educativos, sociales y culturales para uno de los gobiernos locales en Barcelona. Me interesa crear momentos cargados de emoción y significado a partir del trabajo con ciertas personas y grupos que comparten intereses comunes. Hay cineastas que trabajan con temas políticos y sociales desde un punto de vista personal y artístico; yo trato de hacer lo mismo. Para mí, el valor estético de mi obra surge con la creación de este momento formal y emotivo, resultado de un intrincado proceso colaborativo que nace de las nuevas relaciones entre los participantes y de las posibilidades expresivas de sus estilos de vida y actividades.

He llamado *estética de la colaboración* a mi trabajo para diferenciarlo del *relational art*, del *engagement art* o del *participatory art*, que son en mi opinión maneras limitadas de trabajar con la gente, porque mantienen el sistema de autoría en que el artista sigue siendo el señor absoluto de la obra y el resto meros invitados. Algo más: es imposible hablar de este tipo de obras y no mencionar la ética. Muchos artistas, curadores e instituciones manipulan el concepto de ética y a la gente como parte de una agenda profesional o institucional. Arte, gente y ética forman parte integral de una discusión que no se puede seguir postergando.

At the Root:
Humberto Vélez and Panama

Adrienne Samos in conversation with Humberto Vélez

Adrienne Samos: You and I go back a long way. We began working together on countless projects soon after we met, in 1994. Therefore, I am well aware of Panama's significance for your art, and conversely, of how your work has influenced Panama's contemporary artistic practices.

It's been twenty-two years since you left Panama and yet you keep coming back. Sure, you miss Panama: the deep-set memories, the natural pull of family and friends. You also exhibit here occasionally, but there has to be more to it. You seem to be undertaking some kind of stubborn mission.

Humberto Vélez: Panama's people, culture, and idiosyncrasies are the reason I left and, ironically, the reason I keep coming back. Panama is at the core of much of what I do as an artist. My stubborn mission, as you call it, is to help create a widespread awareness of a specific vitality unique to this part of the world, one that needs to be liberated from heaps of apathy and conservative pretense.

In Panama, the lower urban classes have developed a peculiar attitude towards life that is worth reflecting upon in order to redefine it, strengthen it, and share it. It can be as much a strategy for seizing the moment as a tool for resistance and change. We should exploit it in more conscious and critical ways.

Samos: This vitality seems to be linked to a lightness of being, a spirited cunning, and a distinctive sense of humor that give way to an impulsive creativity. After all, Panama is almost a Caribbean island anchored in the mainland. But we're all sorts of other things too, of course.

More than thirty years ago, Roque Javier Laurenza wrote that "the damned geographic determinism and its transit zone, a fact that hangs over all Panamanian existence, has produced a human type that only has eyes for immediate and tangible things." Maybe it's our defense mechanism. Panama's size is inversely proportional to its global importance, so our tiny country has always been coveted and exploited by foreign powers.

Our condition is paradoxical, as are our ways of dealing with it. We have at all times been at the center of world trade and communication routes, and yet nonetheless isolated from our immediate neighbors.

Vélez: Detachment from our immediate neighbors worries me less than our attachment to the idea of the "American way of life." Panama still behaves like a colony. While the United States gave us back the canal and the Canal Zone at the turn of this century, we still have a colonized ideology. Our cultural identity seems so frail that the economic aspect overshadows all other values.

However, we are not and have never been either Colombian or Central American. That is very clear to us. I wholeheartedly agree that Panama is more like a Caribbean island. We have much more in common with both the English and Spanish speaking Antilles than we have with South or Central America.

We have a distinctive day-to-day extravagant behavior that is uniquely ours; a way of expressing and behaving ourselves that is impossible to put it into words. Only if and when we become aware that we are like no other people can we begin to be free. Free to be who we are, to invent our own world, both personally and collectively.

Samos: Artistic practice such as yours often aims to symbolically craft a free society, a sort of potential future community, or in Rancière's bold and beautiful words, a "monument to its expectation, a monument to its absence."

Vélez: Not only artists, but also many writers, thinkers, musicians, and cultural agitators are committed to opening new ways of seeing and feeling and acting. More than ten years ago, we came close to weaving a strong and creative community here in Panama around the cultural magazine *Talingo*.[1]

Samos: For more than a decade, *Talingo* served as a laboratory of ideas and as a showcase for all kinds of worldwide cultural production. Starting in 1994, you wrote for *Talingo* on contemporary art and cinema in a captivating narrative flow packed with erudition and critical insight, helping us—the makers and readers of *Talingo*—to weave the international with the regional and the local; to look at ourselves through diverse prisms, so to speak.

At the same time, you also began to influence artists through your novel practice and mentorship. Many of these young creators did not have a fine arts education, coming instead from high-tech digital professions: graphic design, computer engineering, film and photography….

Other newborn projects were injecting strong energy into contemporary art, such as the Panamanian and Central American biennials, and Virginia Pérez-Ratton's untiring curatorial work based in Costa Rica.

Vélez: Thanks to Virginia I had my first solo show, *Café Tropical*, at the Museum of Art and Contemporary Design in San José in 1996, when she was in charge of that institution.

Samos: A few months later, your installation, *El amor,* was exhibited in the Museum of Contemporary Art in Panama. And in March 2000, you occupied the entire museum with your solo show *Instalaciones* [Installations], which made a decisive impact on an emerging generation of Panamanian artists.

Vélez: Since we're focusing on the big highlights, let's not skip *ciudadMULTIPLEcity* in 2003.

Samos: That project was successful because it didn't land like a UFO. Gerardo Mosquera and I conceived *ciudadMULTIPLEcity* as part of an internal evolution that was already taking place in Panama. The event brought together artists from various countries so they could react to the city and conceive works that could reach people and, at the same time, constitute experimental examples of urban art.

Your performance, *La Banda de mi Hogar,* caused a commotion on several levels. Along with the members of the popular band, you generated amazement and wonder in the streets, and exposed a number of phenomena related to the idiosyncrasies of this city and its inhabitants.

Vélez: It was an excellent opportunity for me. *ciudadMULTIPLEcity* offered me the platform I needed to take the plunge into another kind of art: collaborative public performance.

Samos: Also, I think you delved deeper than ever before into our collective psyche, which informs so much of what you are and what you do. Tell me about your formative years.

Vélez: My maternal great-grandparents were farmers from the province of Chiriquí, and my grandparents emigrated to the capital thanks to the boom generated by World War II. My grandfather, a blacksmith, established his own workshop and upgraded the family to average Latin American lower-middle class status.

My parents, who divorced when I was seven, worked all the time so I was always cared for by my maternal grandparents. I liked seeing the sketches my grandfather made for his ironwork. I remember the gates, windows, beds, tables, and chairs—practically the whole house—were made of iron. My first desk was wrought iron. We still have my grandfather's anvil in our yard, as souvenir and relic.

I studied at *La Salle*, a Catholic school run by priests. I was very shy and kept to myself. I drew comics that my classmates read. I spent much time in the school library. I also saw a lot of television and read books, encyclopedias, and women's fashion magazines that published bestselling serialized novels. I devoured everything I could see or read. Everything.

My father gave me my first job as assistant in his small businesses. He had several kiosks in the city, including one at the racetrack, where I spent the weekends. I believe this experience helped me begin to understand and appreciate popular urban life. When one runs a kiosk near the racetrack or in Calidonia, one has plenty of time to see what happens on the street.

Samos: What about your college days? While studying, you worked as a radio drama heart-throb, right? Did you study broadcasting or did you just throw yourself into the ring?

Vélez: During college—thanks to my years as a theatrical actor and the help of my stepfather who worked for the RPC channel—I started working in radio dramas. It was a wonderful experience. I was 21 years old and the youngest of the actors in the studio, surrounded by the stars I had listened to since childhood. My first role was a victim of the werewolf: I was eaten in the second chapter. I gradually rose to become Solin, noble Kaliman's disreputable assistant. Had these soap operas not been canceled by the economic crisis that Noriega provoked, I would have eventually become the hero Kaliman! More importantly, I learned about the use of sound in narration, scriptwriting, and improvisation. We had to do at least five half-hour chapters in three hours.

Samos: Why did you study law?

Vélez: In Panama the closest thing to a literary profession was law.

Samos: Did you get involved in politics during your college days?

Vélez: Certainly. I even founded a political party, along with two friends: the *Victoriano Lorenzo Student Front*, also named *FE-15* because Victoriano was shot on May 15, 1903. He was the first true Latin American guerrilla fighter, executed as a scapegoat—and for discriminatory reasons. Our party was a means to participate in less dogmatic left-wing politics. There were very few members, but the party managed to survive six years.

Those were intense times for Panama, and for politically engaged youth. This period was marked by strong social protests against the United States' interventionism and against our military dictatorship.

Samos: Language is a key element in your work. Besides being an avid reader you were a poet. What type of poetry did you write back then?

Vélez: I wrote existentialist love poems, influenced by Paz, Bataille, Apollinaire, Schehadé, and my undying reverence for San Juan de la Cruz.

Samos: You decided to leave it all to study filmmaking abroad. Why?

Vélez: I knew I wanted to be an artist, but not a traditional one. My financial situation did not allow me to study abroad, so I had to earn a scholarship. *Escuela Internacional de Cine y TV de San Antonio de los Baño*s in Cuba enjoyed great prestige. I worshiped cinema and felt that learning its mechanisms could serve as expressive vehicles for my future work. So, when I won a scholarship, I didn't hesitate.

Film school helped me to become an international player. We were students from all over the world, all very different, so we had to learn to work together. Cinema is central to my way of practicing art, which is both authorial and collaborative, and involves particular ways of approaching people. In fact, my working method has more to do with documentary filmmaking than with visual and performance art. My work feeds on forces in tension that lead to a conflict. Conflict—which at a certain point is resolved in a climax—is essential to my performances.

Cuba taught me how to interpret contemporary art from a non-Western Caribbean context. It was fortunate for me that Cuba and Panama have many similarities, which made clear the need to make art in Panama, without counting on a rich art historical background such as Cuba's.

The result of my research within the Cuban experience was *Instalaciones.* All the pieces were the product of my reflections on Panama's culture rendered in contemporary media and language.

Samos: No one in Panama had made use of such an array of materials and techniques appropriated from popular, high-tech, traditional, *and* contemporary realms. You tran-scended your early interest in ritualizing social mores in order to explore the ways we relate to our corporal, psychic, and geographical territories. Your formal language underwent a radically reductive conversion in *Instalaciones* vis-à-vis earlier works. Your life abroad was obviously influential to your practice.

Vélez: True. But Cuba was the premier catalyst. Sometimes I feel closer to Cuban artists of my generation than to those of Panama or Central America. They also identify strongly with my work. It has to do with particular affinities: our similar approach to certain concepts, lifestyle, humor, fluency, conceptual rigor, and critical self-awareness, as well as a conscious differentiation from European contemporary expressions.

Samos: So, oddly enough, it's Panamanians' frustrating lack of rigor and self-awareness that keeps you coming back?

Vélez: In these barren times—without the network of activities and communication between artists that we enjoyed ten to fifteen years ago—our isolation and ignorance have increased alarmingly. My most recent scheme has been to launch *Visiting Minds*, an art and education forum that invites international personalities to visit Panama. As you know, Hans-Michael Herzog, my first guest, talked about the pivotal role of collecting Latin American art in daring and conscientious ways. My objective is to maintain a high-level dialogue on subjects of interest, which may motivate Panamanians to live in awareness.

NOTES

1. The Sunday cultural supplement *Talingo*, founded in 1993 by Samos and Alberto Gualde, was published in the Panamanian newspaper *La Prensa* until 2002. Talingo received the Prince Claus Award in 2001.

De raíz:
Humberto Vélez y Panamá

Adrienne Samos en conversación con Humberto Vélez

Adrienne Samos: Nos conocimos en 1994, y desde entonces hemos trabajado juntos en incontables proyectos. Estoy consciente de la importancia que tiene Panamá en tu arte y de cómo tu trabajo ha influido en las prácticas artísticas contemporáneas del país. Veintidós años han pasado desde que saliste de Panamá. Y, sin embargo, sigues regresando. Extrañas tu país, claro: te reclaman los recuerdos de infancia y juventud, la familia, los amigos…. También expones tu obra de vez en cuando. Pero hay más. Pareces emprender algún tipo de obstinada misión.

Humberto Vélez: Su gente, cultura e idiosincrasias son la razón por la que me fui, e irónicamente, la razón por la que regreso una y otra vez. Panamá es el eje de gran parte de lo que hago como artista. Mi obstinada misión, como tú la llamas, es ayudar a crear conciencia de cierta vitalidad propia de esta parte del mundo. Vitalidad que necesita liberarse de montones de apatía y pretensión conservadora.

En Panamá, la clase popular urbana ha desarrollado una peculiar actitud hacia la vida que merece la pena estudiar para redefinirla, fortalecerla y compartirla. Puede servirnos como estrategia para vivir el momento o como herramienta de resistencia y cambio. Habría que aprovecharla de manera más consciente y crítica.

Samos: Yo ligaría esa vitalidad a una condición de ligereza, de astucia traviesa y sentido peculiar del humor que dan paso a una creatividad impulsiva. Somos caribeños, a fin de cuentas. Panamá es casi una isla del Caribe anclada en tierra firme. Pero también somos muchas otras cosas, por supuesto.

Roque Javier Laurenza se lamentaba hace 30 años de que "el maldito determinismo geográfico y su zona de tránsito—hecho que gravita sobre toda la existencia panameña— ha producido este tipo humano que sólo tiene ojos para las cosas inmediatas y tangibles". Tal vez sea un mecanismo de defensa. El tamaño de Panamá es inversamente proporcional a su importancia mundial, por lo que potencias extranjeras sin cesar han codiciado y explotado nuestro pequeño país.

Nuestra condición es paradójica, así como nuestra forma de lidiar con ella. Hemos sido siempre un cruce de caminos y al mismo tiempo, nos hemos mantenido aislados de nuestros vecinos.

Vélez: Nuestro aislamiento me preocupa menos que nuestro apego a la idea del "American way of life". Panamá todavía se comporta como una colonia. Estados Unidos nos devolvió el canal y su Zona a fines de este siglo, pero aún mantenemos una ideología colonizada. Nuestra identidad es tan endeble que lo económico suplanta los demás valores.

Sin embargo, no somos y nunca hemos sido colombianos o centroamericanos. Eso sí lo tenemos muy claro. Estoy plenamente de acuerdo con que Panamá se puede comparar a una isla del Caribe. Tenemos mucho más en común con las Antillas de habla inglesa y española que con cualquier país continental.

Nuestra manera cotidiana de comportarnos y expresarnos es singular, extravagante e imposible de explicar en palabras. Sólo cuando entendamos que somos únicos, podremos empezar a ser libres. Libres de ser lo que somos, de inventar nuestro propio mundo personal y colectivo.

Samos: Prácticas artísticas como la tuya a menudo buscan la simbólica creación de una sociedad libre, una especie de comunidad potencial o, en las bellas y audaces palabras de Rancière, "un monumento a su esperanza, un monumento a su ausencia".

Vélez: No sólo artistas, sino también escritores, pensadores, músicos y agitadores culturales están lanzados a descubrir nuevas maneras de ver, sentir y actuar. Aquí en Panamá hace diez años estuvimos cerca de construir una sólida comunidad creativa en torno a la revista cultural *Talingo*.[1]

Samos: *Talingo* fue durante más de una década un laboratorio de ideas y una vitrina de lo que pasaba en nuestro entorno y más allá. Desde 1994 empezaste a escribir sobre arte contemporáneo y cine en reseñas que sobresalían por esa mezcla tan tuya de erudición, mirada crítica y chispa narrativa. Motivaste a quienes hacíamos y leíamos la revista a entretejer lo internacional, lo regional y lo local … a mirarnos más hacia adentro con distintos prismas, por así decirlo.

Ya desde inicios de los 90, también comenzaste a ejercer un impacto en artistas jóvenes, por el enfoque novedoso de tu arte y por tu voluntad de comunicarte con ellos. A todo esto, se sumaron otros proyectos claves, como las bienales de arte panameña y centroamericana, o la extraordinaria labor aglutinadora y divulgadora de Virginia Pérez-Ratton desde Costa Rica.

Vélez: Gracias a Virginia tuve mi primera exhibición individual, *Café Tropical*, en el Museo de Arte y Diseño Contemporáneo de San José en 1996, cuando ella dirigía esa institución.

Samos: Pocos meses después, exhibiste tu instalación *El amor* en el Museo de Arte Contemporáneo de Panamá. Y en marzo de 2000 ocupaste todo el museo con tu muestra individual *Instalaciones*, que ejerció una influencia decisiva en la generación emergente de artistas panameños.

Vélez: Si vamos a enfocarnos en los proyectos más destacados, el siguiente sería *ciudadMULTIPLEcity* en el 2003.

Samos: Ese proyecto fue exitoso porque no aterrizó cual ovni. El nuevo ambiente artístico en Panamá motivó a Gerardo Mosquera y a mí a concebir *ciudadMULTIPLEcity*. No buscamos presentar arte público en el sentido tradicional: artistas de varios países fueron convocados a crear obras que se relacionaran con la ciudad y su gente, y que a la vez fueran ejemplos innovadores de arte urbano.

Tu performance, *La Banda de mi Hogar*, causó conmoción en varios niveles. Junto con los miembros de la popular banda, generaste sorpresa y extrañeza entre el público de la calle, por una parte, y por otra pusiste al descubierto fenómenos relacionados con la idiosincrasia de esta ciudad y de sus habitantes.

Vélez: Esa fue la oportunidad de oro para lanzarme a hacer mi primera performance pública colaborativa, género que informa buena parte de mi obra en la última década. *ciudadMULTIPLEcity* me proporcionó el empujón y la plataforma que necesitaba para dar el salto.

Samos: Además, creo que te adentraste, como nunca antes, en aspectos clave de nuestra psique colectiva, la cual sustenta buena parte de lo que eres y lo que haces. Háblame de tus años de formación.

Vélez: Mis bisabuelos maternos eran campesinos de la provincia de Chiriquí y mis abuelos emigraron a la ciudad de Panamá con la bonanza que acarreó la II Guerra Mundial. Mi abuelo era herrero y tenía su propio taller, gracias al cual la familia ascendió a una clase media-baja latinoamericana.

Mis padres se divorciaron cuando yo tenía siete años. Siempre estuve al cuidado de mis abuelos maternos porque mis padres trabajan todo el tiempo. Me gustaba ver los diseños que dibujaba mi abuelo y que luego forjaba en hierro. Recuerdo de niño que teníamos las verjas, la cama, las mesas, las sillas, casi toda la casa hecha de hierro. Mi primer escritorio me lo hizo el abuelo a mi medida en hierro. Todavía conservamos el yunque del abuelo en el patio de la casa como recuerdo y reliquia.

Estudié en el colegio católico La Salle. Era muy tímido y me la pasaba dibujando cómics, que mis compañeros leían. Pasaba mucho tiempo en la biblioteca del colegio. Veía también muchísima televisión y mis lecturas no excluían enciclopedias y revistas como *Vanidades, Cosmopolitan* o *Buenhogar*, donde publicaban *bestsellers* por entrega. Devoraba todo lo que podía ver o leer. Todo.

Mi padre me dio mi primer trabajo como ayudante de sus negocios de venta de comida. Tenía varios kioscos en la ciudad, entre ellos uno en el hipódromo, donde pasaba los fines de semana. Creo que esta experiencia forzada me sirvió para empezar a apreciar la vida popular urbana. Cuando uno administra un kiosco en Calidonia o en el hipódromo uno tiene tiempo de sobra para ver lo que pasa en la calle.

Samos: ¿Y tu época universitaria? Mientras estudiabas trabajaste como locutor de radio y galán de radionovelas, ¿no es así? ¿Estudiaste para locutor o simplemente te lanzaste al ruedo?

Vélez: En la universidad—debido a mi experiencia en el teatro y con la ayuda de mi padrastro, que trabaja para el canal *RPC*—entré a trabajar en las radionovelas. Fue una experiencia maravillosa. Yo era el más joven, tenía 21 años y estaba rodeado de las estrellas que había escuchado desde niño. Mi primer papel fue de víctima del hombre lobo: me devoró en el segundo capítulo. Poco a poco fui ascendiendo hasta convertirme en Solín, el ayudante de dudosa reputación apegado a Kalimán, noble héroe. De no haberse cancelado las radionovelas por la crisis económica que originó Noriega, ¡hubiese llegado a ser Kalimán! Aprendí también sobre el uso del sonido en la narración, el guión, la actuación improvisada, y el trabajo rápido y preciso. Teníamos que hacer mínimo cinco capítulos, de media hora cada uno, en tres horas.

Samos: ¿Por qué estudiaste leyes?

Vélez: En Panamá lo más cercano a una profesión literaria era leyes.

Samos: ¿Te involucraste en la política durante tu época universitaria?

Vélez: Claro. Hasta llegué a hacer un partido político junto con dos amigos: el Frente Estudiantil Victoriano Lorenzo, o FE-15, por el 15 mayo de 1903, fecha en que fue fusilado. Victoriano fue el primer guerrillero de América Latina, y por supuesto lo ejecutaron como chivo expiatorio y por razones discriminatorias y clasistas. Para mí el partido representaba otra forma de hacer izquierda, menos programática. Éramos apenas cuatro gatos, pero nuestro partido llegó a sobrevivir seis años.

Fueron tiempos intensos para Panamá y para la juventud comprometida políticamente.

La época a finales de mis estudios universitarios estuvo marcada por el enfrentamiento con Estados Unidos y con la dictadura de Noriega.

Samos: Tus piezas trabajan el lenguaje como componente clave. Además de tu temprana afición por la lectura, fuiste poeta desde joven. ¿Qué tipo de poesía escribías?

Vélez: Poemas de amor, pero de corte existencial, influído por mis lecturas de Paz, Bataille, Apollinaire y Schehadé. Siempre he sido y seré el *fan* número uno de San Juan de la Cruz.

Samos: Lo dejaste todo por estudiar cine fuera del país. ¿Por qué?

Vélez: Sabía que quería ser artista, pero no uno tradicional. Por mi situación económica no podía salir a estudiar por mi cuenta. Tenía que ganarme una beca. La Escuela Internacional de Cine y TV de San Antonio de los Baños en Cuba gozaba de gran prestigio. Adoraba el cine y pensé que estudiar a fondo sus mecanismos me serviría como vehículo expresivo. Cuando gané la beca, ni lo dudé.

La escuela de cine me sirvió para internacionalizarme. Éramos estudiantes de todas partes del mundo, todos diferentes, así que teníamos que aprender, no sólo a tolerarnos sino a trabajar en conjunto. El cine fue fundamental para mi manera de practicar el arte, que es individual y grupal, e incorpora formas muy particulares de acercarse a la gente. De hecho, mi método de trabajo tiene que ver más con el género documental y los cineastas, que con los artistas de artes visuales y performáticas. Mi obra se alimenta de fuerzas en tensión que llevan a un conflicto. El conflicto, que se resuelve en un desenlace, es primordial para mis performances.

Cuba me enseñó una manera de interpretar las artes a partir del contexto caribeño, es decir, de un país no "occidental". Fue una suerte para mí que Cuba y Panamá tengan muchas similitudes porque me quedó clara la necesidad de hacer arte en Panamá; ahora bien, sin el trasfondo o los artistas que tiene Cuba.

El resultado de mi investigación a partir de la experiencia cubana fue la muestra individual *Instalaciones* en el 2000. Todas eran propuestas de arte contemporáneo a partir de mis reflexiones sobre la cultura de mi país.

Samos: Nadie en Panamá había hecho uso de una gama tan amplia de materiales y técnicas apropiados del ámbito popular y digital, la tradición y la contemporaneidad. Tu interés por ritualizar las costumbres sociales trascendió a la indagación en las formas como nos relacionamos con nuestros territorios corporales, psíquicos y geográficos. Tu lenguaje formal experimentó una radical conversión reductora en *Instalaciones*, fruto de tus experiencias en el exterior.

Vélez: Cierto. Pero Cuba fue el supremo catalizador. A veces me siento más cercano a los artistas cubanos de mi generación que a los de Panamá y América Central. Ellos también se sienten muy identificados con mi trabajo. Tiene que ver con afinidades como el acercamiento a ciertos conceptos, el estilo de vida, el humor, la soltura, el rigor conceptual, el autoconocimiento crítico y la diferenciación consciente de las expresiones europeas y las nuestras.

Samos: Pero, ¿justo esa falta de autoconocimiento y rigor te sigue motivando a regresar a Panamá?

Vélez: En esta época de las vacas flacas, sin la red de actividades y comunicación entre artistas que había hace diez y quince años atrás, nuestro aislamiento e ignorancia se han incrementado de manera alarmante. Mi estrategia más reciente ha sido lanzar *Visiting Minds*, un foro de carácter cultural y educativo. Como sabes, mi primer invitado fue Hans-Michael Herzog, quien habló sobre la importancia de coleccionar arte latinoamericano de forma audaz y responsable. El propósito es invitar a personas sobresalientes a Panamá para mantener vivo un diálogo de alto nivel sobre temas significativos, ayudando así a motivar a los panameños a vivir con mayor conciencia.

NOTAS

1. *Talingo*, el semanario cultural fundado en 1993 por Adrienne Samos y Alberto Gualde, se publicó en el diario panameño *La Prensa* hasta 2002. Talingo recibió el premio Príncipe Claus en 2001.

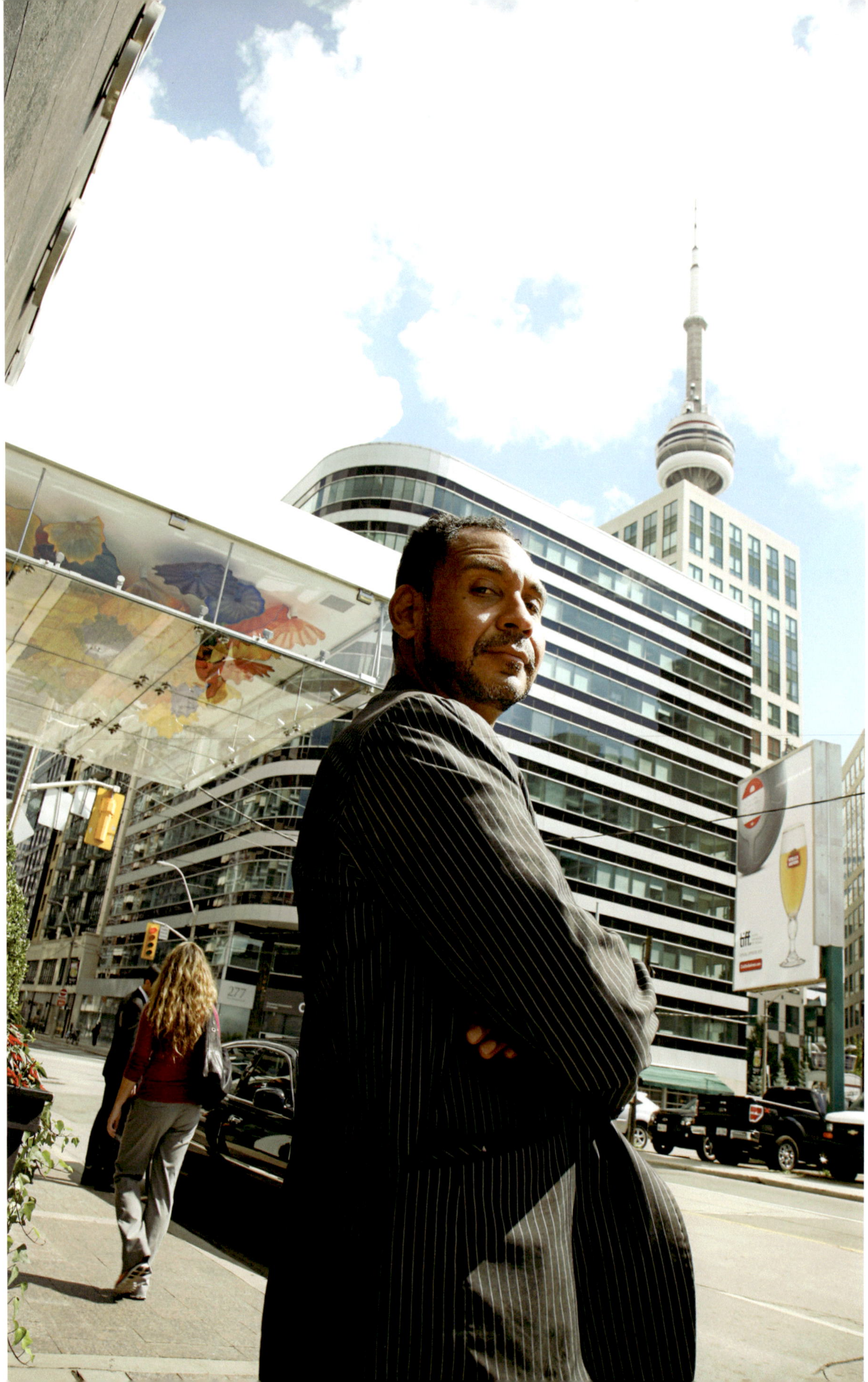

Building Bridges Not Dams: The (re) Awakening of the Canadian Spirit

Emelie Chhangur

Emelie Chhangur: Working on your Toronto project, for lack of a better word for it at the moment, there were obstacles… I mean, I think there's a complexity here in Toronto that's hard to penetrate. Perhaps Torontonians don't…well, they're not willing to commit to certain attitudes they have toward the city they live in, and perhaps they're not really that willing to look at themselves. I learned this through you being here 'cause I think, more and more, part of working with you is also learning about the place where I live. I look at Toronto a bit differently now because of this. But your initial ideas surrounding a performance in Toronto seem to allude to structures or things like…an orchestra, with many contributors all making different noises together, but which results in some kind of unified sound. Is this how you're thinking of Toronto, how you feel Torontonians relate or don't relate to each other?

Humberto Vélez: Well both, and a new thing: I move intuitively in the Toronto project. And my feeling is that I would like to create a project with some people from Toronto to initiate a kind of energy, and it's an energy coming from the people there, who are maybe invisible, young people, urban people, as well as First Nations artists; those people who come from a long tradition as Canadians—the First Canadians, no? And it's because I couldn't make total sense of the history of this Canada or Toronto. I'm not yet sure. I'm trying to draw from what I feel is powerful, or from what I feel I can build a narrative from, a focus, an energy— to create energy, you see. So my small contribution is to energize some places in Toronto through these people. To stop sometimes the flatness of the… yes, the energy, and concentrate people in some big emotions, through actions, and through giving a sense of history or symbolism. It's very basic, nothing more than that, so I think it's gonna be very simple, not simplistic, but a simple way of giving… a direction, a direction of how to feel the city. It's gonna be very sensual, I would say. I'm gonna work a little bit with shock, but not really in a shocking way, no?

Humberto Vélez in downtown Toronto, September 13, 2010.

Chhangur: Oh that shouldn't be too difficult! Canadians are known for their discretion!

[Laughter]

Vélez: Exactly… everybody naked!

Chhangur: Yeah! Everyone'd be like "ooh!"

Vélez: Ooh…. What's your number?

[Laughter]

Chhangur: They're all hiding behind the CN Tower… *almost* willing to expose themselves!

Vélez: Naked!… so maybe it's gonna be the tower, maybe it's gonna be that, what's it called? That big hotel near the tower, it's not that far…

Chhangur: um…well there's the Radisson… A hotel, you say?

Vélez: I think it's a hotel, yeah…. There's a train station as well.

Chhangur: Oh, right… the Royal York. That's across from Union Station, you're right.

Vélez: Exactly. So maybe it's gonna be a kind of energetic procession that could almost be aggressive, but it's not aggressive, it's just gonna impose situations, and it's going to disrupt, I want to disrupt Toronto as well. So that is the feeling of it. I think that…okay, I can tell you about all these meanings, and the context and all that, but I want it to be more an energy, through form, to talk about the *lack* of energy, possibly. So at the moment it's going in that direction. Let's see…and it's got to do with all these senses as well about the people not defining themselves, *never enough*.[1]

MAY 2012
OPENING THE CIRCLE

I am writing this a year after *The Awakening / Giigozhkozimin* performance took place, but it still *feels* like it was yesterday. Going back over all the various stages of the project's development, I found the above transcript almost by accident and it's uncanny to see there everything that manifested itself in those culminating sixty minutes of performance present from the very beginning. Only a *whole lot* happened in between.

Humberto's projects take time—a long time, in fact. Toronto's project took three years

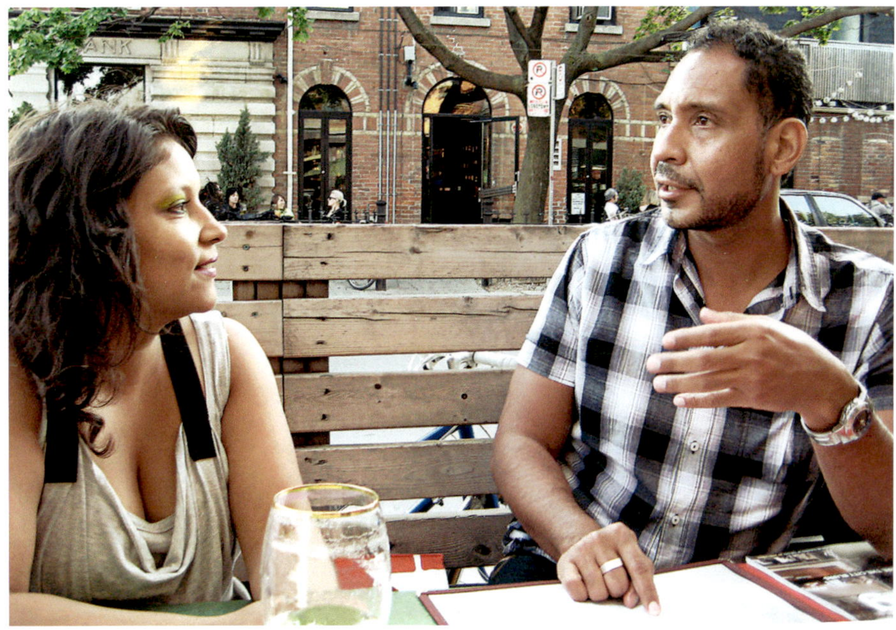

Emelie Chhangur and Humberto Vélez at their very first meeting in Toronto, August 23, 2009.

of preparation: yearly one-to-two month site visits by Humberto, with field trips, bus trips between Toronto and the Mississaugas of the New Credit First Nation Reserve, powwows and parkour meets, workshops and rehearsals—the list could go on. With Humberto's projects, there is always a tremendous lead up to what are comparatively short perform-ances. This disproportion, however, should not be viewed in terms of relative importance. Participatory process and final orchestrated performance are two different beasts, with different significances—the latter with an audience not privy to the former.

Humberto shaped all this into an emotional event, but emotions already were the shaping forces, even within the unspoken relations between people. So in the emotional awakening of writing this text, I must now find an equivalent form to Humberto's practice: to give shape to the story of *The Awakening / Giigozhkozimin*, itself a story about Canadians, from an insider perspective *and* as an objective observer. No easy task, but then I have learned by participating in *The Awakening*. And, in the end, through it, I learned about this place called Toronto.

Humberto's work always begins with people. People are what make the story of each place he works unique. In each of his projects, in every city he's worked, Humberto begins by finding something he can relate to through a common aspiration he shares with the people living there—whether long-time residents, newcomers, or refugees. That is, he first finds something based on his *own* personal story, a foundation for collaboration.

"There's got to be more to Toronto than just an accumulation of communities. You talk of peace and unity but these are also forms of repression. I want to tap into Canadians' voices and I want to know why you don't say anything about who you are!" So Humberto stated in a 2009 talk he gave in Toronto.[2] Toronto wasn't easy to access, let alone assess. In a city declared by the United Nations to be the most diverse in the world, Torontonians avoided

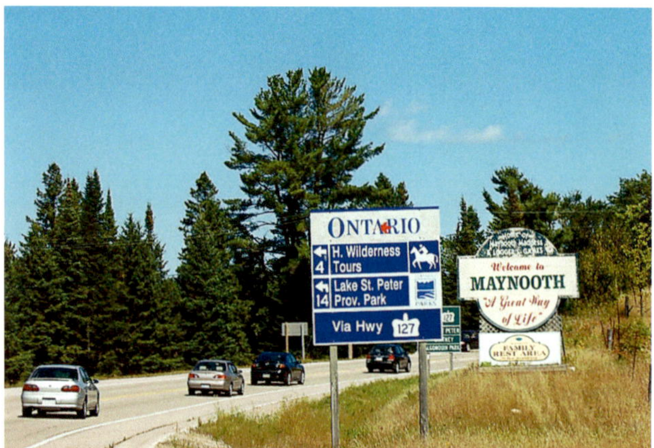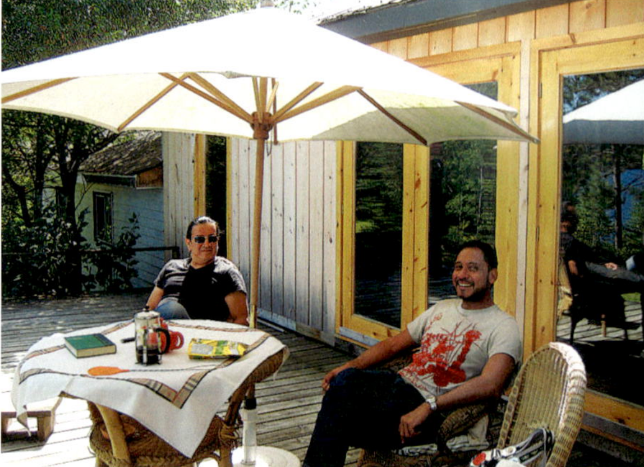

talking about First Nations. On his first site visit, Humberto didn't learn Toronto's story from what people said, or failed to say, but from what they didn't want to say. Moreover, they didn't know what to say because, perhaps, they didn't have the language with which to describe it.

No one could have anticipated that the process leading up to *The Awakening* would be the discovery, or rather *recovery*, of an Aboriginal voice. Or that, in Toronto, Humberto would find his methodologies reflected in Aboriginal ethics and principles. These ethics are based on an ever-expandable, all-inclusive circle premised on mutual dependency, partnership, respect, and fairness. For Humberto, and—as we learned in the process—for our First Nations friends who helped shape *The Awakening*, diversity is a non-racial concept.[3]

Humberto expands *his* circle by working with people who have divergent perspectives. He also works collaboratively with non-artists as a way to undermine authority and ownership, expanding the often-exclusionary circle of the art world. In the past he has connected boxers and dancers (*The Fight*, 2007), spoken word poets and swimmers (*Le Plongeon*, 2010), and he has brought together different groups of asylum seekers in projects that break through racial and class barriers (*The Welcoming*, 2006). This is not an easy undertaking as it involves real people, not just concepts. Bringing people together requires respectful negotiation—first, between the artist and individual members of the groups, then between the artist and the various groups and communities that have stakes in the project, and finally between the individual members themselves. It involves fair compromise and mutual trust. It requires an ethical pact where power is de-centralized. It necessitates finding ways of working together that benefit the individual as much as the group. Although it has been repressed, this *was* the story of Canada.

Perhaps these foundational principles could be re-awakened through our project. It would mean Aboriginals and non-Aboriginals would have to come together again. Together, we would seek our common past. Our common legacy of negotiation, compromise, and fairness would be a guide and, in turn, our project would be an example for future generations of Canadians. Indeed, *The Awakening* was a story destined for the future of Canada.

While Humberto found an avoidance of talk of First Nations in Toronto by the non-

Left to right: Nearing the end of our five hour "road trip" from Toronto to Bark Lake on September 11, 2009; Humberto and Philip Cote relaxing at Duke Redbird's cabin; Duke and Humberto taking in the beauty of Northern Ontario on Bark Lake; AGYU Director Philip Monk and Humberto settling in for a good night's rest.

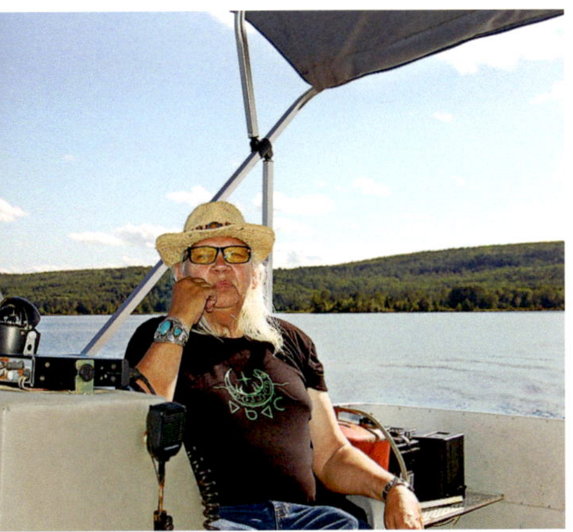 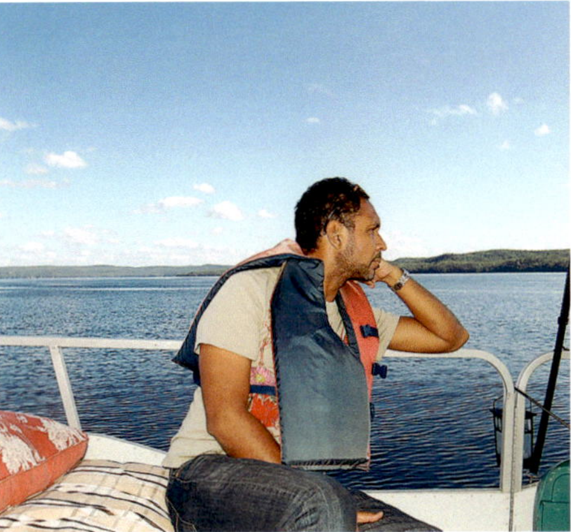 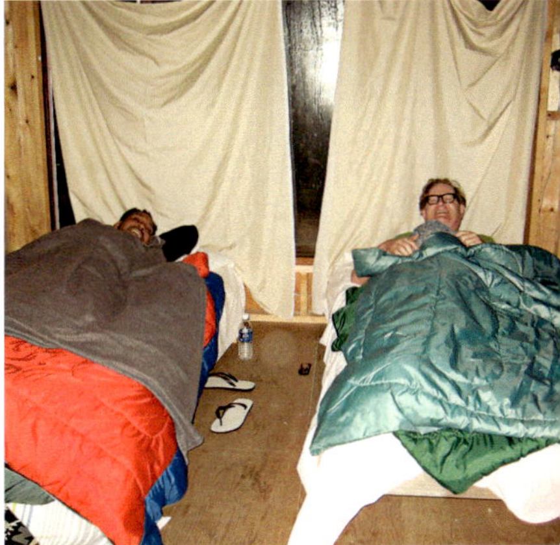

Aboriginal people he met there, Indians openly welcomed him in a pipe ceremony in Northern Ontario.[4] This *is* the Aboriginal way, after all. After we had met the Tecumseh Collective First Nations Community Organization, Toronto-based members and visual artists Philip Cote and Rebecca Baird took us on a road trip to Elder Duke Redbird's property on Bark Lake. There, in addition to the pipe ceremony, we spent a weekend together learning about Canada from a perspective entirely different from what the Canadians among us had been taught in school. Philip and Rebecca opened for us a window into their culture, the first of many over the course of our collaboration. This was a clearing of a methodological path that eventually came full circle to be *the heart* of the performance itself.

STOKING THE FIRE

Humberto found the identity—or spirit—for his project in Canada's Aboriginal history and he sourced its energy—or fire—in a group of young parkour artists from Toronto.[5] In both of these groups he discovered that while they are radically different, they both shared a common philosophy of tolerance and respect.

Parkour, too, are stereotyped and pigeonholed as a sub-culture in society, seen as vandals or hoodlums. But the reality of parkour is reflected in their commitment, training, and dedication to their particular lifestyle, and to athletics in general. This dedication and authenticity to their art is always overshadowed by "mainstream" and media misconceptions of who they are or what their innovative practice of "free running" stands for. For its part, parkour philosophy rather is of a creative physical engagement with the built environment, but without leaving a trace—so much like Aboriginal's respect for the land.

Humberto recognized a common ethos of tolerance and respect—one he also shared in various ways—in Canada's oldest culture *and* in a new generation of young Canadians from many different cultural backgrounds. Here was the energy he sought!

Before leaving Toronto in 2009, Humberto introduced the idea of working together—parkour and First Nations—on an art project for the Art Gallery of York University (AGYU).

Not having yet met, he told each about the other and of the possibility of bringing his new "Toronto friends" together through this project. It was an opportunity for *all* of them to show Torontonians who they *really* were. He was certain that each group wanted to get to know one another, and he proposed it as such. Feeding off each other's energy eventually would be the force that Humberto harnessed to shape *The Awakening*. Finding ways of bringing these "solitary" communities together to learn about, but also from, each other would be next year's challenge for "Toronto's project."

In Humberto's absence, the AGYU became the project's "fire keeper," so to speak. We kept the project's spirit alive by maintaining contact with, on the one hand, the Tecumseh Collective through Philip and Rebecca, and, on the other, the group of young parkour artists through Dan Iaboni, who owned and directed the Monkey Vault Parkour Gym where the group trained. Like all of Humberto's collaborators, the gallery had to find its "position" in relation to the project. Given the two groups Humberto had chosen to work with, this position obviously couldn't be too *institutional*. In Humberto's collaborative projects, *how* one chooses to participate in the group dynamic says a lot about the individual. In the case of the AGYU, our choices reflected the type of organization we wanted to be.

For Humberto, understanding the role an institution plays in the development of his projects is really about testing the institution's willingness to be open to new ideas. And to take risks. On the one hand, he does this by carefully observing the institution's social dynamic and professional role (both in relation to him and within the local cultural context); on the other hand, he observes how the institution frames his project in relation to its other programming. After a decade of creating participatory performances, Humberto knows that some aspects of his practice are institutionally valued over others. Most institutions want a slick performance…but not the messy process, nor the unpredictable outcomes. Many want Humberto to engage different audiences or demographics (to serve its education goals or mandate to "outreach" to "marginalized" communities), but don't themselves want to get too involved *with* "*those* people." Humberto, however, sees these implicit demands on him instead as ethical battles; he actively resists the institution's desires in order to support his collaborator's *needs*. Projects are guided by Humberto's vision and each project's internal logic—or impassioned drive—which also includes the long-term significance the performance will have for his collaborators—not by institutional interests. In Toronto, this would become doubly complicated. *The Awakening* would be staged at an entirely different institution—with a different set of interests and priorities—than the one that commissioned it.

AWAKENING MANITO (THE SPIRIT)

"My people will sleep for one hundred years, but when they awake, it will be the artists who give them their spirit back," Métis leader Louis Riel proclaimed in 1885, not long before he was executed for treason. Although barely visible amidst the other Aboriginal artifacts

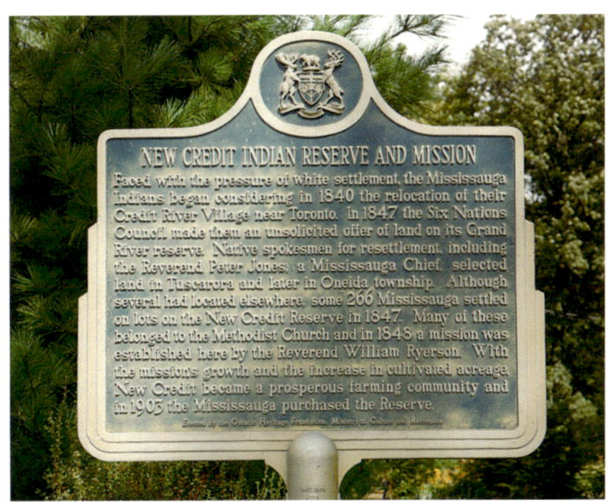

NEW CREDIT INDIAN RESERVE AND MISSION
Faced with the pressure of white settlement, the Mississauga Indians began considering in 1840 the relocation of their Credit River Village near Toronto. In 1847 the Six Nations Council made them an unsolicited offer of land on its Grand River reserve. Native spokesmen for resettlement, including the Reverend Peter Jones, a Mississauga Chief, selected land in Tuscarora and later in Oneida township. Although several had located elsewhere, some 266 Mississauga settled on lots on the New Credit Reserve in 1847. Many of these belonged to the Methodist Church and in 1848 a mission was established here by the Reverend William Ryerson. With the mission's growth and the increase in cultivated acreage, New Credit became a prosperous farming community and in 1903 the Mississauga purchased the Reserve.
Erected by the Ontario Heritage Foundation, Ministry of Culture and Recreation

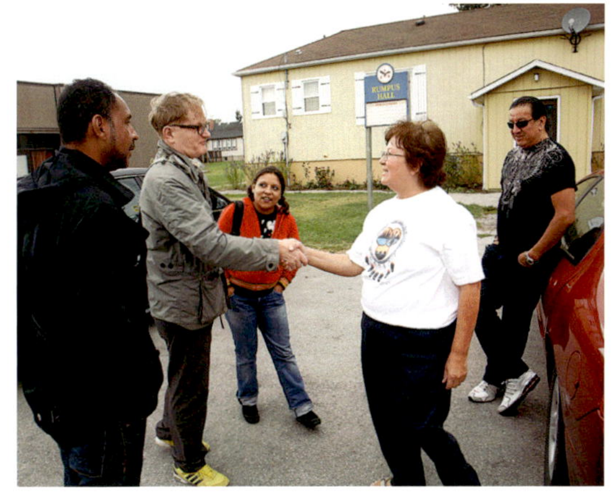

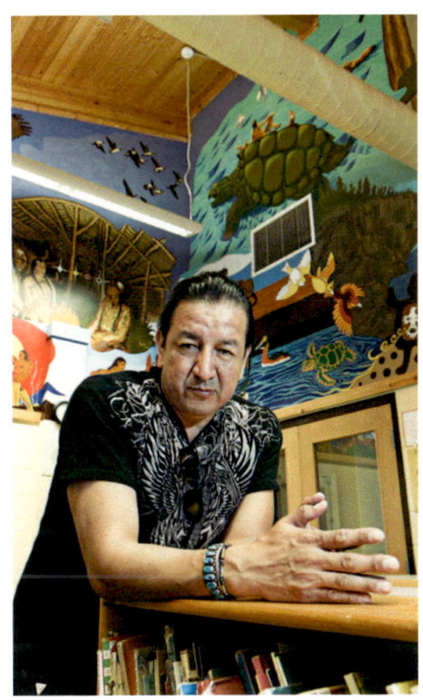

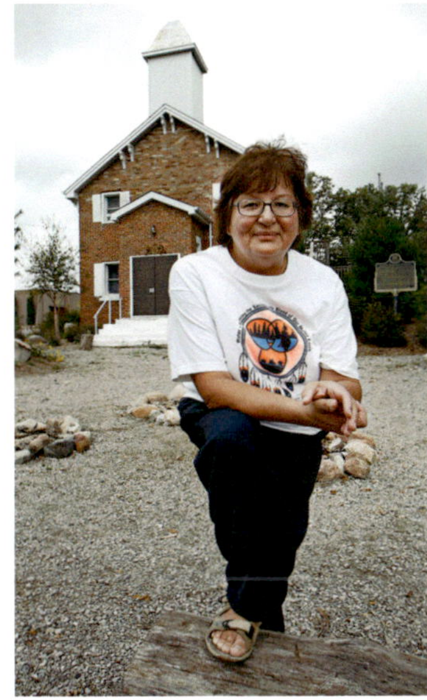

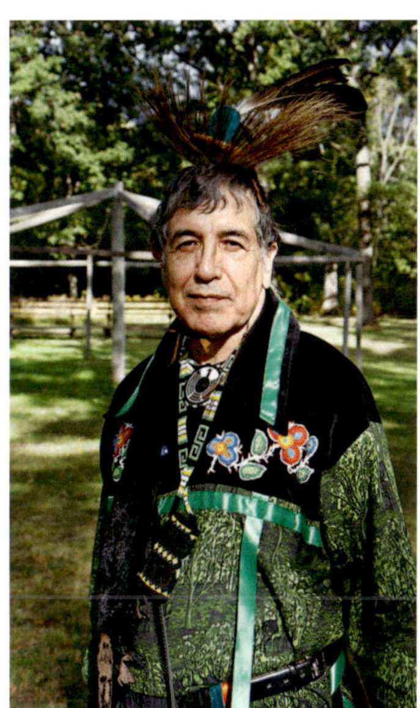

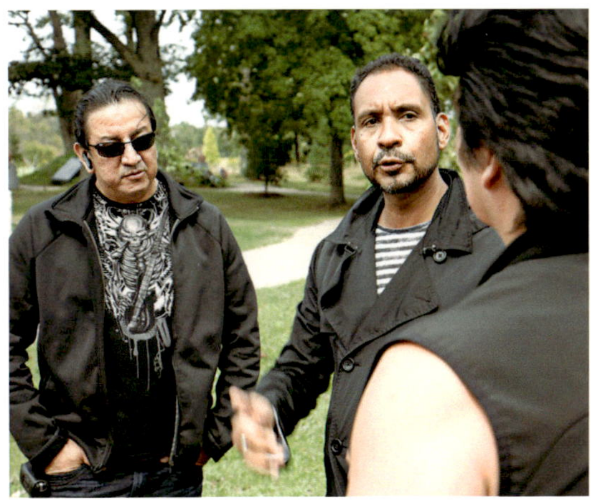

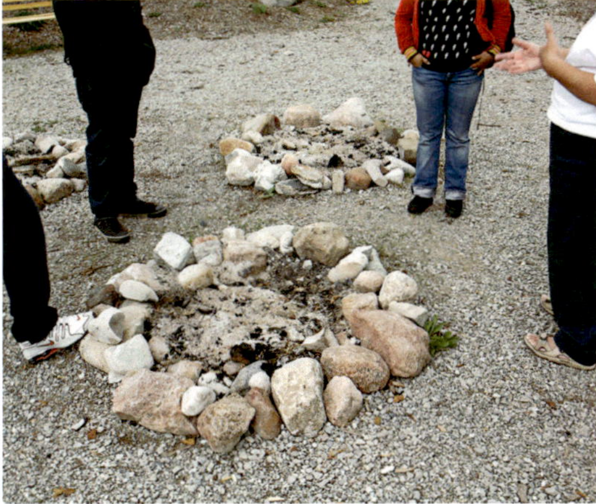

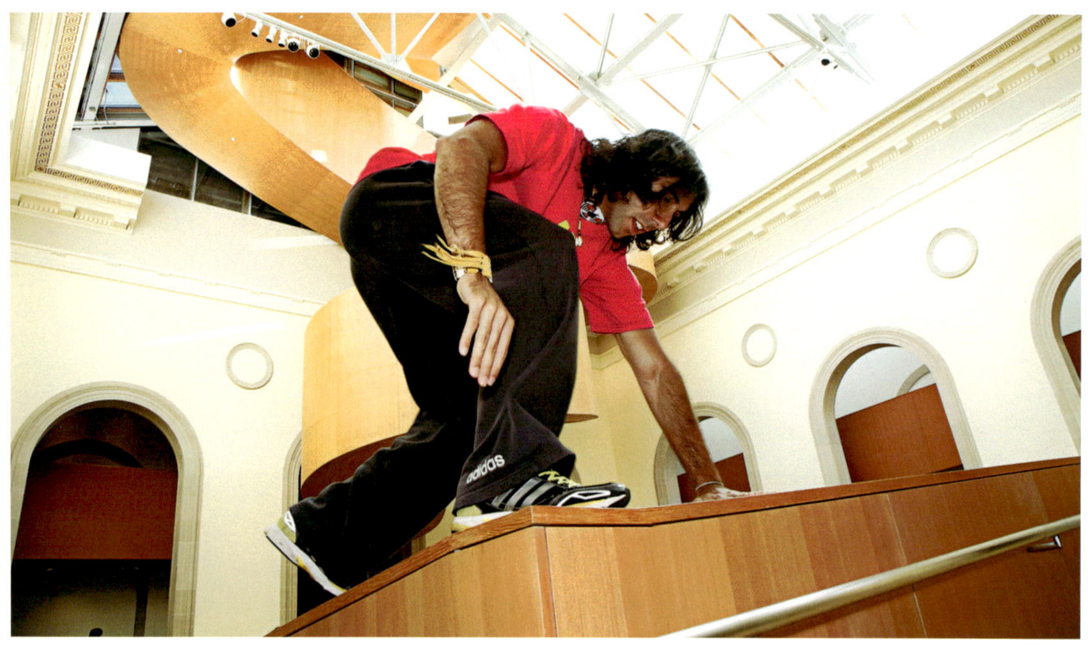

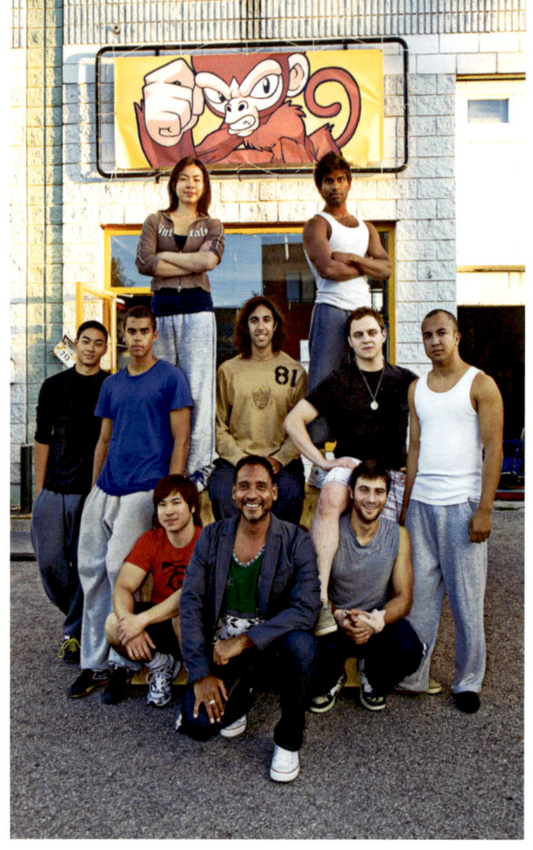

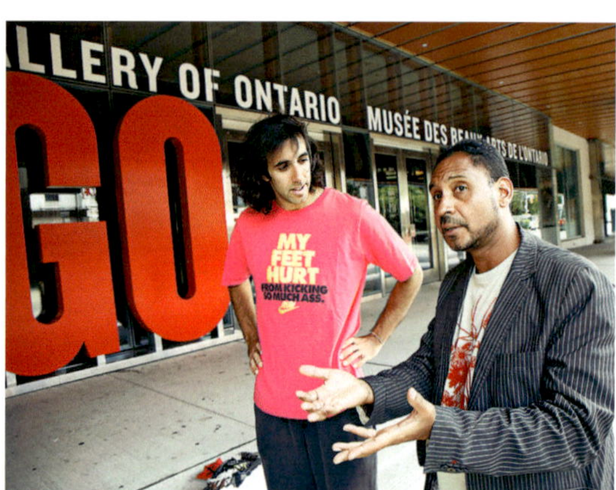

LLERY OF ONTARIO   MUSÉE DES BEAUX-ARTS DE L'ONTARIO
GO
MY FEET HURT
FROM KICKING SO MUCH ASS.

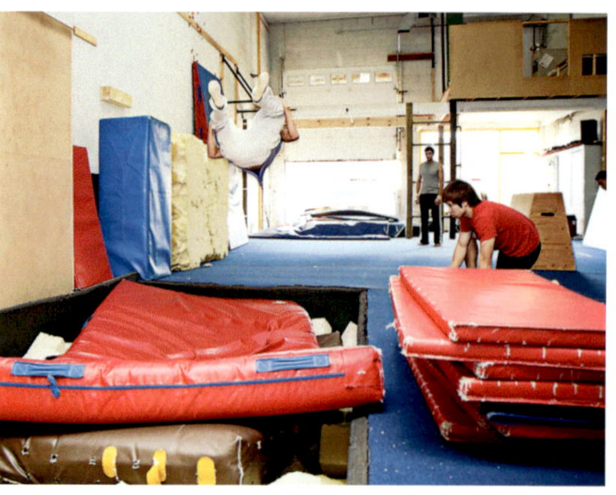

installed in a narrow corridor at the Art Gallery of Ontario (AGO), this short quotation, typeset on a small piece of paper, seemed to jump out at Humberto as if written in flashing neon lights. Finding this quotation on a casual visit to the AGO in 2010 was a *eureka* moment! There and then, we found a common language to describe *our* awakening of thought, history, and collaboration. A refreshed beginning that would ensure another one hundred years of cultural hibernation would never have a second opportunity. It was time to give Toronto back its spirit through an artistic action that was distinctly *Canadian* precisely because its origins were Indigenous.

Riel's quotation underscored the fundamental role that artists play in shaping, or, more to the point, *reshaping* the social imaginaries of a place. Itself so fully entrenched in Aboriginal culture, the interconnectedness of art and life was absent from the alienating "display" practices of most museums, including the Art Gallery of Ontario, Toronto's symbolic centre of visual culture.[6] This balance certainly was foreign to the western, market-driven conception of art today. Now was the time to animate Riel's words: to bring Toronto to an awakening that would bring the past into the present and so bring art's spirit back by mixing the contemporary with the traditional.

We immediately told our parkour friends about our important "find" at the museum, and we found something else out from them in exchange. The AGO had symbolic significance for them, too. Of all the buildings in Toronto, this was the *one* place that Dan and the parkour were dying to jump on—but were forbidden to! Even though Dan was convinced that Frank Gehry's renovation, with its thick ledges and smooth, multi-layered forms was purpose-built for *them* to jump, crawl, and flip on, parkour were kicked off it by AGO security every time they tried. They couldn't even get away with a little side-flip on the outdoor Henry Moore sculpture on which everyone else sits for photographs, or even slides through!

All of this was going to change, however. Humberto encouraged us to dream *big*. *The Awakening* was an artistic adventure! If Humberto got his way, and eventually he did, instead of jumping *off* the building, the parkour would jump *within* it. Similarly, First Nations cultural artifacts no longer simply hang static on the museum's walls, they would awaken, their powers activated through the lived cultural presence of their customary owners. Their contemporary cultural presence would come *alive* through performance and be *experienced* as an important Canadian art form: front and centre. The AGO would be the site of *The Awakening*. There, we would *all* have the prestige of being *present*.

During Humberto's second visit to Toronto, the AGYU's role shifted from fire keeper to *peacekeeper*. Since Humberto wanted *The Awakening* to be staged at the AGO, we needed to broker a relationship with the AGO: firstly, to get their commitment to "host" the performance, and, secondly, to mediate each group's particular needs to this symbolic centre of culture *and power*. Here was a very different role for an institution in Humberto's collaborations. It was unprecedented that the commissioning institution (the AGYU) would be an equal collaborator along with Humberto and his working groups. As such, institutional practices generally would have to mirror Humberto's own as well as specifically, in this case, follow Aboriginal principles and ethics. Humberto was a spark that re-ignited the flame in all of us.

Riel's prophecy was to be the project's guiding spirit: recasting the past as the present's possibility, and its hopeful future. For Humberto, *The Awakening* had to be a living, pulsing energy entering into and flowing out of *the heart* of the museum—as if it, too, was re-awakened *and shaken (free)* by the prophet's words. Frank Gehry's façade, reminiscent of an overturned whaling ship, would no longer be landlocked: this boat would become an integral part of our symbolic *parcours* into the spirit world. The First Nations were our spirit guides now on the water's edge. Together we would storm Walker Court, the AGO's symbolic neoclassical core and, through the melding of participatory art and First Nations cultures and traditions, return its grounds to a ceremonial meeting place. Now we just had to get everyone on board....

THE THREE FIRES

Our artistic adventure was only just beginning. We would have to go backwards before moving forwards, however. Creating a ceremony dedicated to the future of art and to the awakening of a new spirit fire for future generations of Canadians meant following in the footsteps of our Aboriginal ancestors. In Toronto, following the footsteps of the original inhabitants who lightly graced this land led us to the Mississaugas. Toronto *is* Three Fires territory. The Three Fires are the Mississaugas.[7]

The Mississaugas *are* the spirit of Toronto but their history here has been obscured, as they have long been exiled from their original inhabitation. In 1805, under much duress, they surrendered to the British most of what is now metropolitan Toronto for ten shillings. More than two hundred years had passed, but their spirit still burned strong, when in 2010 this historical misdeed finally resulted in a land-claim settlement with the Canadian Federal Government—although the Mississaugas continue to reside on a reserve an hour-and-a-half outside Toronto.[8] So it was auspicious to acknowledge their spirit-claim over the land— the land on which the AGO was built—by way of a ceremony created in the present as art but that also generously brought together Toronto's original inhabitants and today's urban youth and new Canadians. In creating a new ceremony as a work of *contemporary* art, we nonetheless looked to the Mississaugas of the New Credit First Nation in order to learn from their traditions of respect, their art of music and dance, and their joining of generations— not to mention their patience, perseverance, and tenacity.

MISHOMIS [9]

Not everything was smooth sailing on our metaphorical boat journey into *The Awakening*.

With two very different groups in tow, and within one of these two groups, sub-groups—the Tecumseh Collective and the Mississaugas—the inherent complexities and contradictions of the project were just beginning to surface. We would face some rough waters as we navigated Canada's troubled past before we were able to find an appropriate working relationship that fairly respected, and duly represented, the perspectives of everyone involved.

After Confederation in 1867, through its imperial policies of assimilation, the Canadian government took away Aboriginal land and attempted to eliminate their languages. These policies resulted in a slow and insidious annihilation of Aboriginal culture under the auspices of a so-called "unified" Canadian identity and the establishment of the destructive 1876 Indian Act. The brutal effects of these policies still remain today. As a consequence of this and the general lack of knowledge around a *collective* history, the fear of doing or saying something wrong in relation to the First Nations people is deeply embedded in the Canadian psyche. Going from tiptoeing around each other to the full stomp of powwow dancing together was certainly not going to be easy![10]

Obviously, this project was not going to solve social issues so deeply entrenched in the collective consciousness of Canadians. Nor was it going to undo historical misdeeds. *The Awakening*, however, would bring this history out into the open, to be dealt with head-on through collaboration and conversation—two important political and social tools. "We've got to make a space for getting into the ceremony—mutually. *Between* the creators, the organizers, the Mississauga community, and the artists," Humberto said to Philip, Rebecca, Dan, and myself when finally he brought all of us together in late summer 2010. "Especially now that we are going to the powwow in New Credit, we are going to see the possibility of how you can interpret what that experience means from your own point of view. We have to find ways of talking to each other and if you make a mistake, that's fine. If you are trying to teach someone your skills you can transmit your feelings about your situation too, just as you will learn from theirs. We are trying to learn something about ourselves in this project as well. Sometimes we are so divided we don't know how to talk to each other, so I just want to say that this collaboration is really about unity, and we need to talk to each other because we are the core of the project. We can't ask others to come along if we aren't willing to share our skills, our thoughts, and our feelings. We have to always think: how can we help each other? In which way can we support each other?"[11] Humberto's transparency throughout the process was a way to connect the ethical concerns of the project with its production.

Humberto had spoken about creating an "art ceremony" together and he had devised a preliminary script for the performance, but it was only a framework. He would need all of us, and especially the Mississaugas, to contribute the content and bring it to life in order for us to own it *as Canadians*. We would need to find a balance—a reciprocal relation—in between movements and moments at the interstice of the invented space of performance and the reality of our everyday lives. This would be a *Canadian project*, not just Humberto's project *for* Canada.

HANGING IN THE BALANCE

Half Aboriginal and half European, the Métis were all about balance. They figured out how to have the best of both cultures, which made them stronger by being mixed. Along with First Nations' concepts of unity and balance, the amalgamation of forces would be a guiding principle in *The Awakening* and mixing would become an integral way toward understanding our commonalities and accommodating our differences.

Both parkour and powwow dancing developed from emancipatory impulses. Both are forms of cultural and political resistance to the hegemonic structures and repressive policies of mainstream society, albeit at different times and for different reasons.[12] In other words, both the parkour and Aboriginals already understand "*the Man*" and the institutions that have attempted to define and control their existence. So their ethos of building strength through community, sharing, and learning, and their use of the body as an expressive form of non-verbal enunciation already were shared strategies of resistance as much as they are a form of cultural celebration. It was time to teach the parkour to dance and the First Nations to jump!

Careful not to jump in with both feet first, we began slowly, learning more about each other's practices and traditions in the contexts each felt most comfortable. Here would be an opportunity to let experience gently guide our perceptions of each other, and not just presumptions and prejudices.

At a parkour demonstration at Cloud Park in downtown Toronto, Dan mentioned how the parkour often imagined themselves as animals as they leapt through, flew over, or hung from the architectural structures that restrictively condition our everyday movement in the city. This was not something, however, they would openly say. But it intrigued Philip, who in turn told the parkour about how, in Aboriginal culture, one was born into a Clan named after an animal. A connection was made! Even though the parkour weren't yet aware of the origins or significance of the clan system to the First Nations' holistic view of the earth, the parkour's own non-hierarchical identification with and respect for the natural world was a way of *feeling* First Nations culture. A later workshop on the New Credit Reserve would deepen this understanding for the parkour, but for now the personification of the animal world was an essential, non-verbal way for the two groups to communicate with each other. The eagle shared the sky and the monkey, the earth. But the First Nations were also the earth and the parkour, the sky. The horizon was a balancing line between worlds and cultures.

The next step was to take the parkour to the powwow in New Credit. Our interpreters of the momentous day's events would end up being the Tecumseh family, who, along with the Mississaugas, would be key performers in *The Awakening*. The Tecumseh Collective First Nations Community Organization were ambassadors, just as Tecumseh had been in the past, echoing this First Nation leader's own dream of a united people composed of many ages, nations, and interests. Let's introduce them: Philip's niece, dancer Cotee Harper, Shawnee Lakota Potawatomi Ojibway Cree and member of the Mistawasis Band,

Opposite page: The 2011 workshops in New Credit and at the Monkey Vault Parkour Gym as participants learn powwow dancing and parkour moves to incorporate into *The Awakening*.

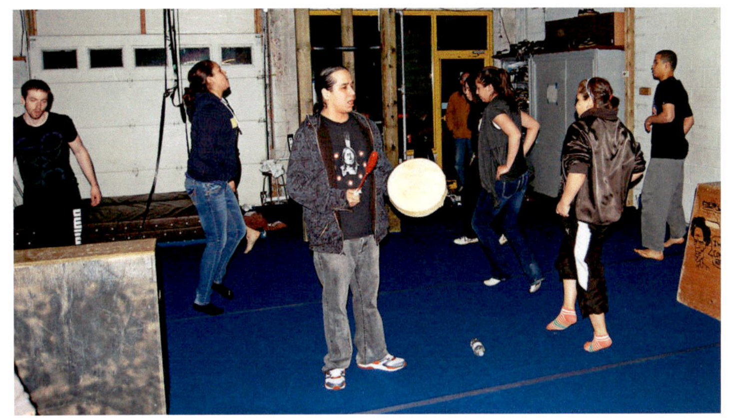

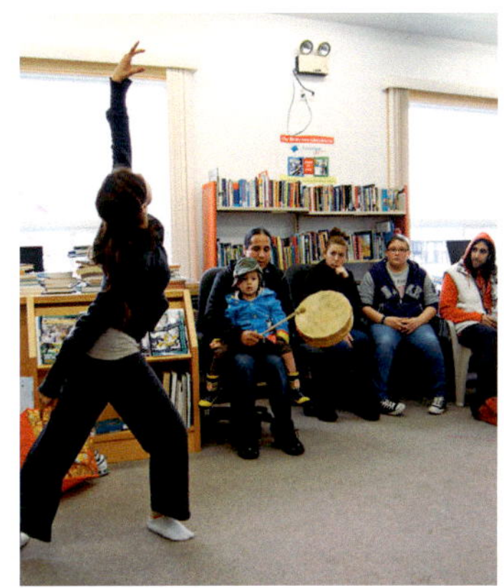

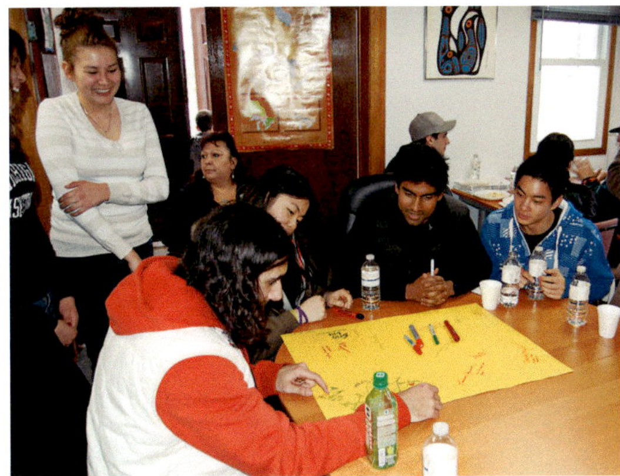

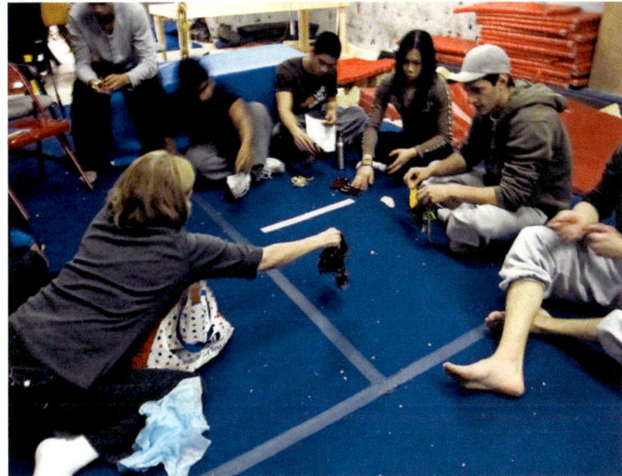

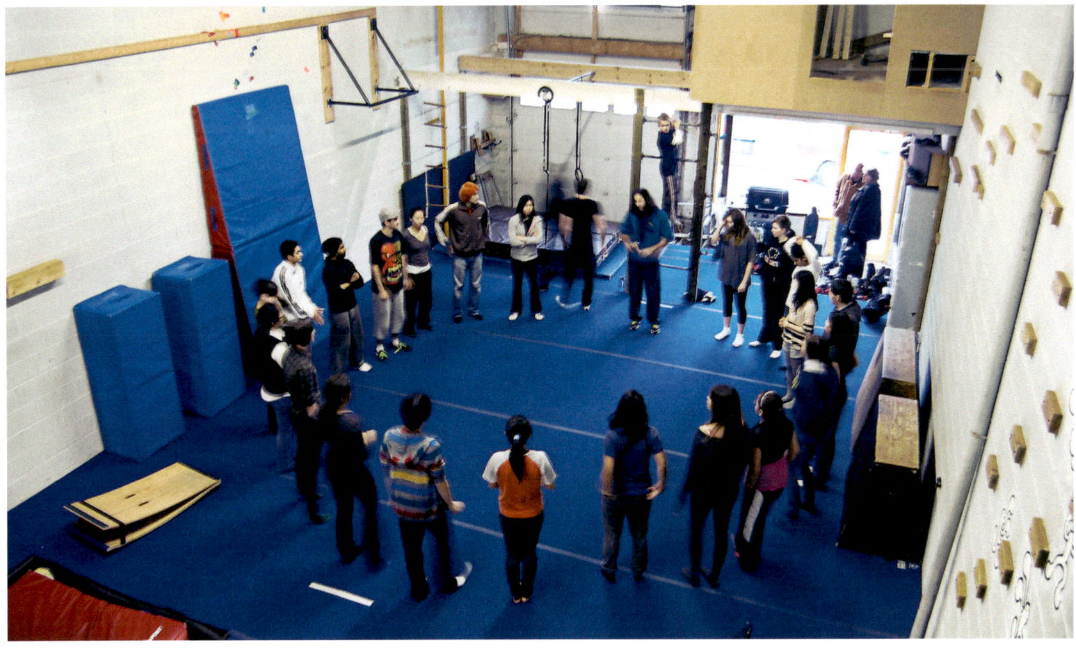

Saskatchewan, and her partner, musician Theo McGregor, Ojibway, Odawa and member of the Wikwemikong First Nation, Manitoulin Island. They differed by living off reserve, in the city of Toronto. They mixed traditional forms with their contemporary interests: Cotee was a graduate of the National Ballet School; Theo sampled found and digitally generated sounds and mixed these with traditional hand drumming and live chanting, creating hybrid musical genres that brought together Aboriginal and non-Aboriginal musicians in its making.

In a sense, the two were what Humberto called "Fire Spirits," a role they eventually represented in the performance, and as such they differed from the Mississaugas. They were freer than all of us: freer than even the free-runners. The Fire Spirits navigated an in-between territory, always already armed with the perspective of the duality so important to what *The Awakening* was all about. They were perpetually suspended in-between moments in time, able to move effortlessly between the traditional and contemporary by balancing both. Opposition was always hanging in the balance. Whereas the parkour—despite their creative disregard for the oppressive grid-lines of the cityscape with their gravity defying leaps and jumps—always moved strategically from point A to point B, acutely aware of being in the present moment, each successive movement, by necessity, a carefully considered advance forward.

The Fire Spirits opened a meandering system of interlaced passages going into and coming out from First Nations culture and, by implication, Canada's past and present. Pathways patted out of tall grass growing for far too long, like the Grass Dancer of the Eagle Clan who stomps the grass down in preparation for a ceremony, calling up the spirits with his movement and, at a powwow, clearing a passageway for the Grand Entry with each new footstep.

… And the singing begins. Singers crying out to the spirits. Ancestors asking to be heard. Their hearts beating in a call and answer to the sound of the drum. A drumbeat felt deep in the chests of everyone—regardless of history, creed, culture, or class.

… And the traditional dancer takes one step forward and another step back, his movements the narrative in a story-telling dance. One foot into the past and the other into the future: the precarious present hanging in the ever-fleeting moment in-between each step that tenderly touches the earth before moving forward and backward, again and again. Ritual time is cyclical.

After the Grand Entry and traditional and fancy dancers, the circle of dancing was opened and others—including non-Aboriginals—were welcomed to join the powwow's festivities. Eager to participate, some of the parkour rose to the challenge when the Master of Ceremonies announced the Potato Dance. Putting the potato between their foreheads and trying not to let it fall, Dan and Leslye danced together. Ten minutes in, they won the competition and subsequently the respect of the First Nations dancers. It was a foreshadowing of what was to become a series of serendipitous moments that brought the parkour's fire and the Mississaugas' spirit closer.

JUMPING THROUGH HOOPS

In late 2010, as we moved into the project's production phase, there were two major hurdles to overcome: obstacles that even some of the most sophisticated parkour jumps wouldn't help us get over and that powwow moves just couldn't dance around. We needed to cross the implicit borders these obstacles represented. Gaining access to the AGO meant adhering to their institutional protocols, while full access to the Reserve meant following the Mississ-augas' cultural ones. Incommensurable to each other, both would take time to negotiate before we could guarantee that a performance actually would take place.

At the AGO, it was the seemingly impenetrable bureaucracy, its own kind of perverse circle, with paperwork begetting more paperwork, meetings leading to even more meetings, and concerns escalating from the bottom to top and back down again: everything from health and safety, to building management, to plant operations, to facilities, and, of course, security. Each level, we were repeatedly reminded, was powerful enough to put an abrupt stop to the project if we weren't willing to accommodate their particular demands, which often frustratingly contradicted one another. Then there was the looming threat that Walker Court could simply be taken away from us to serve the interests of the gallery's development department. Even a wedding rental would usurp our performance! With each small step forward, it seemed as if new barriers were being erected, designed to keep a differing culture *out* of the museum: the type of culture brewing up through Humberto's project, that is.

As a consequence, the AGYU was forced into an awkward position. We would either have to succumb to the demands of the AGO and severely compromise the project or we would have to fight it, tooth and nail, on behalf of the interests of "the people," the integrity of the project, and *our* artist. *As* another art institution nonetheless! At times, it seemed impossible to find a balance in this preposterous opposition, even when as an art gallery ourselves we necessarily sympathized with such institutional protocols.

Not everything could be so open and free if the project was going to take place at the AGO, so we accommodated some of their requests but left them hanging with regards to others. Trying not to prematurely make decisions, or permit the AGO's demands to guide the project's development, we bided time with our delays. Time, again, was needed to allow for negotiations that would ensure that the performance was shaped by the *participant's* points of views.

On the reserve, protocol acts as a way of preserving First Nations culture. Gaining knowledge of protocol on the reserve means gaining access to the self-governed social structure of reserve culture. Protocol and culture are one. So, learning the protocols—on the one hand, offering tobacco to an Elder or, on the other, understanding the role a Band Council plays in the social order of a reserve—meant learning *how to learn* from First Nations traditions when we weren't necessarily being told the rules. First Nation's cultural protocols would have to be incorporated *into* the project if the Mississaugas were able to *fully* participate, that is, if we were to ensure that their culture was upheld, and respected.

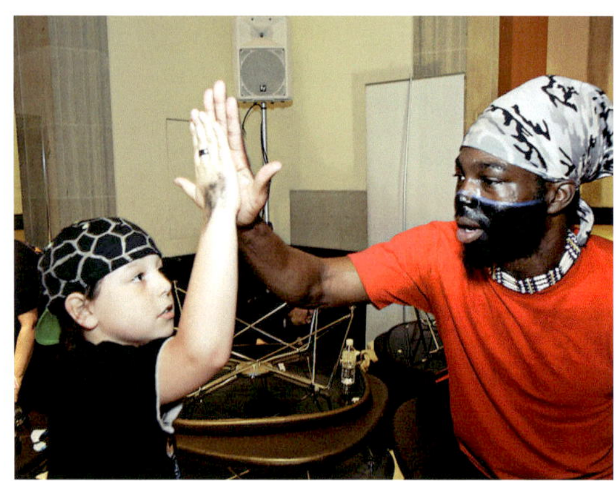
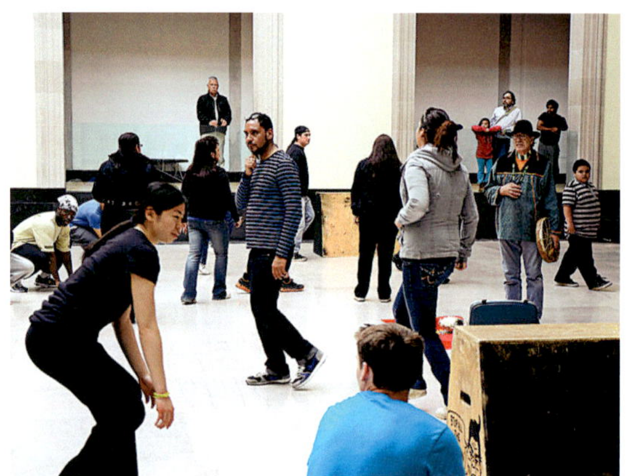
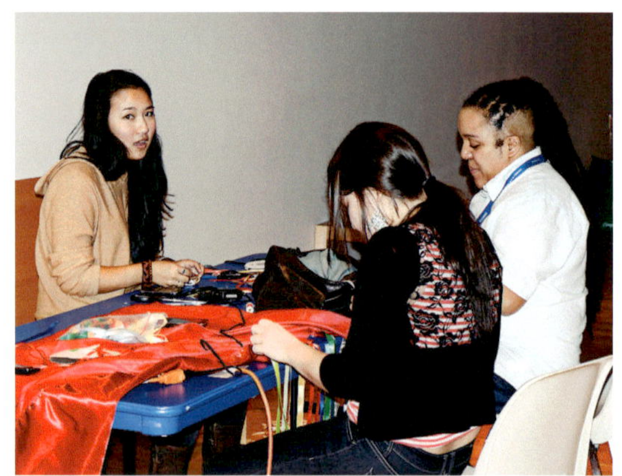
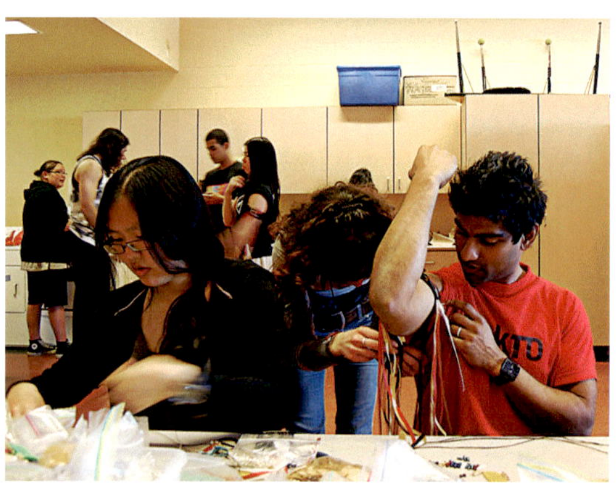
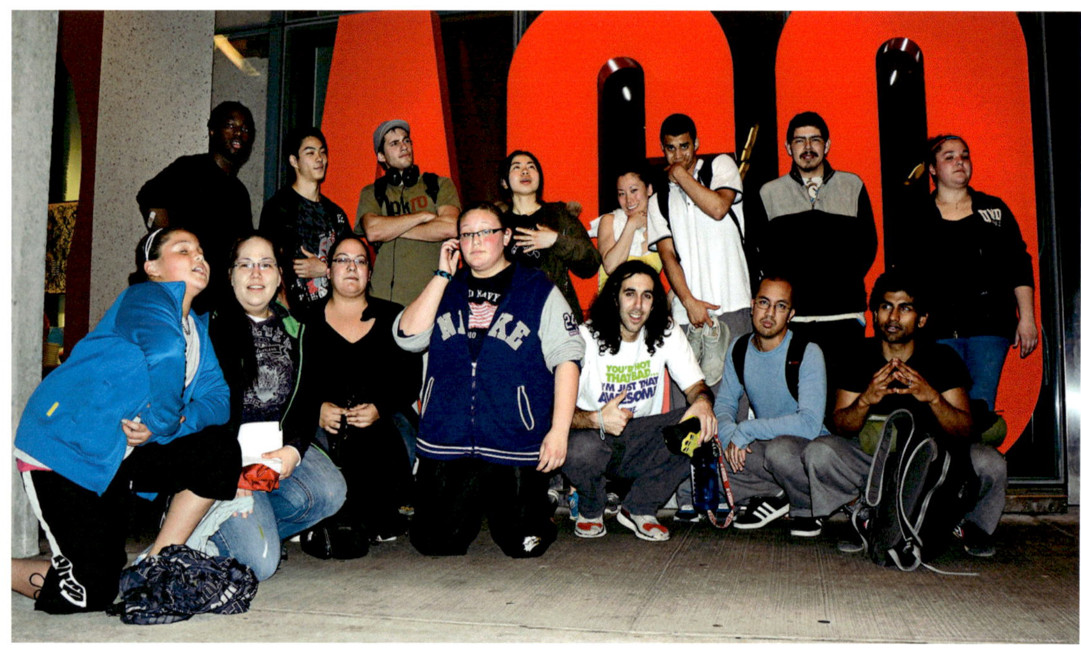

But we had to prove our commitment to learning about the culture before the Mississaugas would commit to teaching us the protocols.[13] We had gone through a canoe-load of tobacco by the time we finally unraveled this riddle.[14]

All of this back and forth was worth it, though. Our subordination at the AGO and our persistence on the New Credit Reserve paid off in the end when, on the day of the performance, Humberto asked Philip Monk, the Director of the AGYU, to lead the procession with Mississaugas' Chief Brian LaForme. The two "chiefs," symbolically made equal, headed the metaphoric "storming" of the institution and entered the AGO alongside the Mississaugas and parkour artists for everyone to witness. It was a new (Canadian) rendition of the classic depiction of "liberty leading the people." This action might have been symbolic in terms of performance but the kinship was real. When the procession entered the AGO, that gallery's staff opened the doors to all of us! But…that too was part of Humberto's "script."[15]

COMING FULL CIRCLE

Ongoing negotiations revealed that the project's significance lay in its process of becoming: not where we were going, per se, but rather, more importantly, *how* we were getting there. Acknowledging the differing forms of knowing that this process would take (from Aboriginal to institutional to somatic) was a first step toward communicating with each other. Knowledge, in this context, was not what we already knew, for our frames of reference were so different from one another's anyway, but how we came to know our differences and our similarities when confronted by the challenges presented by this project.

None of this really mattered to the youth, who, in the end, blew right through all the obstacles, perceived or otherwise, with their openness. Without owning the burden of history, the youth were free to jump and dance or, learning from each other, fearlessly combine both in a single leap of faith into unknown territories. Thus, midway through the project, a youth exchange developed between the Youth Councils of New Credit and the AGO. Being relatively the same age, the parkour were also part of this exchange. Week after week, buses travelled between the New Credit Reserve, the AGO, and the Monkey Vault Gym where knowledge was shared between the participants and locales in a free and open way. Youth would have a role not only in performing in *The Awakening* but in shaping it. They would choose their own roles: whether as jumpers, or dancers, or drummers. Some would choose to be production coordinators, working alongside AGYU and AGO staff to gain valuable experience working in contemporary art. (The AGO Youth Council was like a Trojan Horse: they already knew how to navigate the many layers of the institution, having hosted a number of their own events there.) Youth would bring the project together and make the performance a ceremony destined for the future of Canada, reversing tradition by passing something up to older generations. As Humberto would ask: "what are we teaching with this project?"

In the three months leading to the performance, every Saturday was spent in workshops in New Credit, and every Wednesday at either the AGO or the Monkey Vault Parkour gym. On the New Credit Reserve, interest in participating in *The Awakening* grew exponentially, with new faces, young and old, joining each week. We had weekly feasts, organized and prepared by one of the young Mississauga women studying culinary arts at George Brown College in Toronto. Significantly, through these, other members of the New Credit Reserve, who were not participating in the project, came to know and trust us. The AGYU was happy to pay for these feasts knowing that the money helped fund a Youth Council trip to British Columbia that summer.[16]

Speaking of money, at the very first workshop in New Credit, cutting right to the chase, singers Minga and Raini threw a five-dollar bill on the floor and told the parkour that when they're bored at a powwow here was a game they would play. A challenge: whoever won, kept the money. The stakes were high! The goal was to pick the bill up with your mouth, unassisted by your hands, without falling over. The challengers danced, lowering themselves closer and closer to the ground. After this demonstration, Leslye stepped into the circle to give it a try. Everyone chanted and cheered as she picked up the bill with ease! Then the parkour upped the ante and changed the rules of the game. With a bill in his mouth, Max, threw it up in the air, did a back-flip, and caught it in his mouth again, both feet fully planted back down on the ground. Minga and Raini were in awe. By the end of the day, both youth groups had built an enormous amount of respect for each other's particular talents. (As I said, the youth would bring us together, especially the First Nations youth, who would mix it up, merging pop culture with their own traditions, as if to say to us: "Lighten up; it's not so precious that we can't have fun at the same time.") Later, in the rehearsals, we would see some of the young people go off on their own, giving private lessons to each other as they honed their new found skills. In one such instance, I overheard one of the young Aboriginal dancers tell a parkour artist struggling to learn a powwow dance step: "just move your feet to the beat of the drum, don't be shy… most of the time we make it up anyway!" All of a sudden protocol flew out the window.

At the parkour gym, Dan was a natural leader, his face beaming with pride as he passed along *his* "tradition" to his new peers, teaching everyone how to jump, flip, and fall. Dodging the young bodies flying akimbo through the air, parents laughed and cheered as they watched their sons and daughters off the reserve at home with other youth. Whether on the reserve or at the Monkey Vault Gym, it was natural to make the other welcome, passing on one's own traditions through a process of exchange and respect. Being the same age meant they already had common ground to share. No one was expected to be anything different from what they were. Minga and Raini had freed the parkour and now the parkour enabled others to participate playfully outside their comfort zone. Now no one was afraid to ask each other the tough questions we adults danced around. Suddenly, embarrassment disappeared, whether singers doing their first side-flip or athletes beating on their first hand drum… or, later, entering the AGO as artists with Humberto.

Throughout the workshops, Humberto wrote his script, revising it based on the new possibilities arising from the youth's enthusiasm. Humberto constructed five distinct movements, or "acts," that structured the dramatic action of the performance but it was the participant's emotional authenticity that brought each to life. Each "scene" also became a pedagogical opportunity that deepened the significance of the performance's production process. Elder Garry Sault taught us how to prepare the altar according to the old rituals and the four cardinal points, which would become the opening sequence of the performance. Young boys, who would lead the smudge ceremony to purify the thoughts of the audience, learned how to mix their own medicinal herbs.

The performance became the present's cyclical return to the past, which was brought back again into the present anew. When the parkour finally mastered powwow dancing and combined it with their leaps and jumps, this, too, was skillfully incorporated into Humberto's script. Playing the part of the spirits, the parkour's hybrid movements marked the moment of joyous celebration. Dan descended from the sky and joined the circle of parkour below, each offered tobacco in gratitude for hearing our petition to them.

The moment of awakening had finally arrived.

GIIGOZHKOZIMIN

Faith Rivers, one of the members of the New Credit Cultural Committee, wrote to me in an email two days before the performance: "I am very overwhelmed with all the involvement the team has had with our First Nation and I just have to say Chi Miigwetch which means a Big Thank You in Ojibway…. I love Humberto's energy and his passion for what he does and he is a beautiful person inside and out. I can feel people and I get good feelings from everyone on your team, thanks for that. I know it is a lot of work for you and your team and I can empathize with you, just don't forget to breath … on Saturday we can give a huge sigh of relief and say yes! We did it!" *Together*, we had come a long way.

On the morning of May 14, 2011, in New Credit, Len Grant—a photographer from Manchester brought to Toronto specifically to document the performance—headed out by taxi to the Reserve at 8 am to document the Mississaugas' journey to Toronto for the "big day."[17] When the Mississaugas arrived at the AGO we greeted them with tobacco ties made by the members of the AGO Youth Council.

Behind the scenes was complete chaos. Feathers were flying this way and that as everyone furiously suited up to perform in Walker Court. Parkour were helping smudge boys put on moccasins while the young Mississauga women braided the parkour's hair. Some of the Elders were sewing and stitching, putting the final touches on the banner that had been made specifically for *The Awakening*.[18] Around Walker Court, friends, family, and complete strangers gathered by the hundreds in anticipation of "Toronto's ceremony."

The performance began with a procession outside and the simultaneous preparation of the altar inside Walker Court. At the front doors of the AGO, where Philip Cote was blessing everyone with sweet grass, the gathering of fifty-plus Missssissaugas, Tecumseh

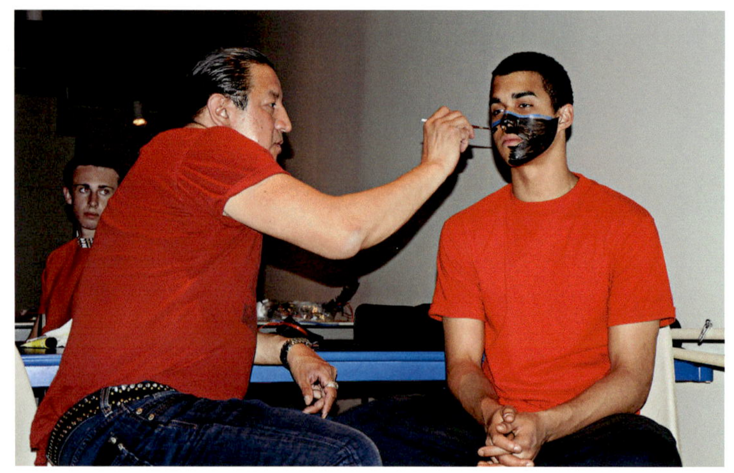

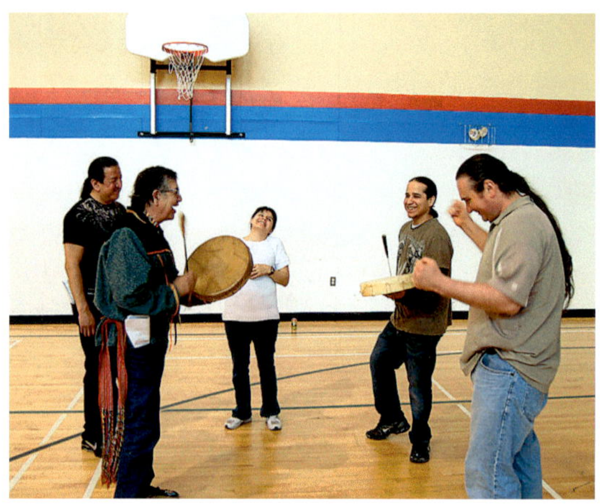

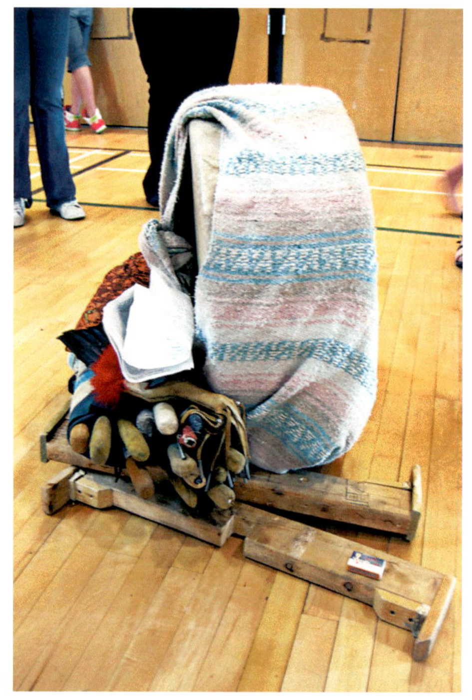

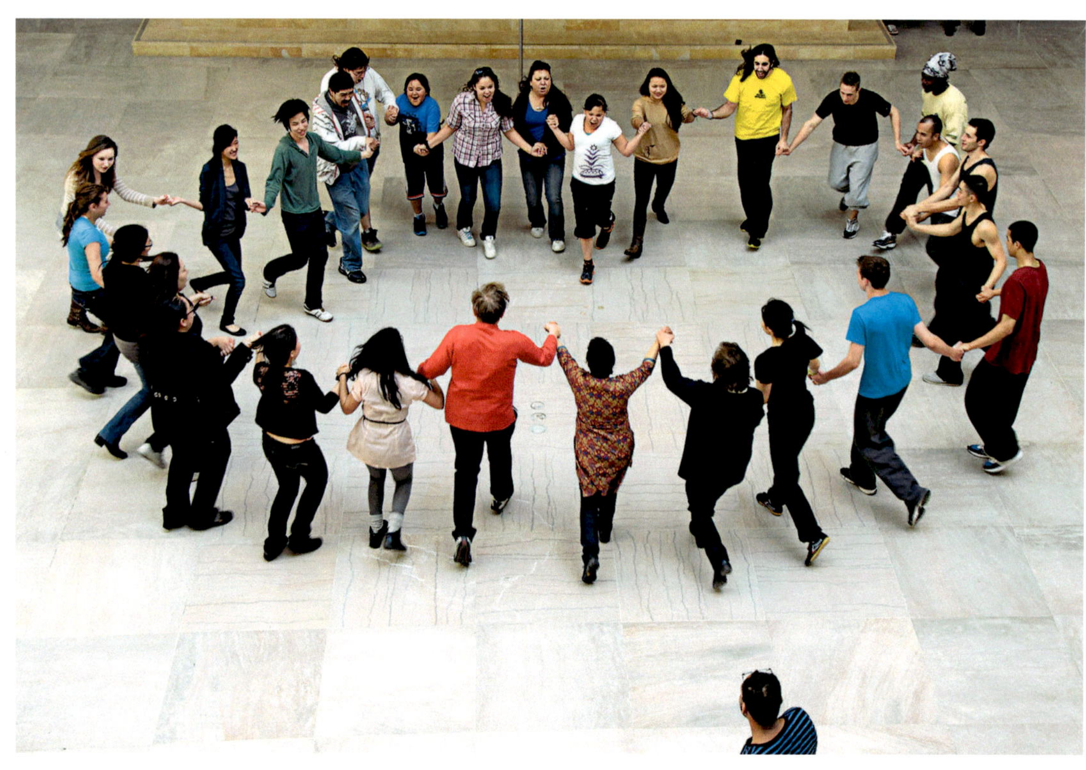

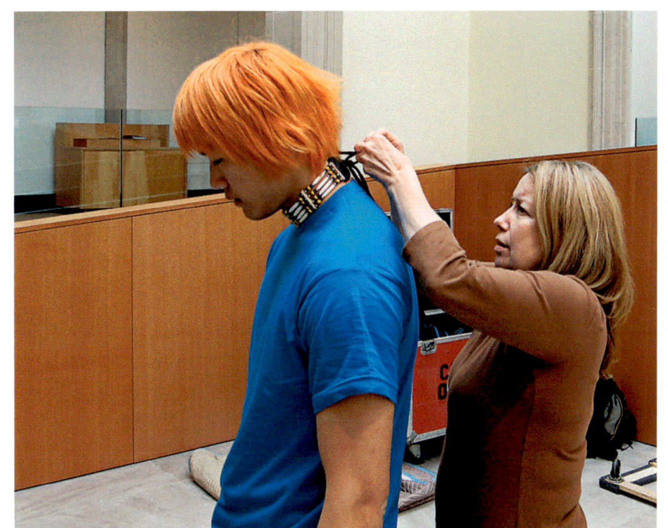
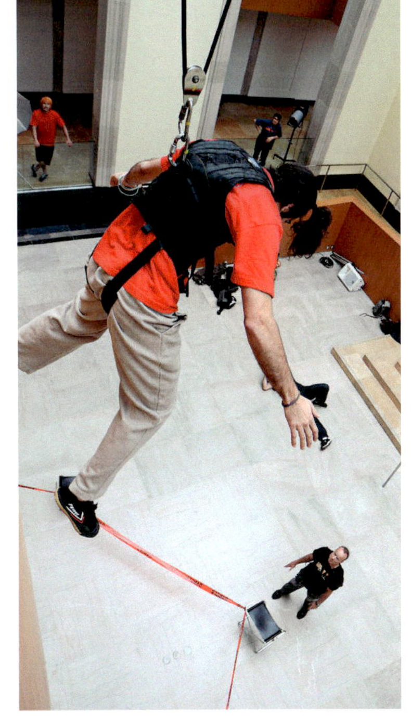
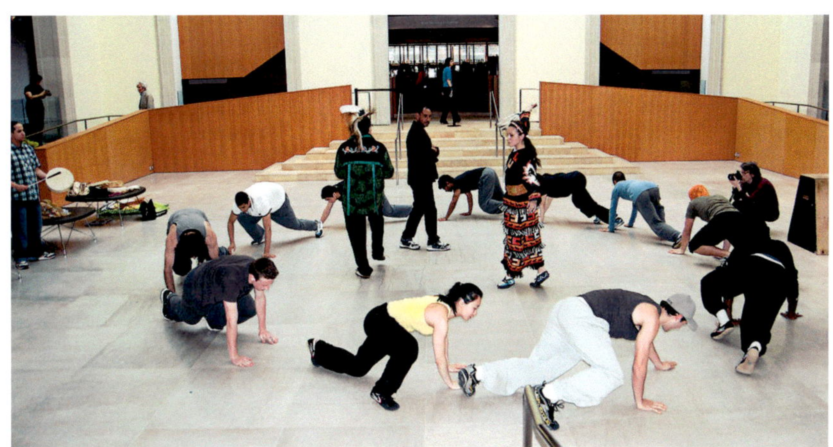
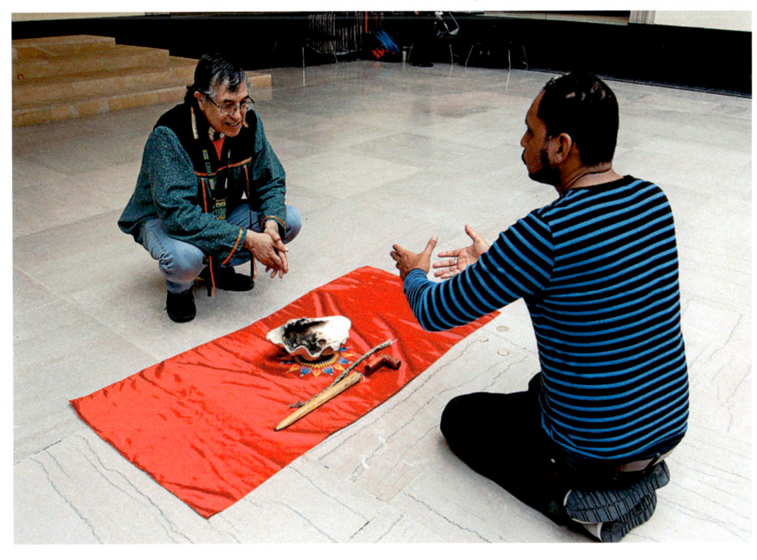
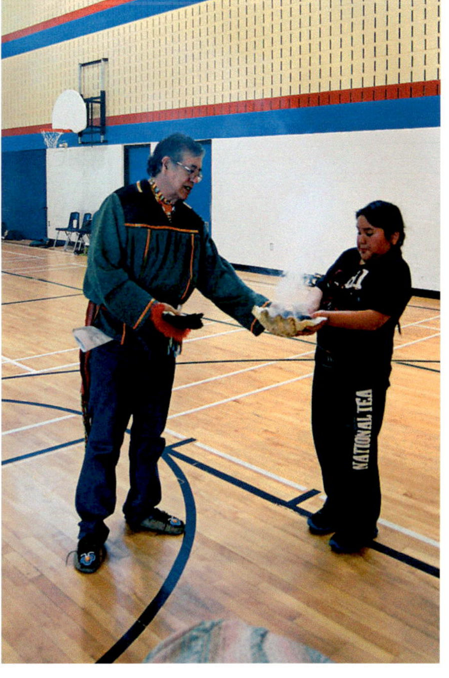

family members, the two youth councils, First Nation Elders, gallery staff, and young parkour artists certainly was surreal. Curious on-lookers took photographs of this unlikely charged "political" image of contemporary Canada coming together in a new association. Inside, an Aboriginal Elder in full regalia, lighting a smudge pot, smoke rising upward in Walker Court, the smell of sweet grass filling the galleries, was an equally uncommon sensory experience that disrupted the usual serenity of the AGO.

Following the Fire Spirit dancer (Cotee Harper), the Chief of the Mississaugas carried the Sacred Eagle Staff, followed by a representative from each of the youth councils carrying our banner. The parkour, youth councils, Tecumseh family members, Mississauga dancers, and drummers maneuvered their way through the ramp that snakes its way through the AGO lobby toward Walker Court. With all the performers settled in position, a magical silence filled the space. Philip Cote, the Masters of Ceremonies, his voice echoing through the galleries surrounding Walker Court, announced:

> My people will sleep for one hundred years, but when they awake, it will be the
> artists who give them their spirit back. This ceremony is our call for a new time.
> A time of understanding, respect, tolerance, unity, and imagination. We would
> like to light a new fire for the future, invoking the spirits of our ancestors.

The energy in Walker Court suddenly shifted. *The Awakening* was not *just* a performance at an art gallery. After all, this ceremony was *real* for both the Mississaugas and the audience.

Halfway through the performance the audience was called upon to help the Aboriginals reach out to the spirits. The entire room, in unison, repeated the word "awakening" in Ojibway, the Mississaugas' mother tongue:

Giigozhkozimin
Giigozhkozimin
Giigozhkozimin
Giigozhkozimin

Perched atop Frank Gehry's massive, snaking spiral staircase that towers over Walker Court, Dan, Shawn, and Gerome catwalked up and down the wide ledges of the staircase, their movements becoming more frantic as energy built toward a climatic peak. The time had arrived: the eagle descended in one fell-swoop from the staircase and joined the Mississauga dancers and the rest of the parkour in celebration. The sprits had heard our call! Elder Garry Sault thanked the "Parkour Spirits" by offering them tobacco. The spirits danced alongside the Fire Spirits. And then the Fancy Dancer (Cheryl Trudeau) and Grass Dancer (Dan Secord) entered the circle to join in celebration.

After the performance, Elder Garry Sault explained what the parkour's role meant to him, "They typified the spirits that are around us in our everyday lives but people don't pay

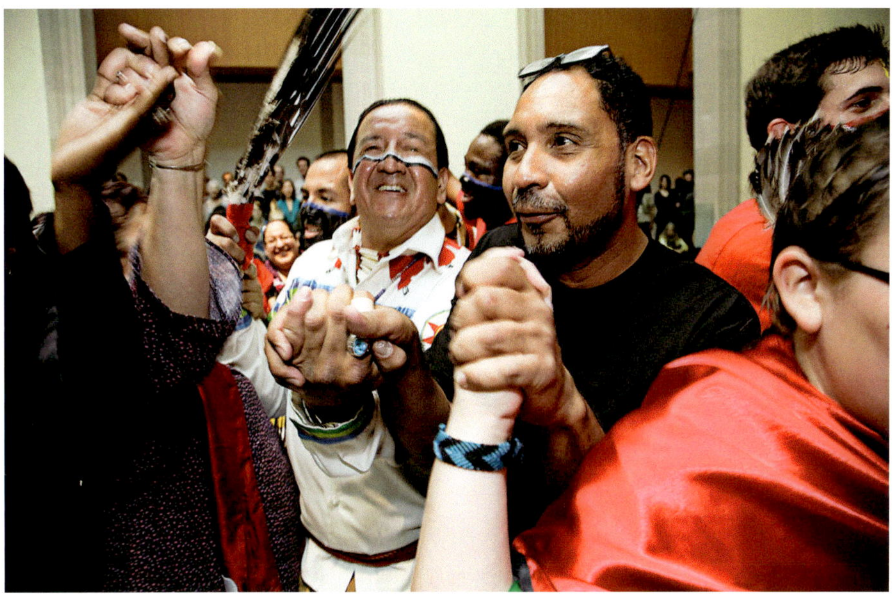

attention to them. So by calling to them, they appeared … in full focus. We're calling on the rest of humanity to come awake because that time is here."

At the end of the ceremony, the audience was invited to join the circle of drumming and dancing.[19] Everyone poured into Walker Court, almost trampling one another in their enthusiasm to participate in this unique celebration. Aboriginal youth taught strangers to powwow dance. Other parkour in the audience back-flipped off the high ledges…. chaos… after about fifteen minutes, over a loudspeaker, AGO staff asked everyone to leave. No one left. All the participants were *so* proud. Everyone was crying. *The Awakening* struck an important emotional cord with Torontonians. It reminded them again of who we are as Canadians, a mix of so many different people, places, and traditions *present* both across time as well as in our current historical moment. After being full of people from all different cultural backgrounds, ages, and abilities, dancing, drumming, and singing together that day, the spirit in Walker Court would never be the same.

Before the Mississaugas boarded the bus to return to New Credit, one of the young Mississaugas gave Humberto a sacred eagle feather: the highest honour one can receive from First Nations.

The Awakening had been for the people, not the institutions. For the parkour, the art institution was no longer a nameless, faceless entity that was off-limits. On behalf of all urban youth, they owned their presence at the official museum that day and felt validated by being allowed to be themselves there. "It was a really good opportunity," Dan said after the performance was finished. "It was a bit scary going into it but once we met [the Mississaugas] and realized how welcoming they were, they took us in and fed us and treated us as one of their own. It was super positive, we want to go and hang out and invite them back to Toronto. We've built a really good bond between us. It's really opened my eyes about other people. When we first began, Humberto kept calling us artists, which I didn't understand until right now." Two days after the performance Dan texted me the following: "the [parkour] group got together yesterday and I just wanted to say that we *already* miss the project—A LOT!"

The Mississaugas were tired of always only belonging in the historical section of museums and being kept in the past by ethnographers and anthropologists. Chief Brian LaForme said, "The performance sends a message to the people of Toronto that we're still here, our presence is still here and we're not going anywhere soon. It's great to see, you can feel the energy here—the place has been transformed by us." Reflecting on the event, Josh Shanush, one of the young Mississauga dancers, said, "I couldn't sleep the night before… I was so nervous! But it was fun, and I'm glad I came and was part of such an historic event."[20] Indeed, it was a historic event for everyone who attended that day, whether participant or audience. Maybe even for the AGO.

The Awakening restored the art gallery as a site for bridging communities and as a catalyst for defining national identities not as an authoritative representation but as an emergent moment.

The Awakening was not only about the affective possibilities of participatory art, however. Nor was it solely about the participants' experience during the process, or the audience's reaction at the performance. Taken together, *The Awakening* was about how Canadians could approach nation building in the future. As a "newcomer" to Toronto, on his very first site visit, Humberto said, "It's a Canadian legacy for the future that we need to look into with this project." To this day, the collaborators, including the AGYU, are still in communication each other. And Humberto is one of my dearest friends. Projects like these change those involved and those who bear witness to them. They don't just end when the artist goes home: we continue to have an obligation towards one another. Humberto's projects have a deep effect on their participants; the enabling is the real purpose of his projects after all.

NOTES

1. This is a transcription from a Skype interview with Humberto in December 2009, not long after his first site visit to Toronto. This transcript reveals something about the nature of Humberto and my relationship: our unabashed goofy-ness, sense of humour, and the sheer fun we had together. But the dialogue, while silly in one regard, also shows how Canada's cultural history is embedded in place names throughout the city of Toronto. For example, the hotels: the Radisson, named after the seventeenth century French explorer and coureur de bois Pierre-Esprit Radisson, and the Royal York, formerly called the "Queen's Hotel," named after the English city of York. The name Toronto is derived from the Iroquois word *tkaronto*, meaning "place where trees stand in the water."

2. Transcript of a public talk given at A Space Gallery in Toronto, organized by the AGYU as part of Humberto's 2009 site visit.

3. For an in-depth discussion of the role that Aboriginals played in shaping Canada as a country based on principles of tolerance and respect see John Ralston Saul's *A Fair Country* (2008), a book neither Humberto nor myself were aware of during the making of *The Awakening*. The book subsequently has had a profound influence on my understanding of how *The Awakening* could be considered a "Métis" project.

4. On a personal note, both Humberto and I are mixed raced people. In part this is why this essay (and the project itself) frames the Métis as a strong, positive identity-shaping force in Canada and a symbol of what it means to be part of the "Americas," though I am aware that the Métis faced discrimination and racism from Canada's formative years through to today.

5. In Canada, "Aboriginal" signifies First Nations, Inuit, and Métis. In this project we were working with Status Indians, who are First Nations. Parkour can be likened to a type of urban gymnastics, popularized by major Hollywood films such as in the opening sequence of *Casino Royale*. The Toronto parkour, who stayed committed to the grass-roots ethos and origins of the activity, particularly impressed Humberto.

6. This statement is not intended to discount the work of AGO curators Gerald McMaster, Georgiana Uhlyarik, or Richard Hill, whose presence in the Canadian Historical department has, over the years, marked a shift in the way in which First Nations art and culture has been represented/displayed in the contemporary galleries. The alienating display practices I am referring to are widespread structural issues, rooted in and inherent to institutional practices of museums in general. I bring this up in the essay to highlight Humberto's interest in exploring the role art plays in First Nations culture as a way of introducing other perspectives to the contemporary art world through his art project, alternatives to those privileged by the Western canon.

7. The Three Fires is symbolic of the Mississaugas' traditional and political alliance with the Ojibway, Odawa, and Pottawatomi Nations.

8. The Mississaugas of the New Credit First Nation presently occupy territory located on the periphery of the much larger Six Nations of the Grand River Reserve. New Credit was gifted to the Mississaugas by the Six Nations in 1847, and was officially confirmed as the Mississauga Indian Reserve in 1903.

9. The Ojibway name for "grandfather" is *mishomis*. It can also refer to "beginning."

10. From the early "Wild West" shows in the 1800s, to mainstream Hollywood movies, to the "timeless" children's role-playing game of "cowboys and Indians," the performance of "Indian as other" (for a non-Aboriginal audience) is fraught with its own problematic history. *The Awakening* would have to contend with this history even though the project was foremost intended to reassert the Indigenous perspective on art and culture in Canada. Following First Nations ethics/teachings and incorporating Aboriginal methodologies into the project were some of the ways we attempted to overcome this conundrum, though it repeatedly reared its ugly head throughout our process. With the audience not privy to the process leading up to the performance, the exoticization of First Nations culture through performance was the central criticism made by the Canadian audience at *The Awakening*. Was this because they were still unable to see Aboriginal performance outside our vexed historical context, or because they were unable to reconcile the images created by Aboriginals and non-Aboriginals performing together—the First Nations' participation in the performance seen as "cultural appropriation." Or, and perhaps more poignantly, was it because they were unable to see First Nations cultural expression as a viable source for contemporary art practices?

11. Transcript from audio recording taken during initial group meetings. All stages of the development of *The Awakening* was documented through audio and video recording, making the project the most comprehensive opportunity to examine Vélez's working practice.

12. Powwows allowed Aboriginal peoples to create large-scale cultural gatherings where the intergenerational sharing of dancing and drumming was a form of teaching, learning, and passing down to future generations the traditional way of life through repetition in performance. The powwow was a means of keeping their traditions alive while subverting Canadian Government sanctions of their cultural activities—sanctions that forbade First Nations from practicing their cultural traditions as well as, in the repressive (and devastating) residential school system, speaking their languages. Intended to assimilate First Peoples into European Canadian society, the residential school system, which separated children from their families and reserves (i.e. communities), has been referred to as Canada's cultural genocide. Powwows also built allegiances between the various groups of First Nations located in different parts of Canada, further building strength amongst their peoples.
Originating in the infamous Paris suburbs, known as banlieues, parkour developed as a reaction the placelessness

that characterized the urban cityscape. Attributed to two French suburban youth from banlieue Lisse, David Belle and Sébastien Foucan, parkour was a form of overcoming the alienation and powerlessness of their urban reality and a means of reclaiming it on their own terms. For Dan Iaboni, who studied with Belle before founding the Monkey Vault Parkour Gym (the only parkour gym in North America), the practice represents a refusal to succumb to the capitalist driven conception of "success" of life in the city. Parkour is an alternative life-style characterized by a direct, physical engagement with the structures that condition the practitioners lives as a way to navigate, and understand, them in a wholly different manner, simultaneously building community, claiming a sense of ownership over their city and their bodies, and challenging stereotypes people have about teenagers in urban centers. Dan would also say that parkour is a form of play.

13. On the reserve, everyone has to be able to share his or her perspective, which most times were told through the narrative of storytelling, such as a fable. As a consequence, there was an entirely different sense of time in New Credit, one that was more spatial than linear; at times at odds with the way the project's timeline had to develop in the context of the AGO.

14. Of course protocol would be learned through trial and error as well: we had paid Philip, Rebecca, Cotee, and Theo a fee for their contribution to *The Awakening* and felt that the two main Mississauga dancers, Dan Secord (Grass Dancer) and Cheryl Trudeau (Fancy Dancer), should also receive a fee. When we asked for their payment information they became extremely upset, however. Paying them, they explained, made them feel they were being put on display. Their culture didn't have a "price tag." It took sometime for them to understand that payment to artists was a protocol of ours, not intended to undermine their cultural contribution to the performance. In the end, the solution was a donation made to a language camp taking place on the New Credit Reserve later that summer. It was a token of our gratitude but also a symbol of our respect for their culture, negotiated on their terms.

15. How art, artists, and communities enter the "art establishment" is a central concern in Humberto's practice. To this end, many subtle and subversive actions and images are incorporated into his performance scripts.

16. Of course paying for these feasts, as well as other expenses on the Reserve became a entirely different kind of problem for the payment protocols of York University, who insisted in obtaining tax ID codes or HST numbers, or insisting we pay companies through invoices rather than individuals through reimbursement. These protocols went against the ways of the reserve (Status Indians do not pay federal taxes on reserve, for example). While cash is the preferred method of payment on the reserve, York University, as a major Canadian institution, insists on having an official paper trail for all transactions. Furthermore, it takes four-to-six weeks to obtain a cheque from York University, which

was counter to the unpredictability and last minute needs of the project's production phase.

17. Len Grant, who has documented a number of Humberto's past projects, has developed a collaboratorative documentary photography practice with non-artists, usually focusing on social issues in England. Len came to Toronto in 2010 to meet Humberto's collaborators and had subsequently built personal relationships with them. Thus, when it came time to document the rehearsals and performance in 2011 everyone already knew and trusted him. Integrating "the documenter" into the participatory frame of the project is an ethical strategy in line with Humberto's way of working.

18. The banner travelled to all the workshops and rehearsals and had contributions from all the participants. It was also used as a teaching tool for beading and sewing. This is also true for the necklaces and armbands specifically created for the parkour to wear in the performance.

19. Humberto had asked Carolyn King, former Mississauga Chief and the one who really helped to broker our relationship with the Mississaugas, to "direct" and lead this part of the performance in order to acknowledge the role she played in bringing people together. As Humberto would say, "Carolyn is a star." On another note, Val King (Minga and Raini's mother, Bear Clan), another one of the many strong women of the Mississaugas of the New Credit First Nation whose role was instrumental in the production of *The Awakening*, was my "star," playing the real role of spirit advisor, helping me to properly and respectfully obtain the community drum, smudge pots, and other traditional items needed for the performance as well as teaching me the appropriate protocol around these items without hesitation or prejudice.

20. All unidentified quotes in this section come from interviews David Sharpe conducted with the participants on the day of the performance in preparation for his front page article on *The Awakening* for the *TEKA Times*, the official newspaper of the Mississaugas' and Six Nations' Reserves. David not only attended the performance, he followed the entire process, attending a number of the workshops in New Credit. While his expertise is not necessarily in contemporary art, his observations and editorial about *The Awakening* and the subversive potential of Humberto's practice was bang on, more perceptive than the contemporary art writer of *The Toronto Star*, who also covered the performance.

Tal vez este proyecto es un intento
artístico de abordar las construcciones
nacionales y las múltiples ideas
del arte que existen en nuestros
países y de experimentarlas en lo
contemporáneo. Como siempre he
dicho, tenemos que enfocarnos en
el legado de Canadá para el futuro.

Humberto Vélez (noviembre del 2011)

Maybe this project is an art attempt of approaching the national constructions of the Americas and also the multiple existences of ideas of art that we have in our countries and to experience it in the contemporary. As I always said it is the Canadian legacy for the future that we need to look into.

Humberto Vélez (November 2011)

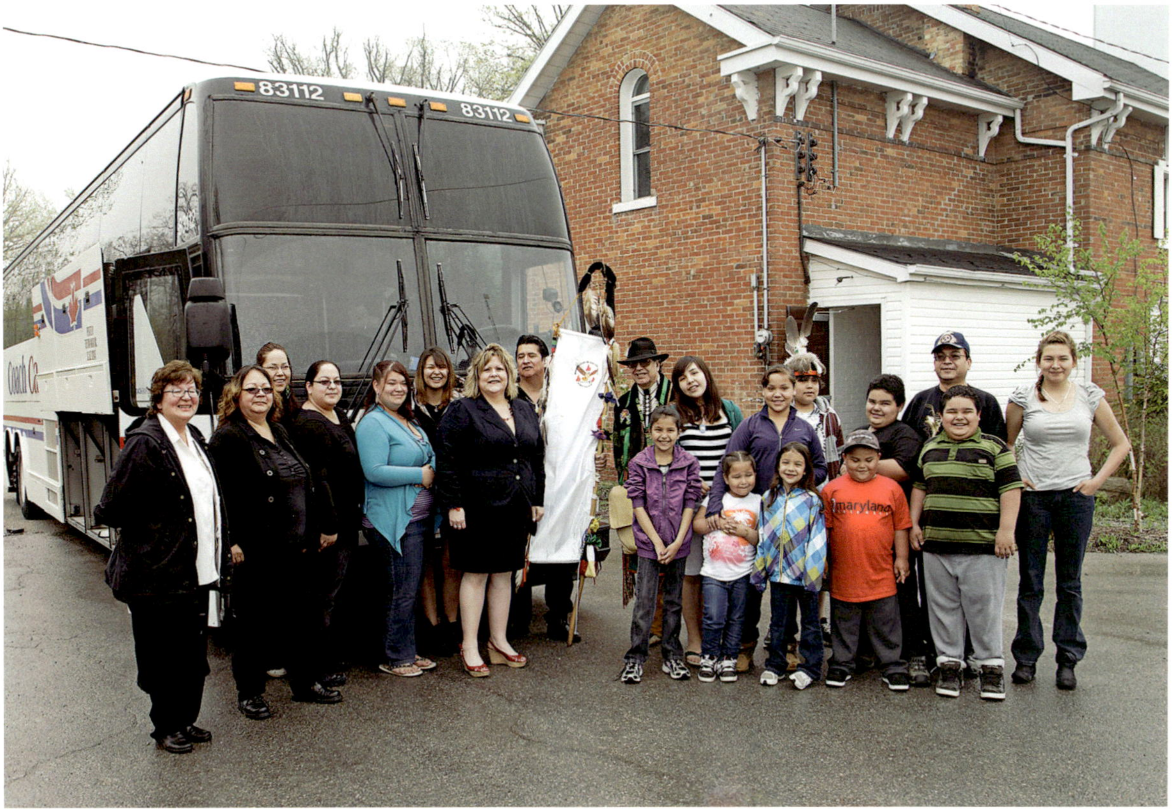

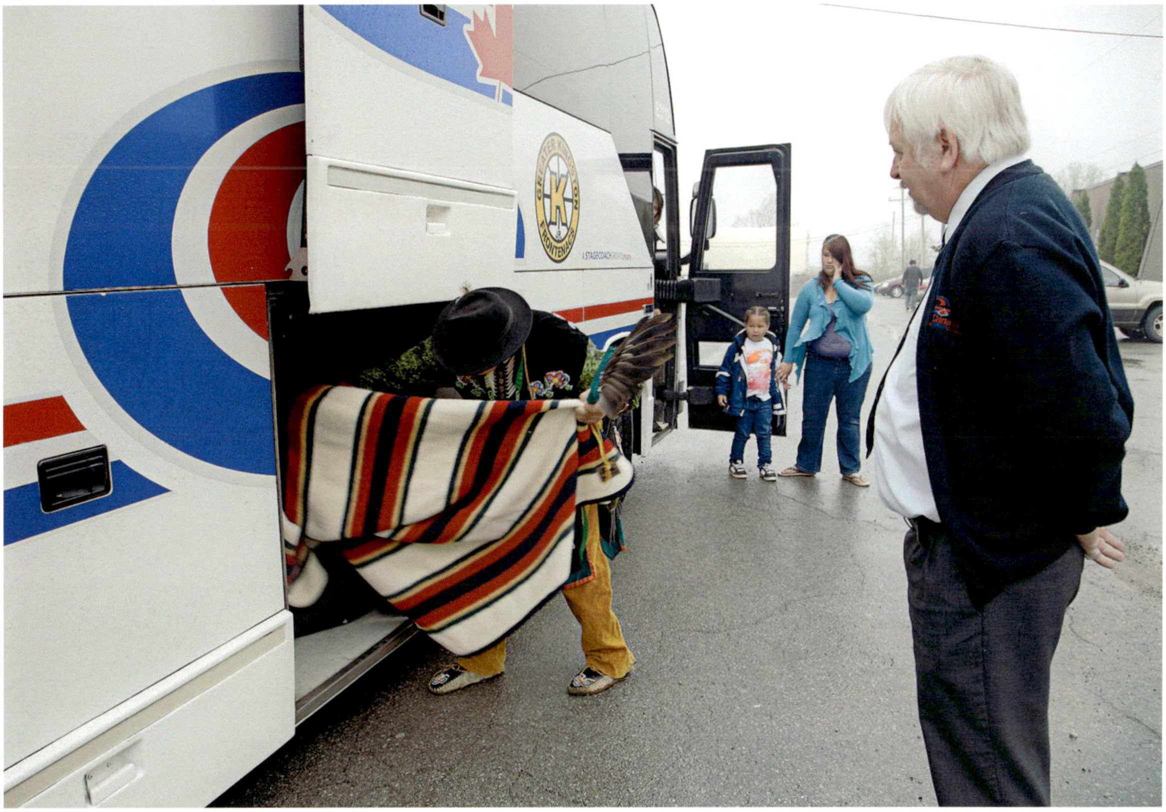

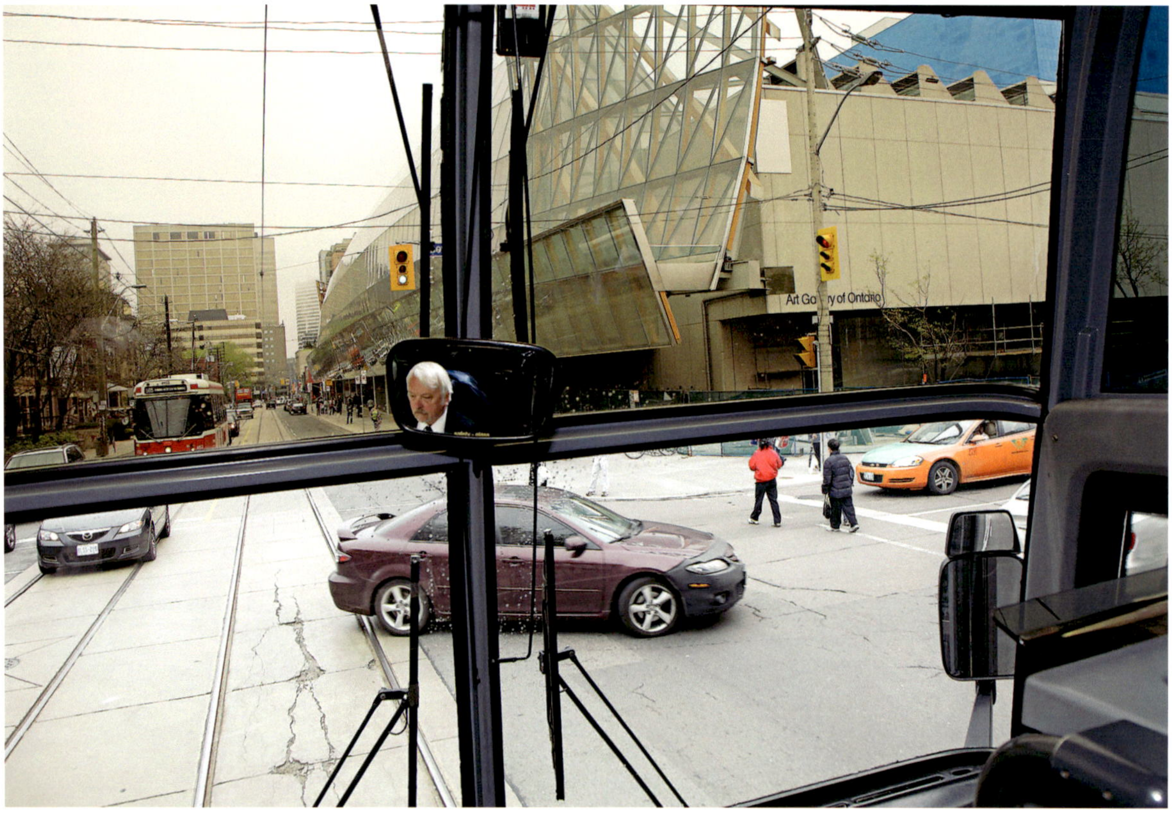

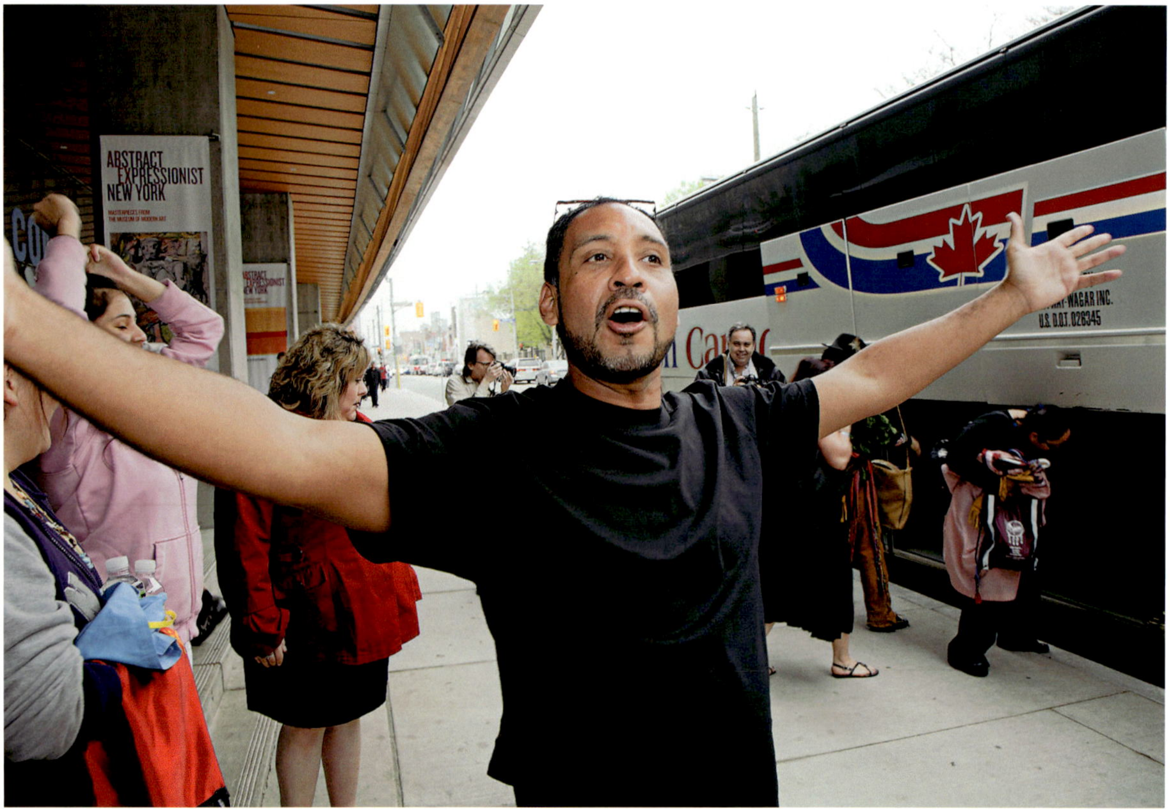

Art Gallery of Ontario

ABSTRACT
EXPRESSIONIST
NEW YORK
MASTERPIECES FROM
THE MUSEUM OF MODERN ART

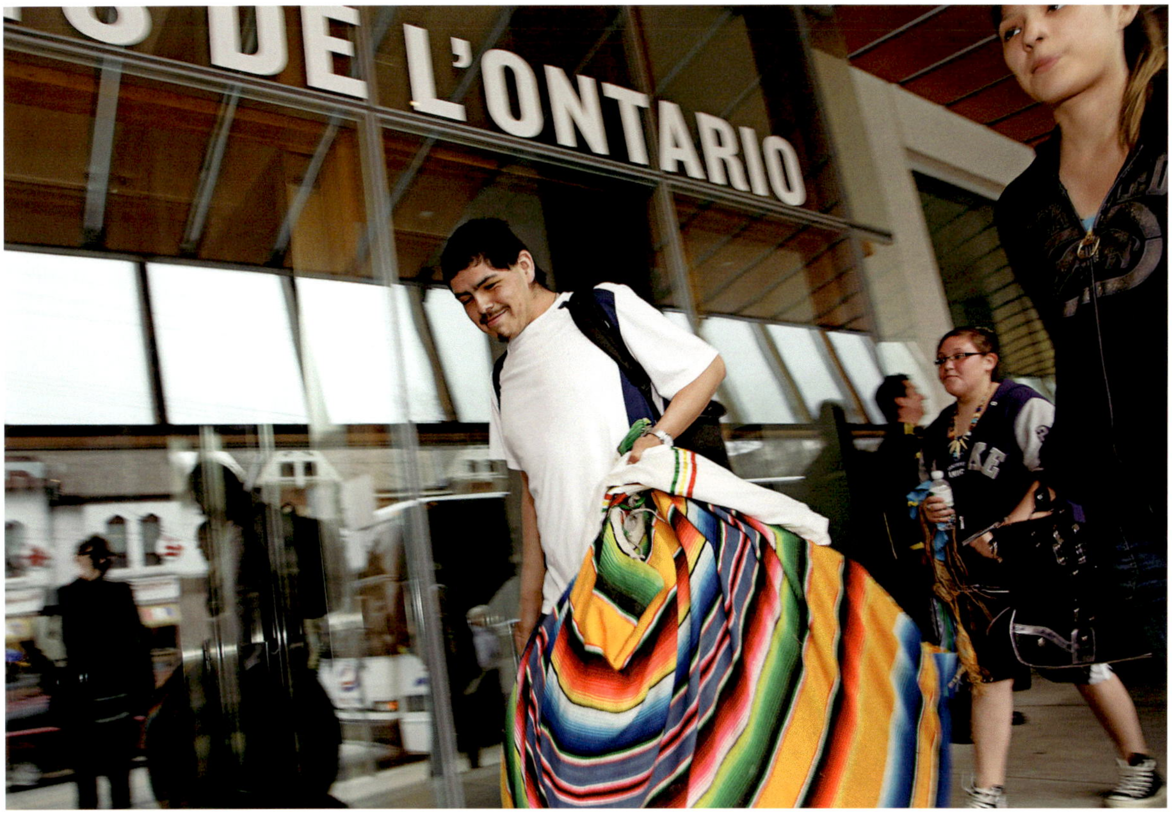

S DE L'ONTARIO

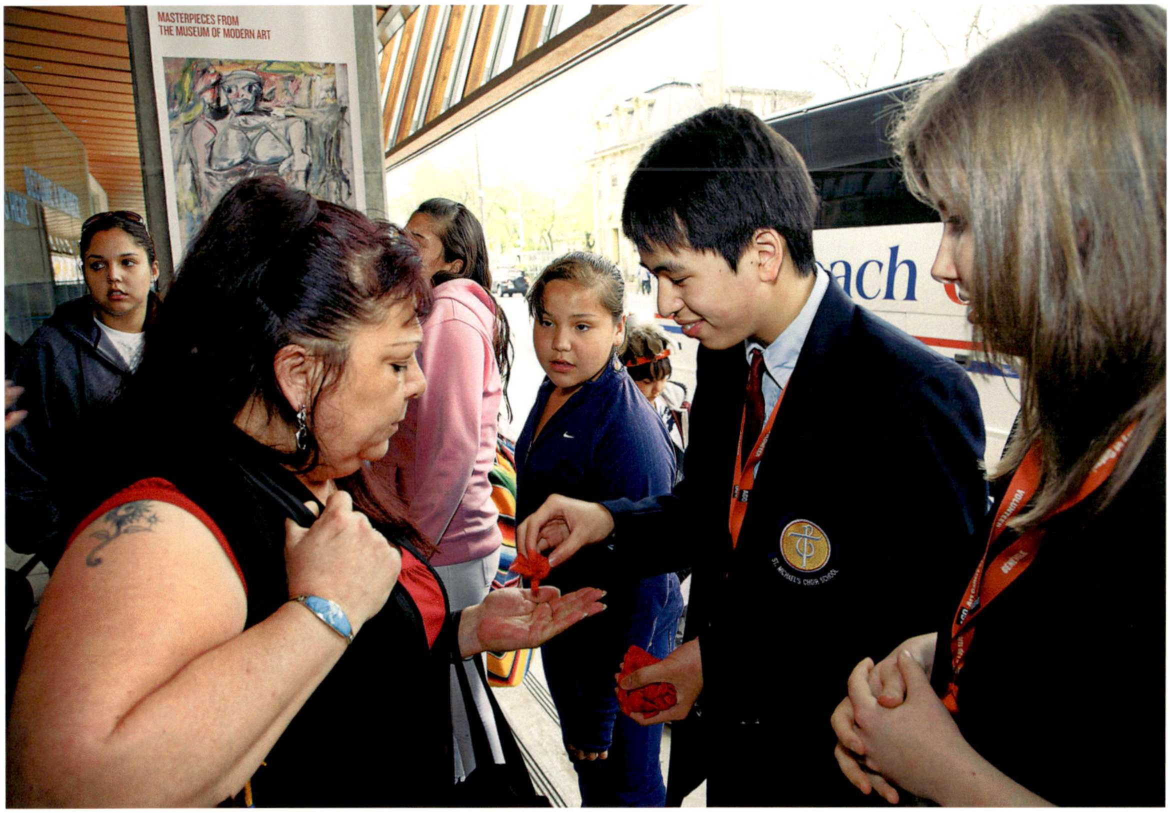

MASTERPIECES FROM
THE MUSEUM OF MODERN ART

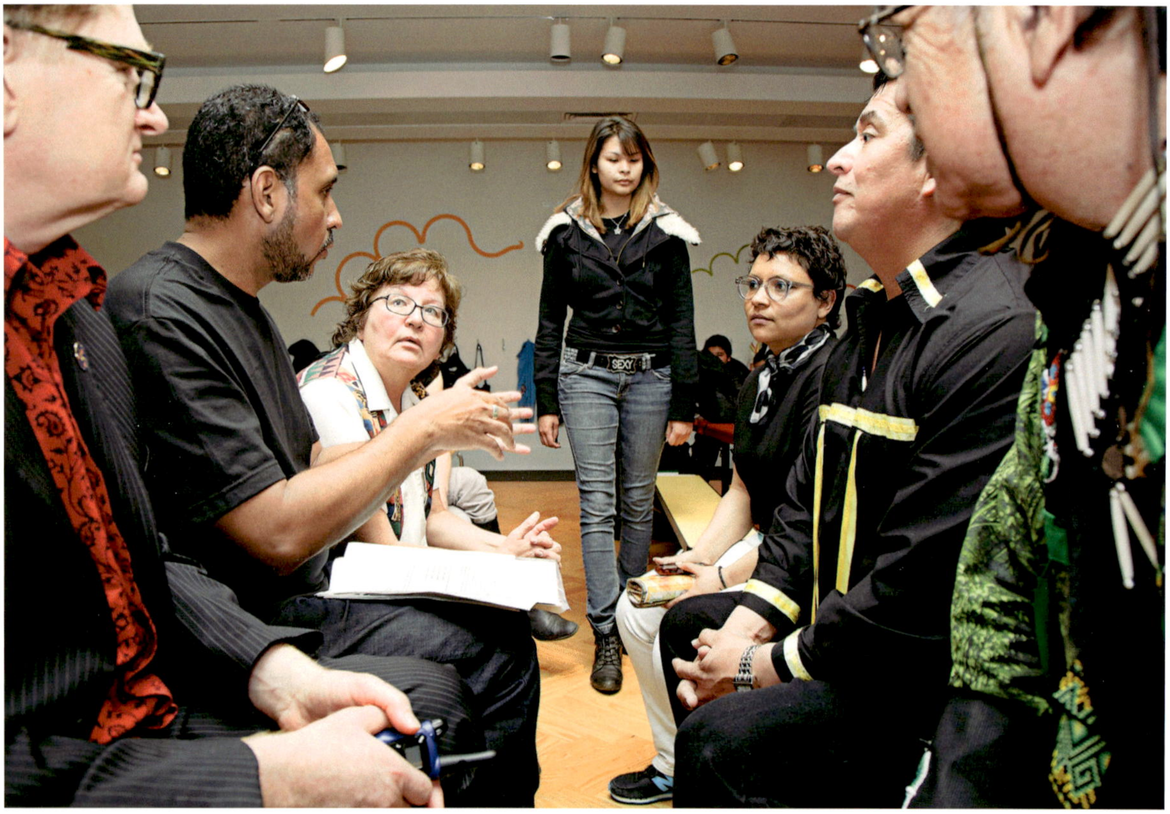

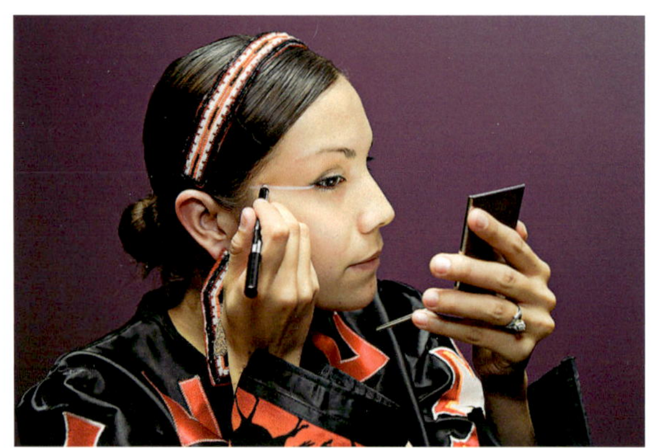
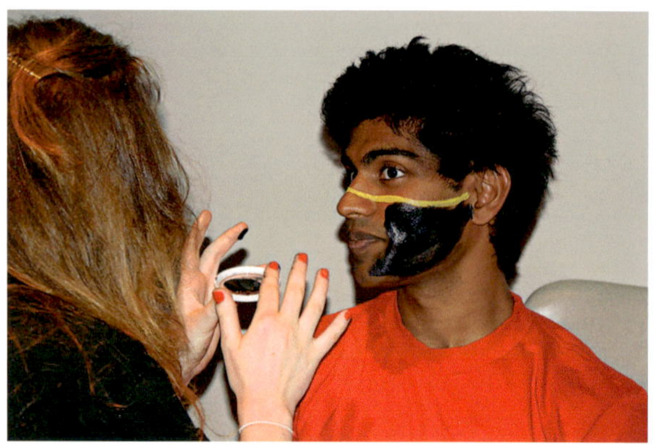
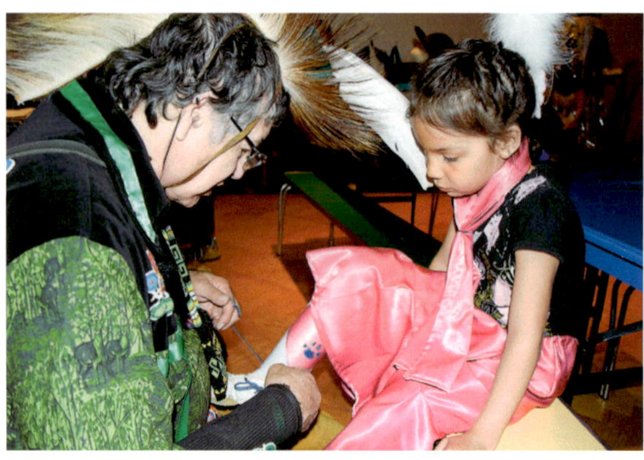
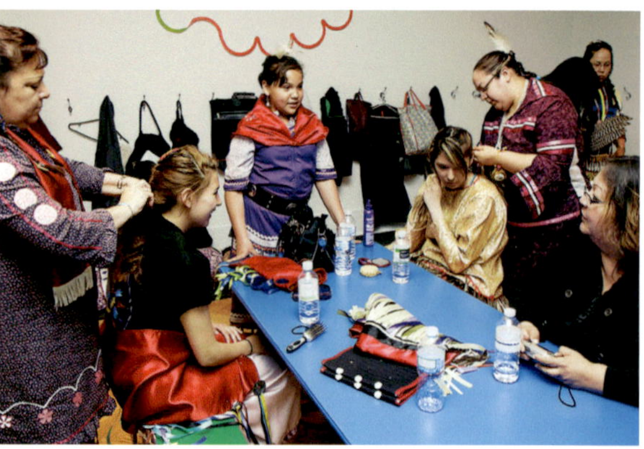

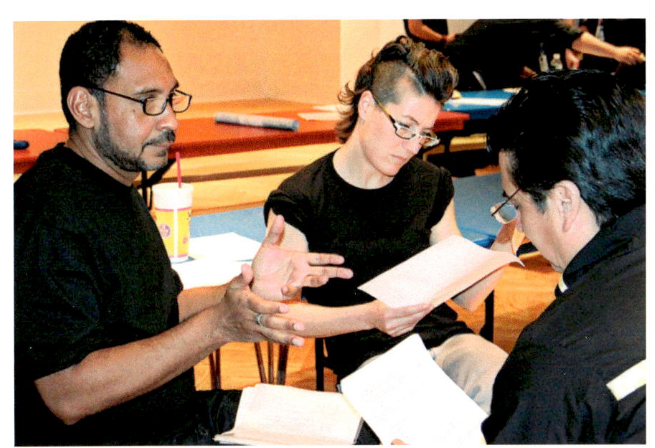

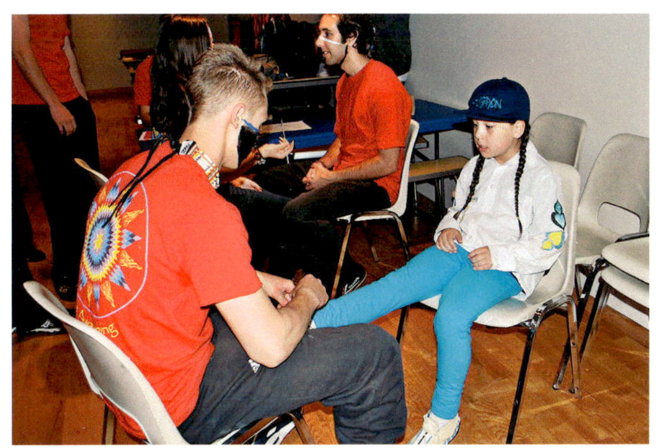

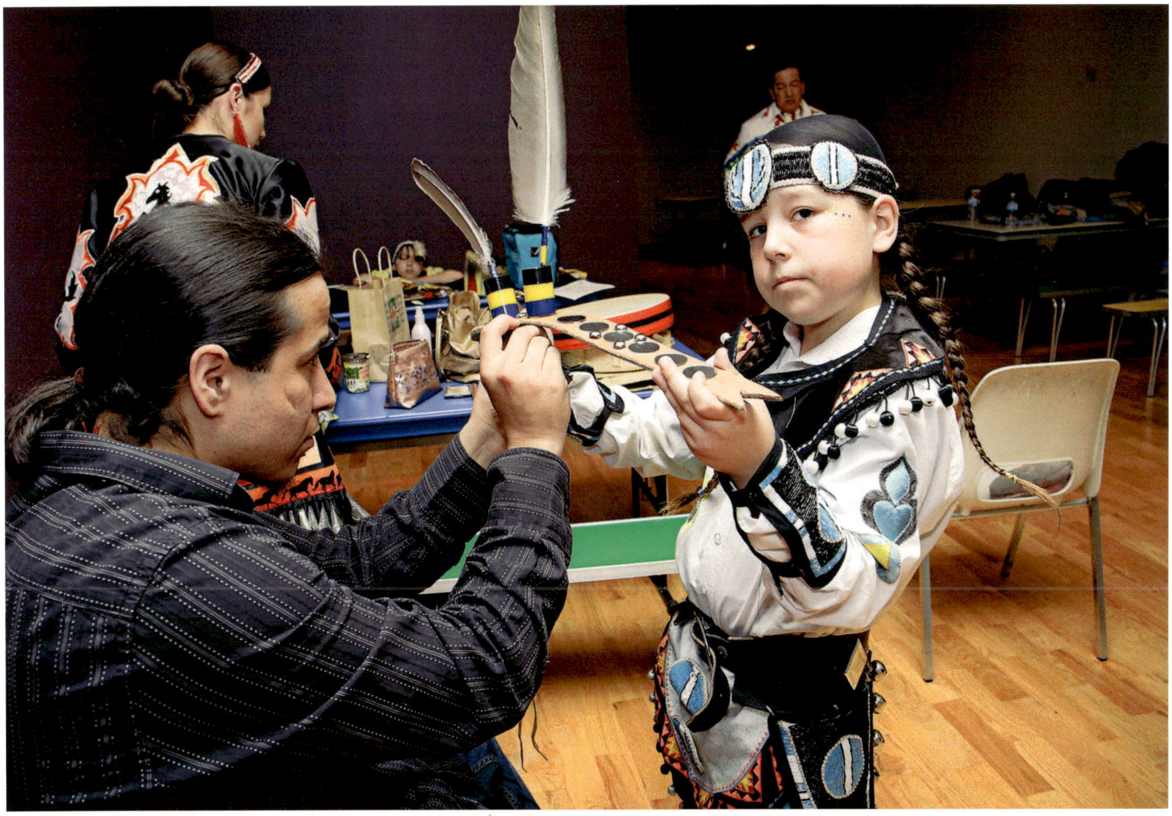

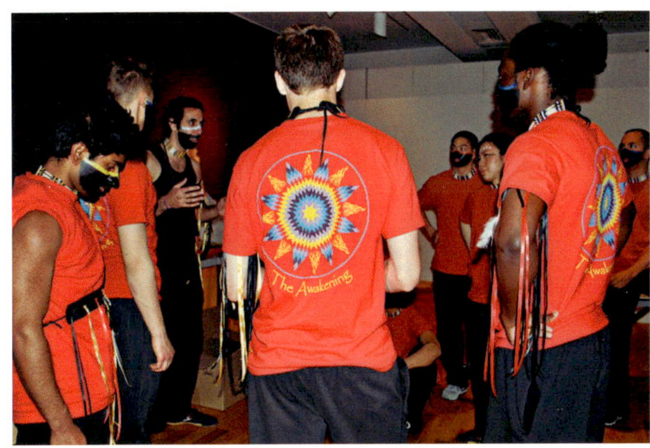

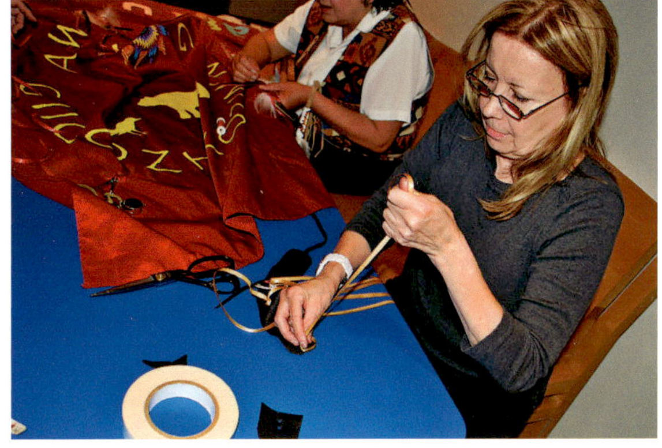

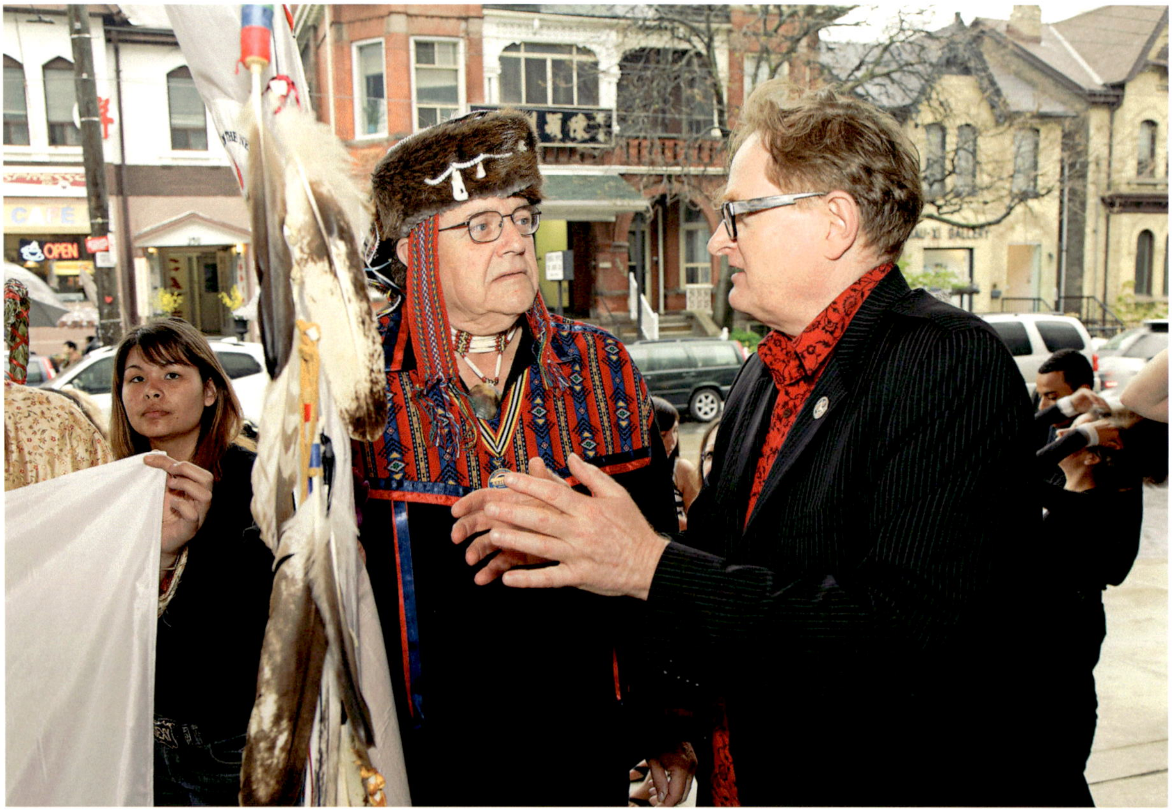

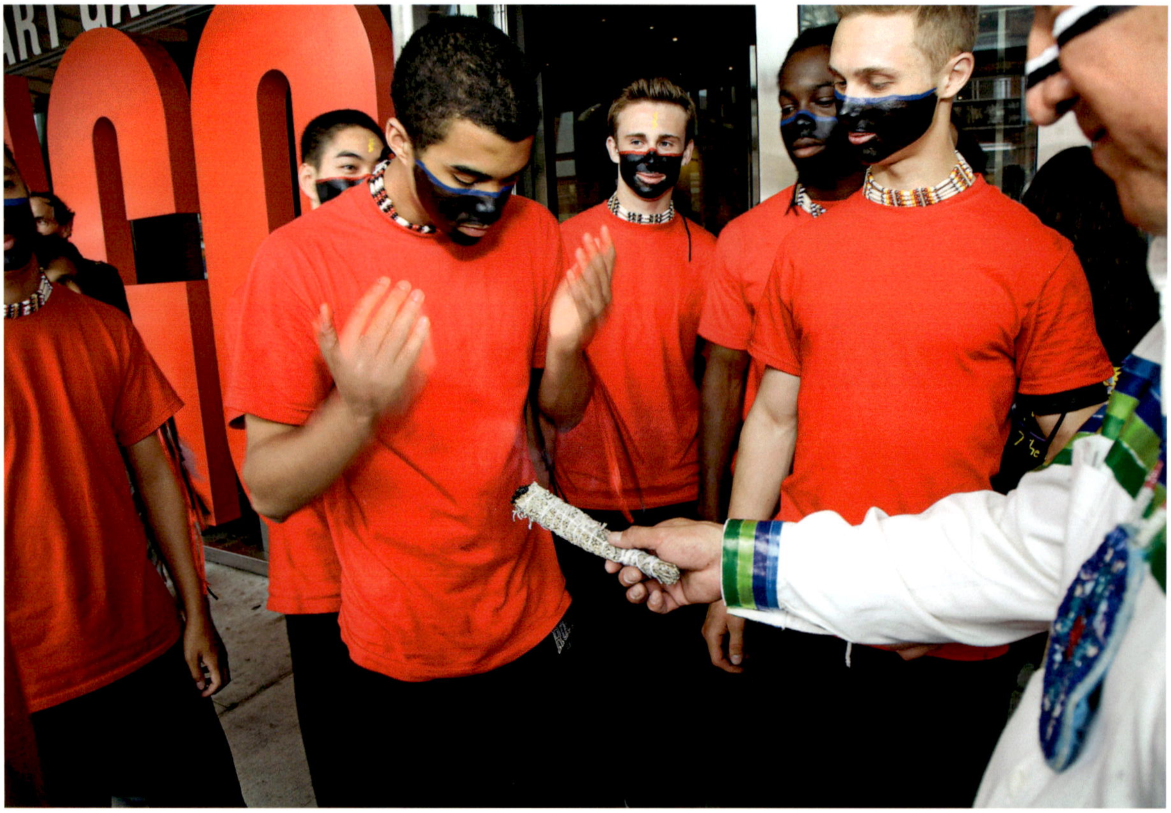

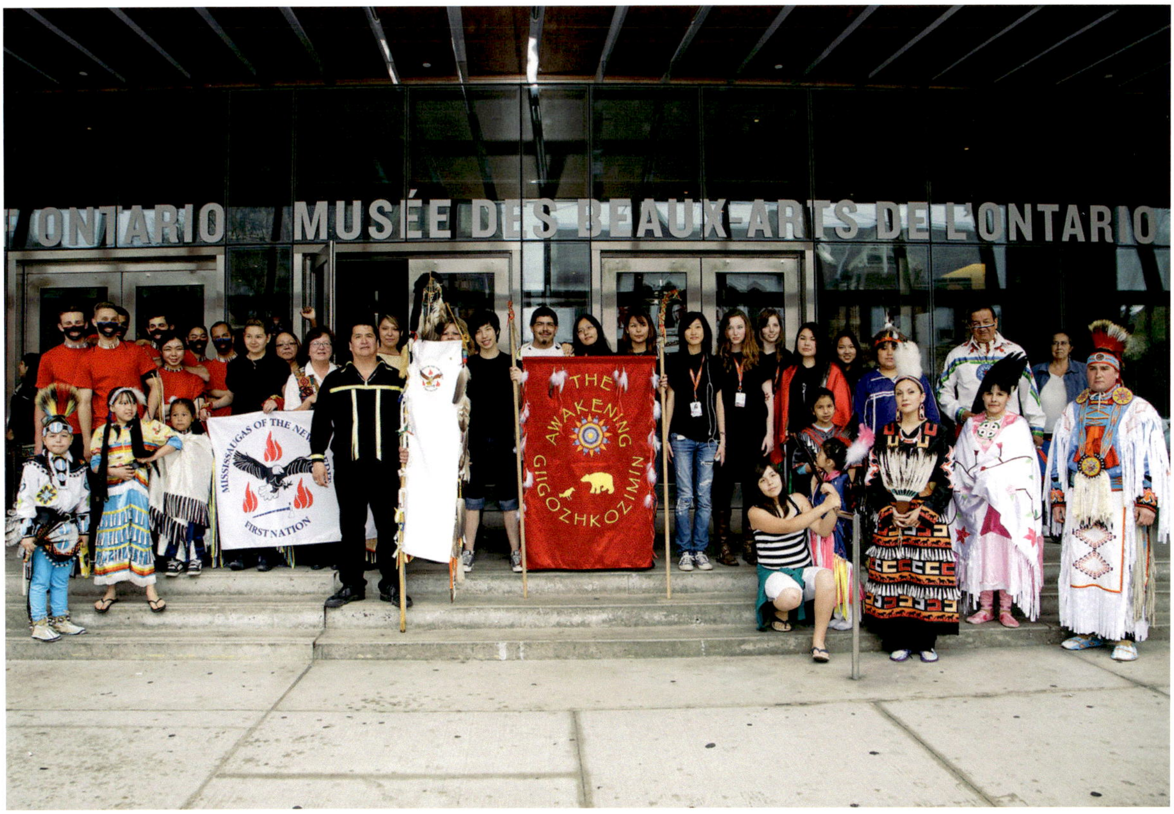

ONTARIO
MUSÉE DES BEAUX-ARTS DE L'ONTARIO
MISSISSAUGAS OF THE NEW
FIRST NATION
THE
AWAKENING
GIIGOZHKOZIMIN

MUSÉE DES
UX ARTS DE L'ONTARIO
The Awakening

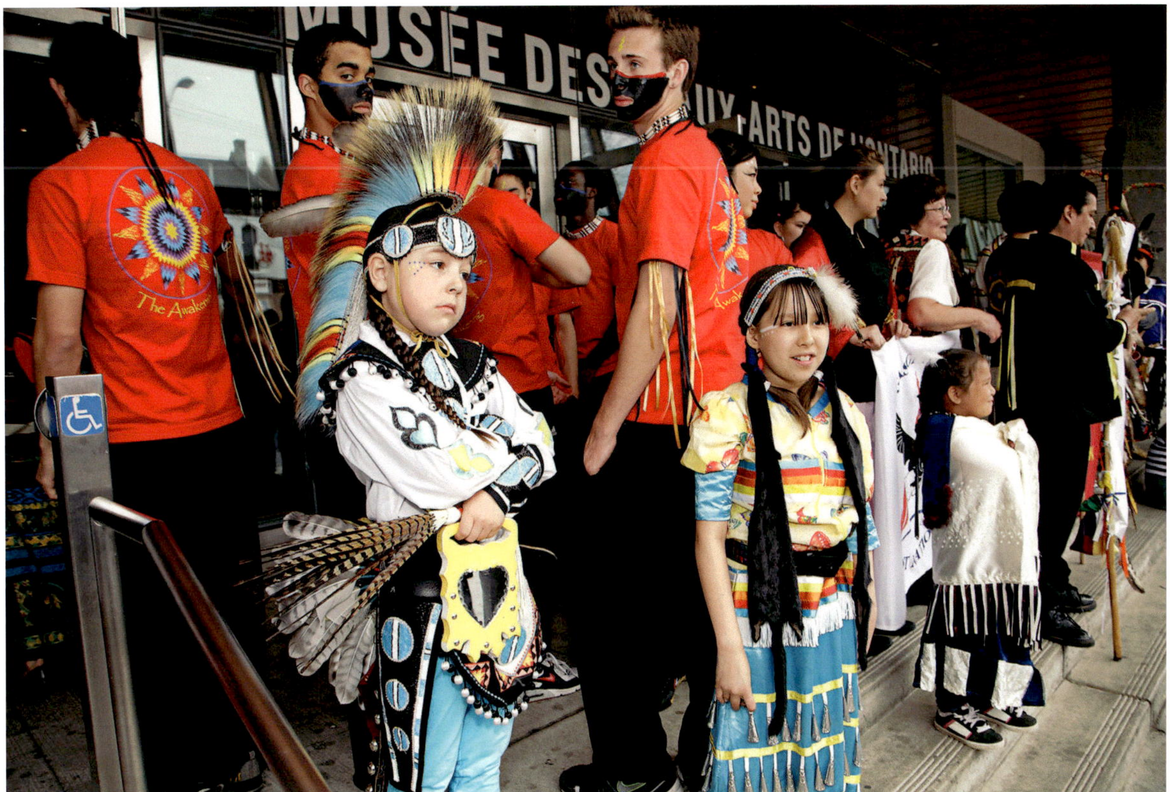

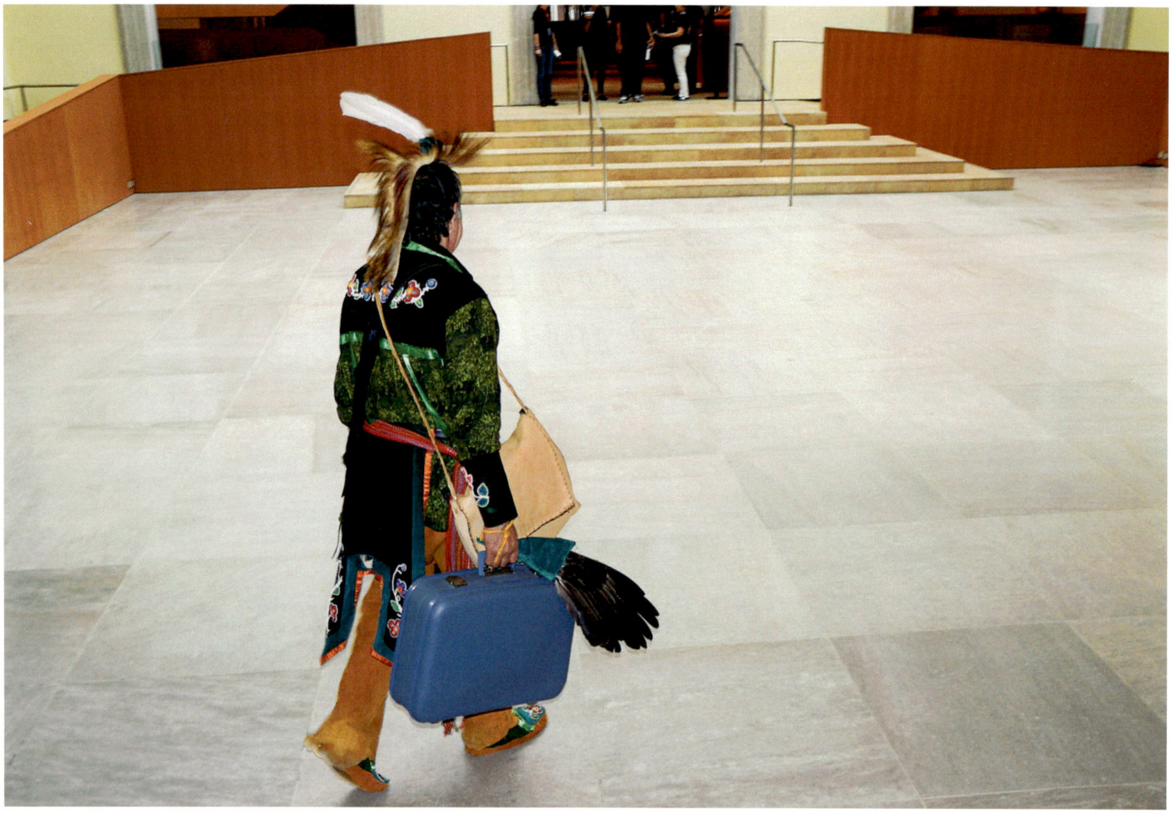

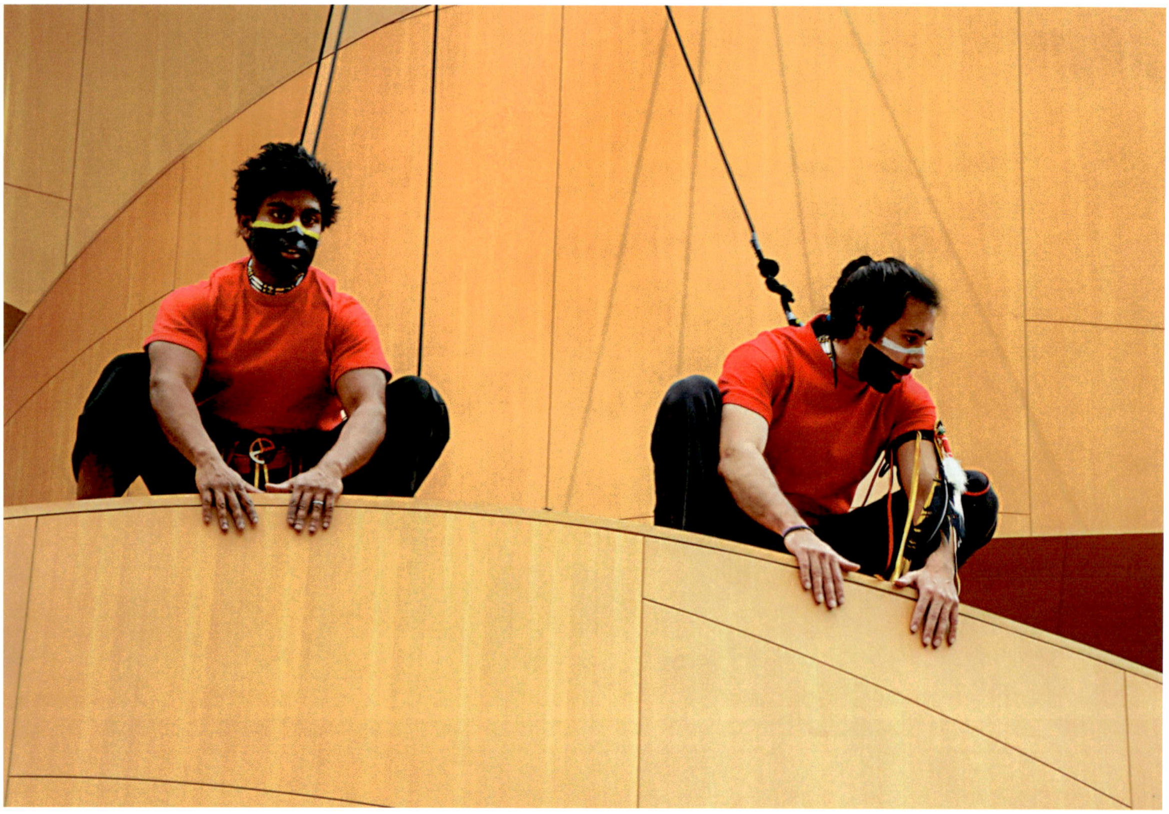

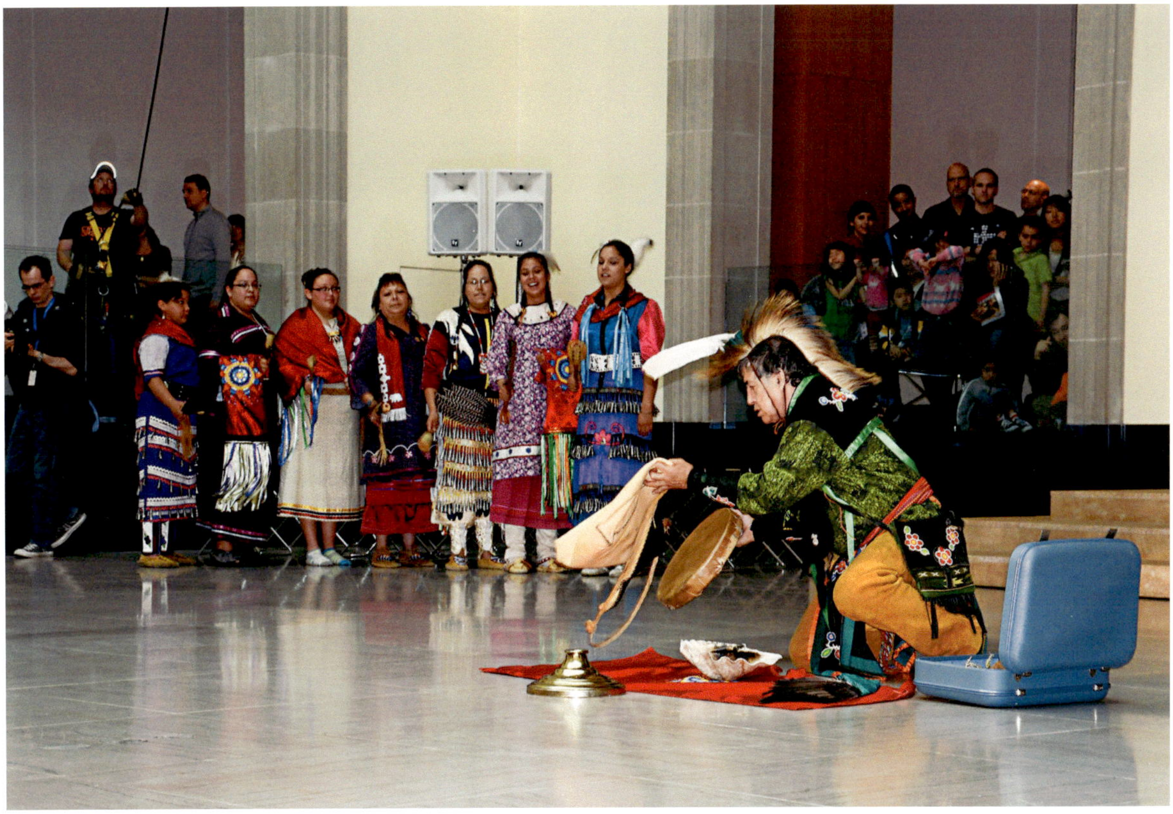

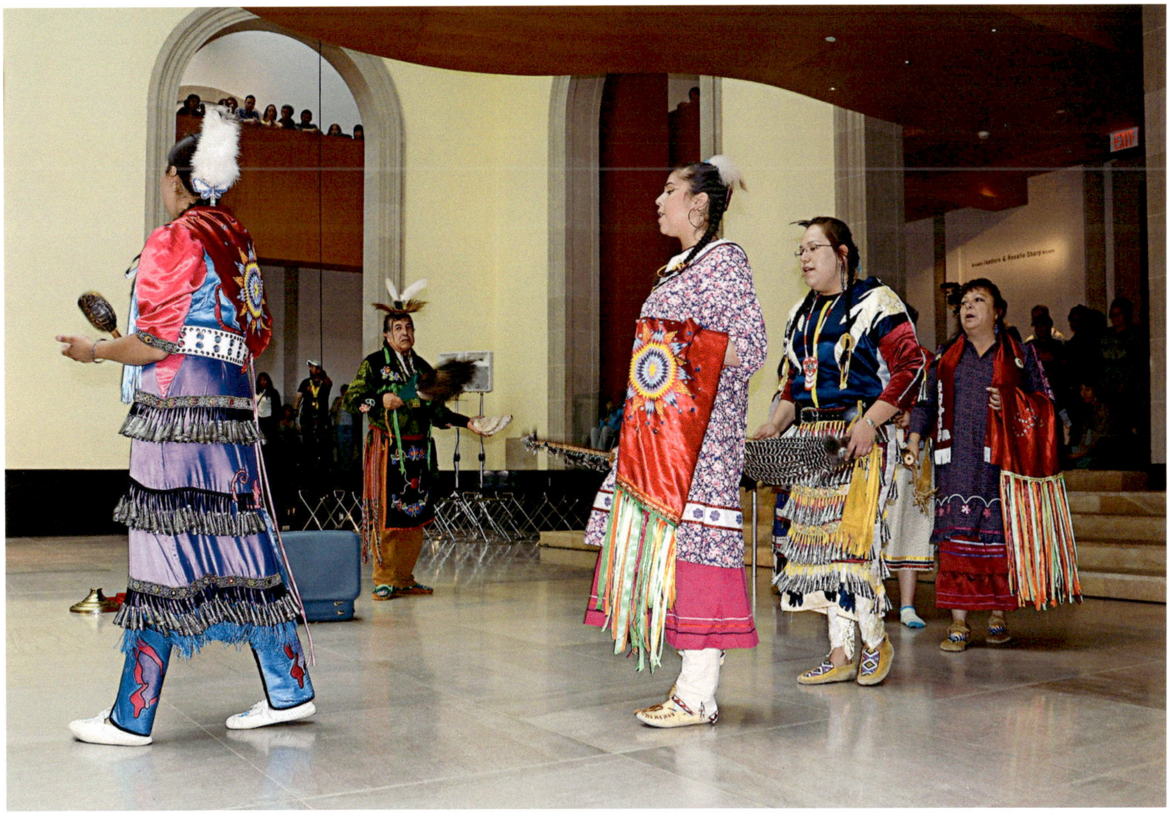
EXIT
Isadore & Rosalie Sharp

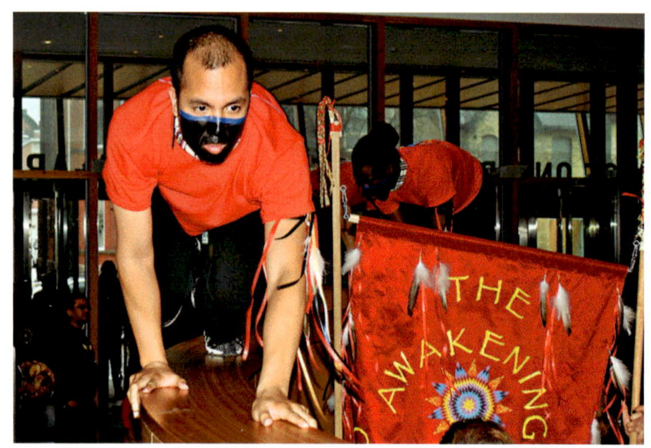
THE
AWAKENING

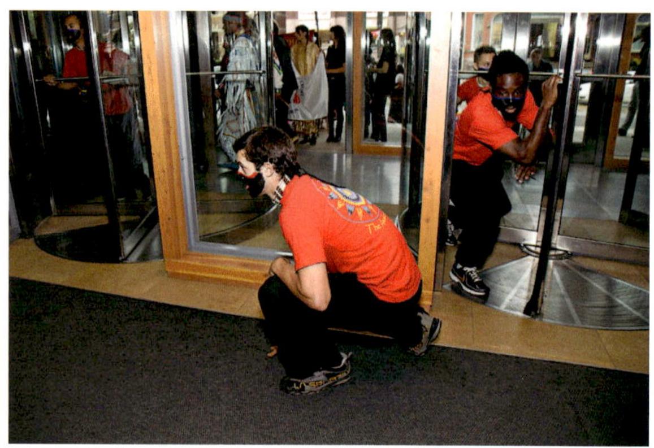

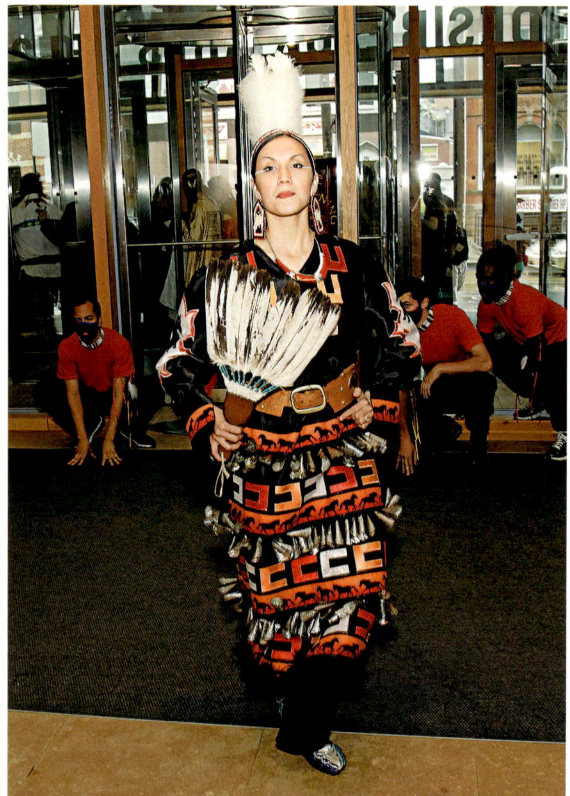

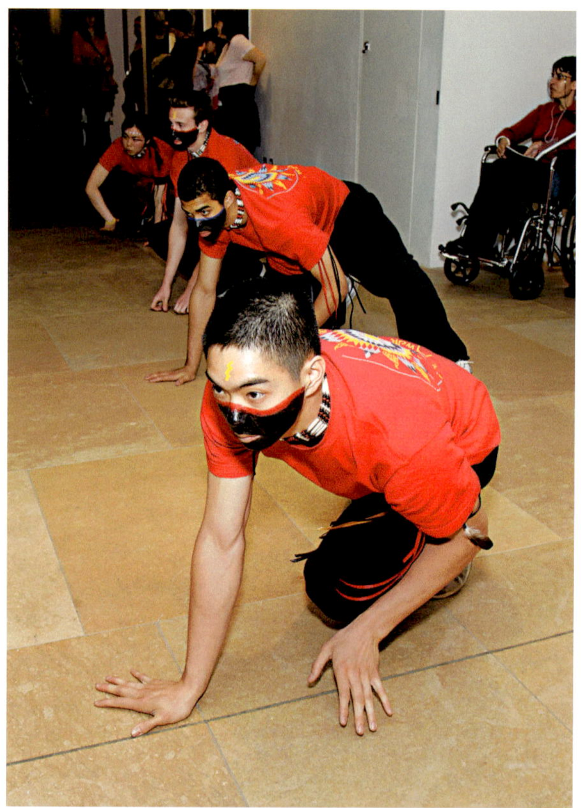

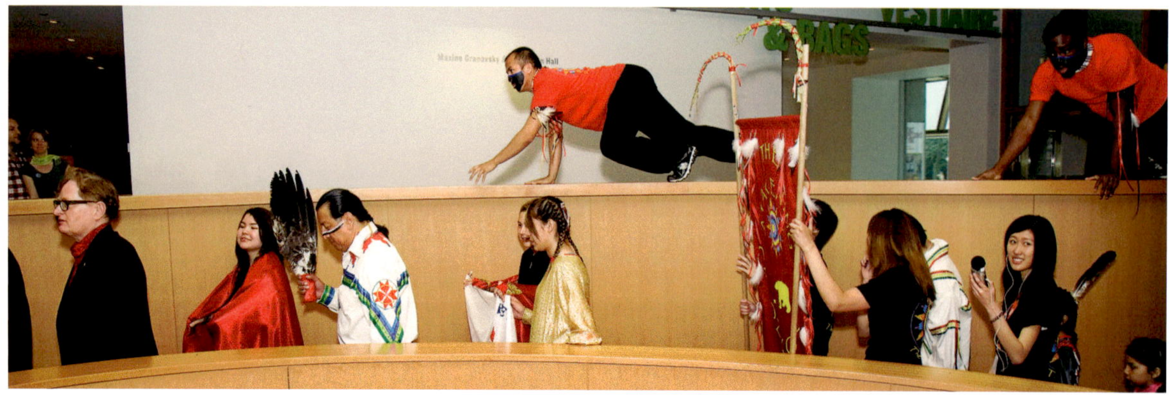
& BAGS
VESTAIRE

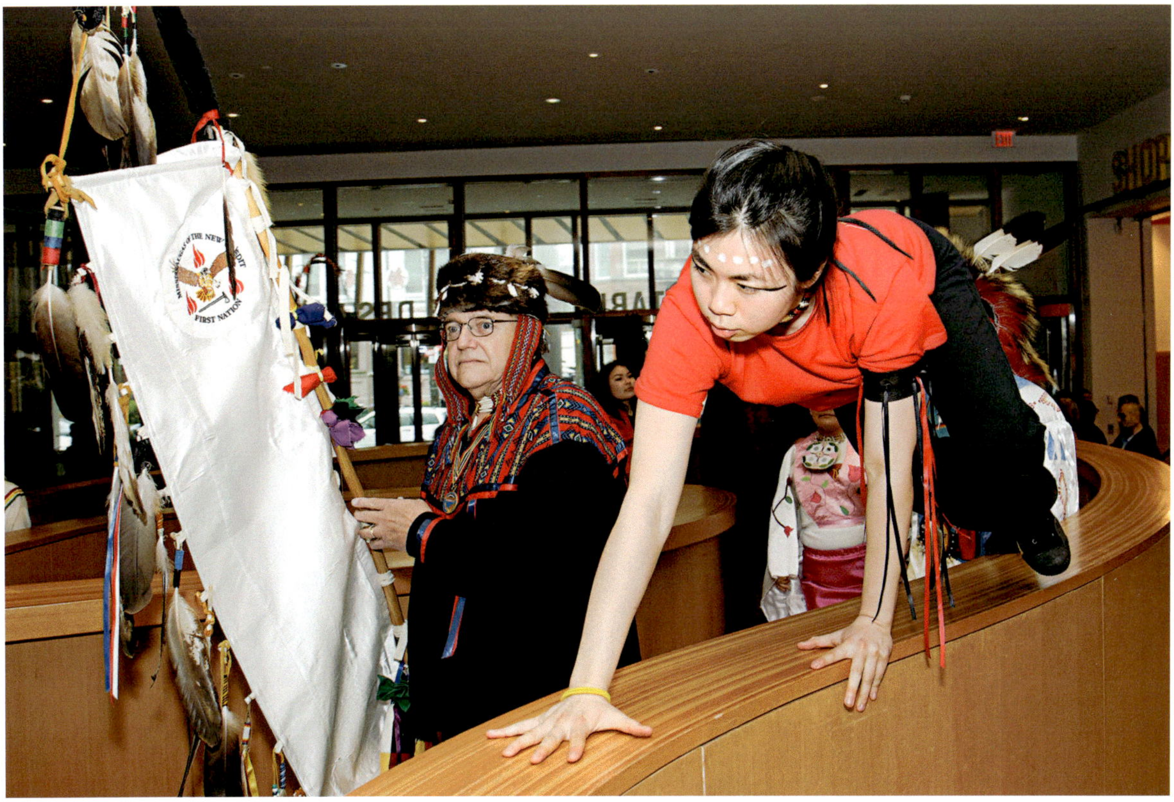

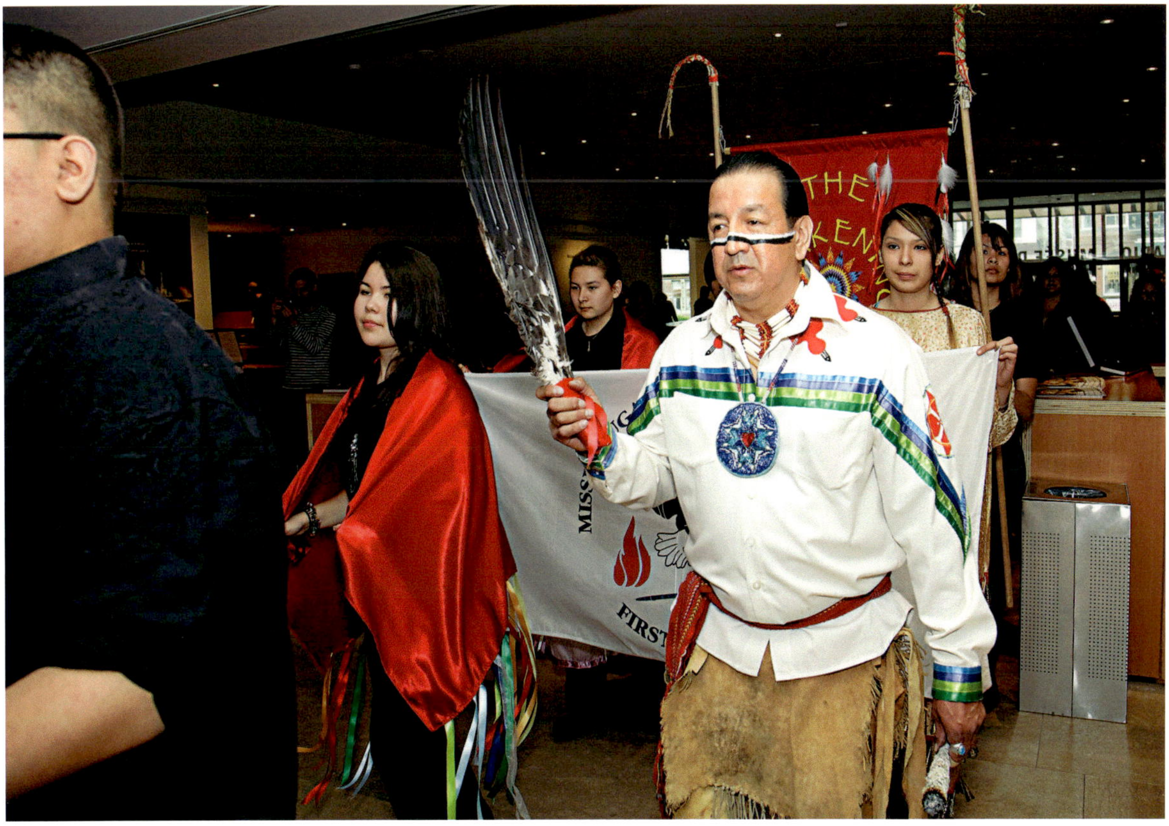

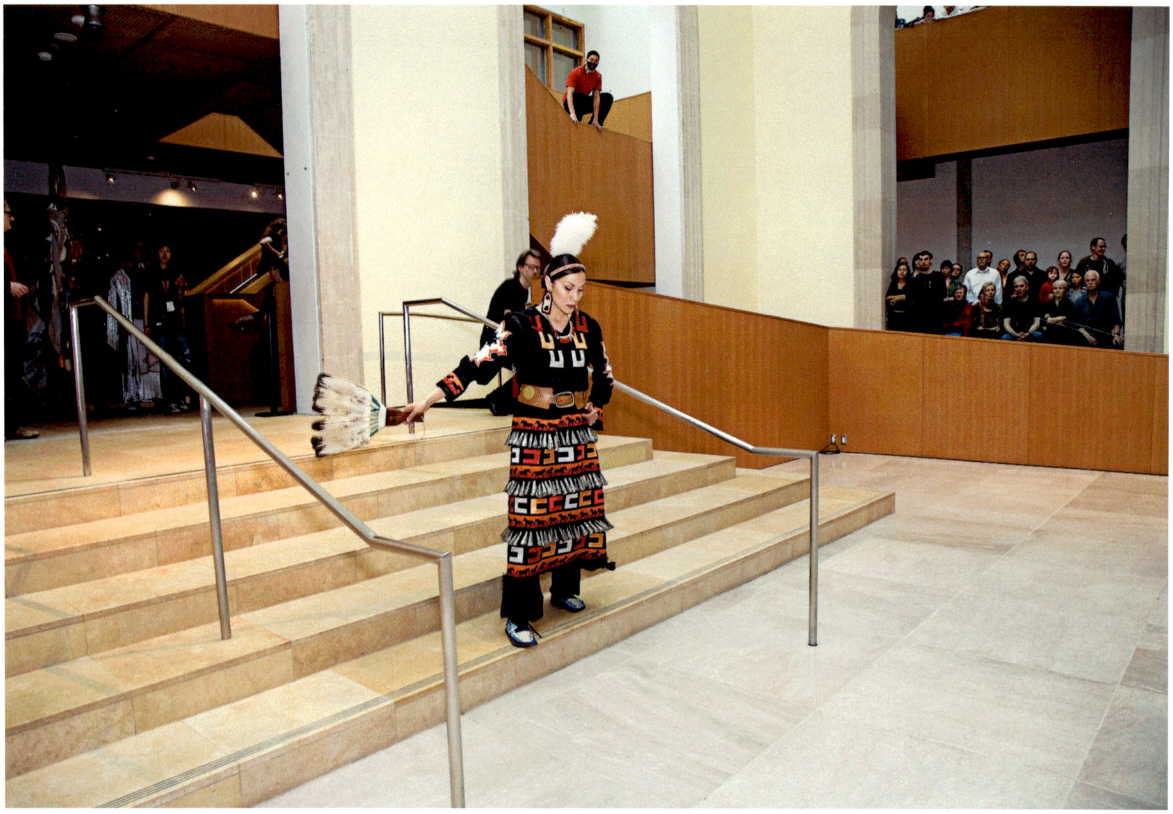

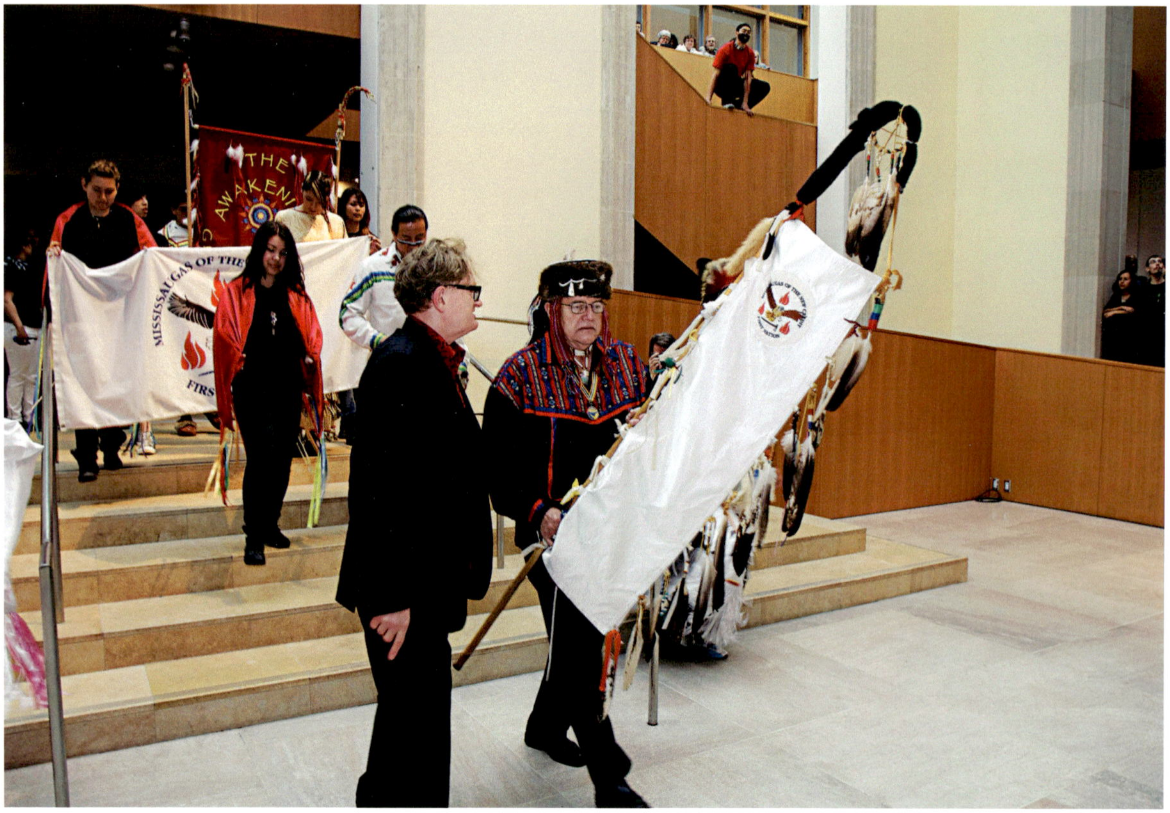

THE AWAKEN
MISSISSAUGAS OF THE
FIRST

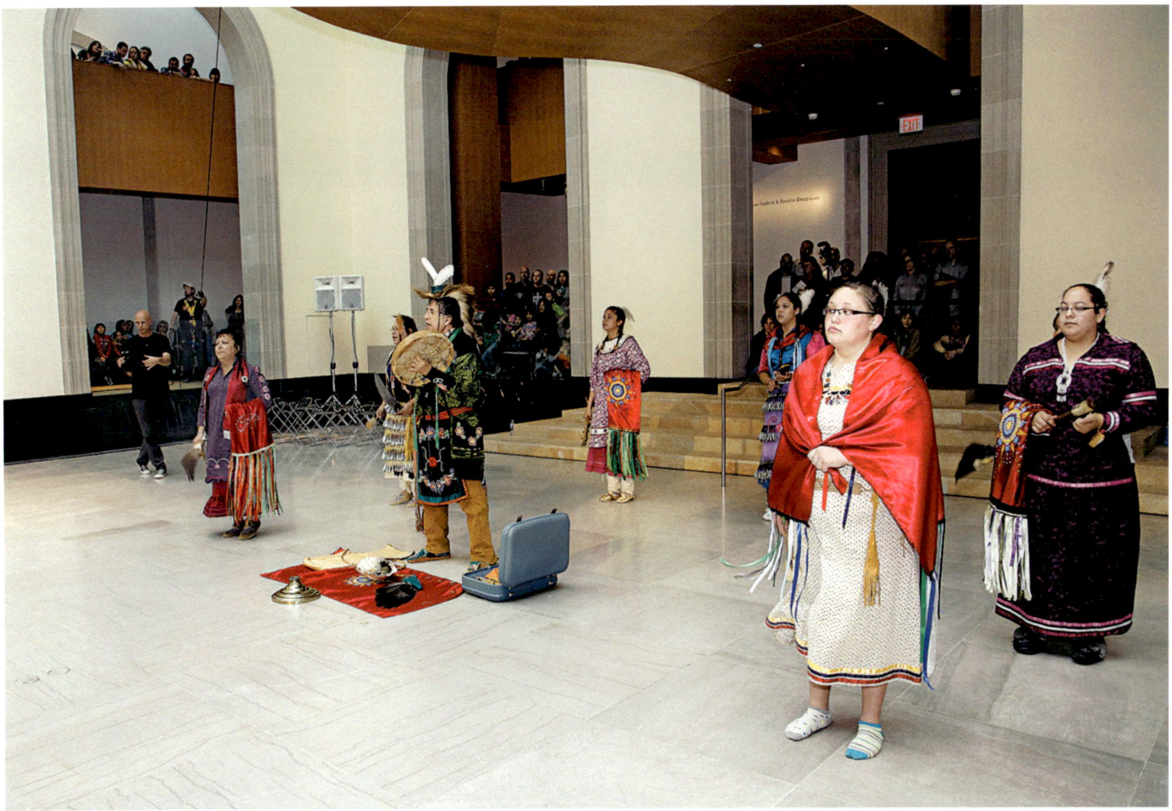

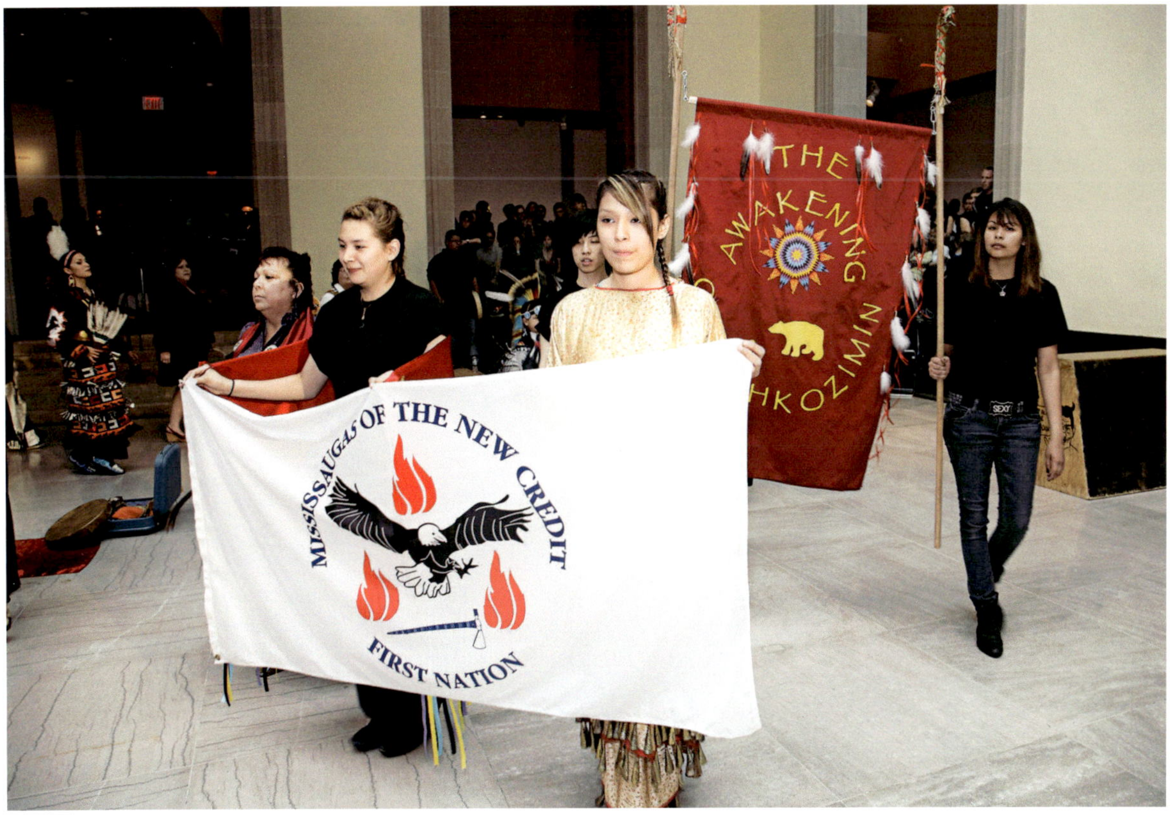

THE AWAKENING
HKOZIMIN

MISSISSAUGAS OF THE NEW CREDIT
FIRST NATION
SEXY

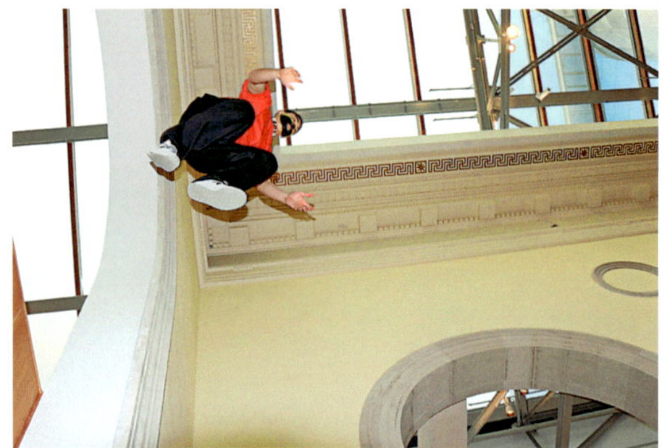

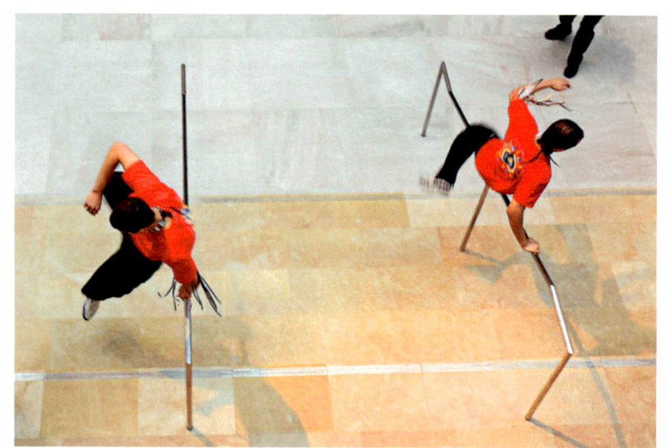

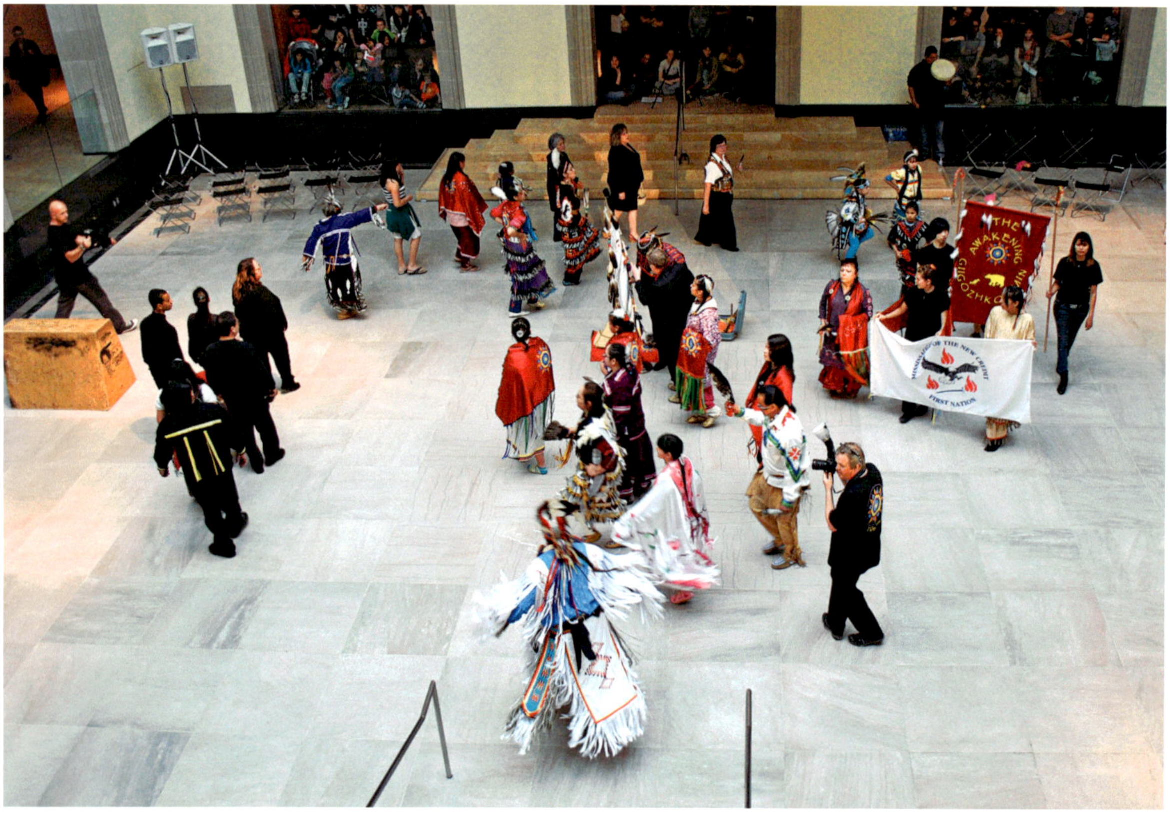

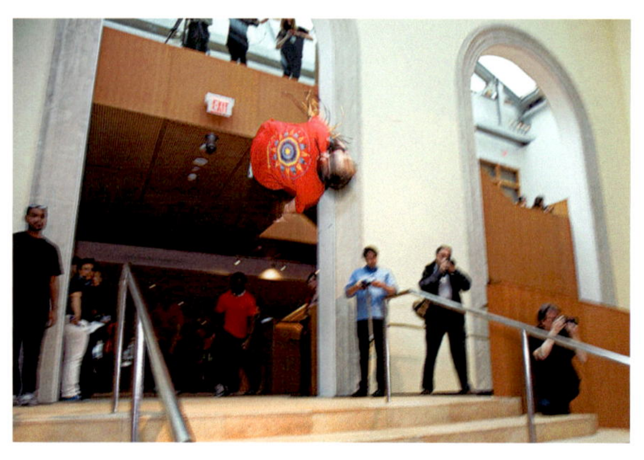

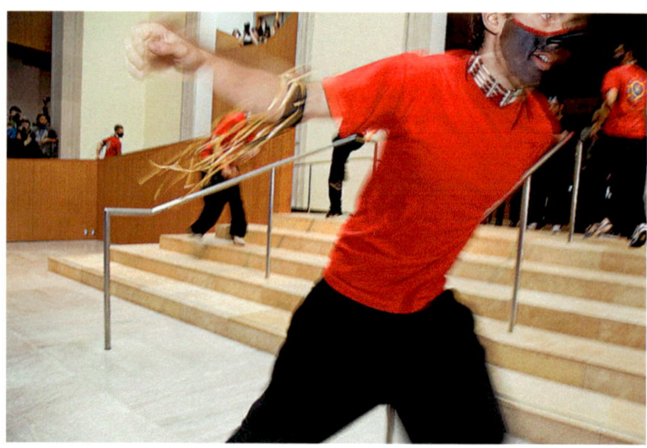

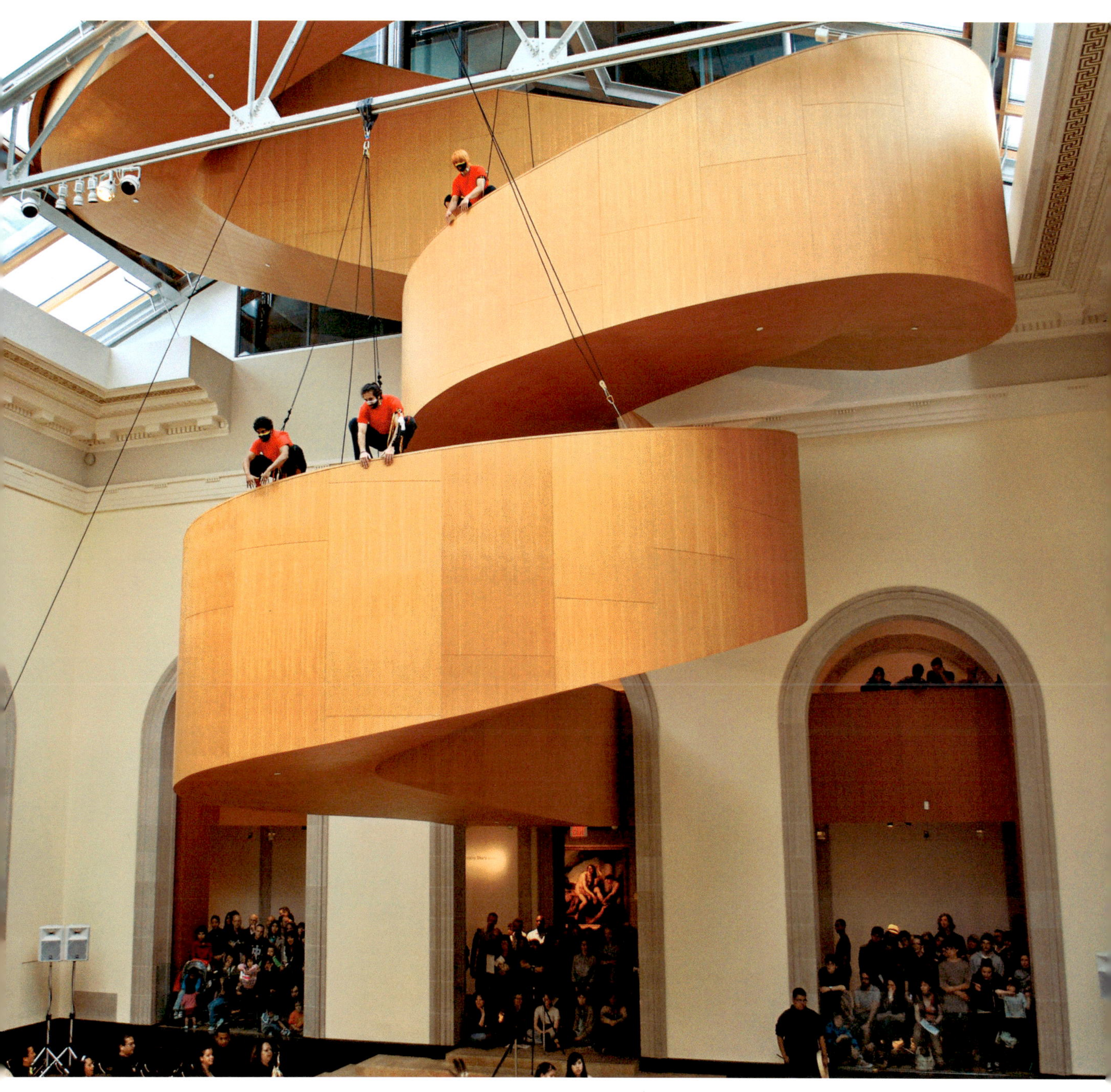

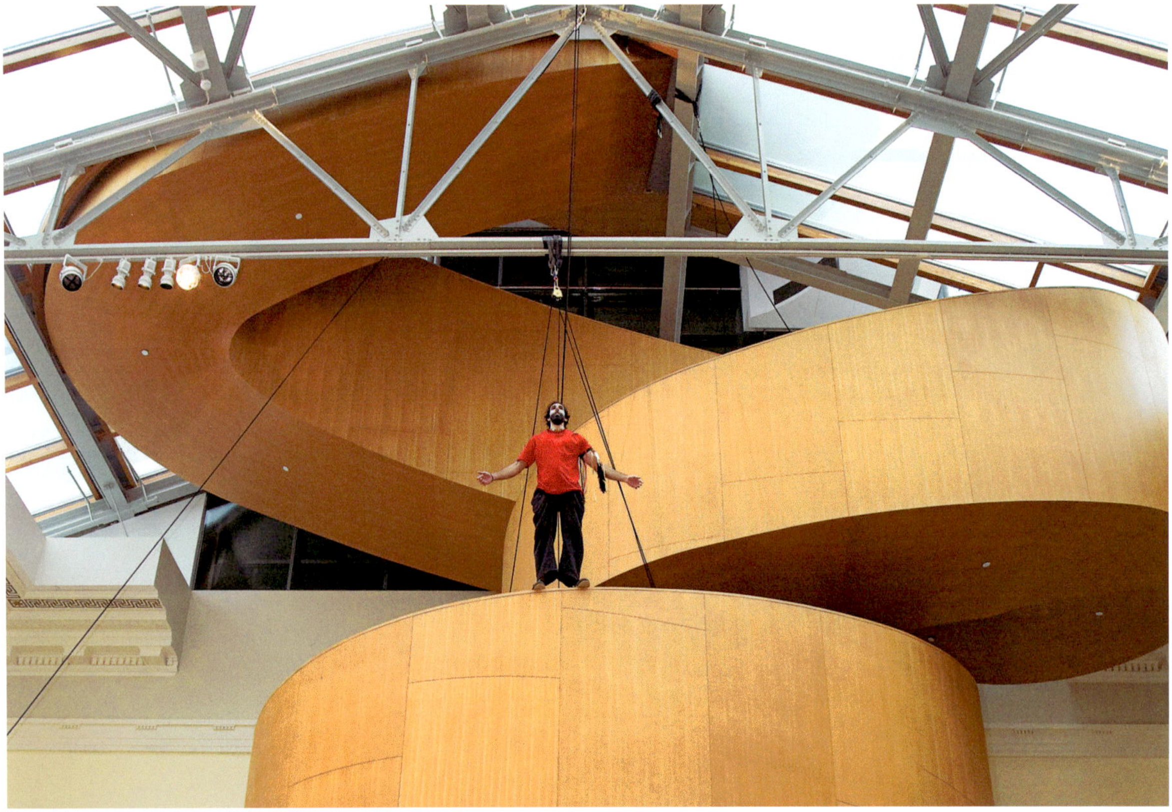

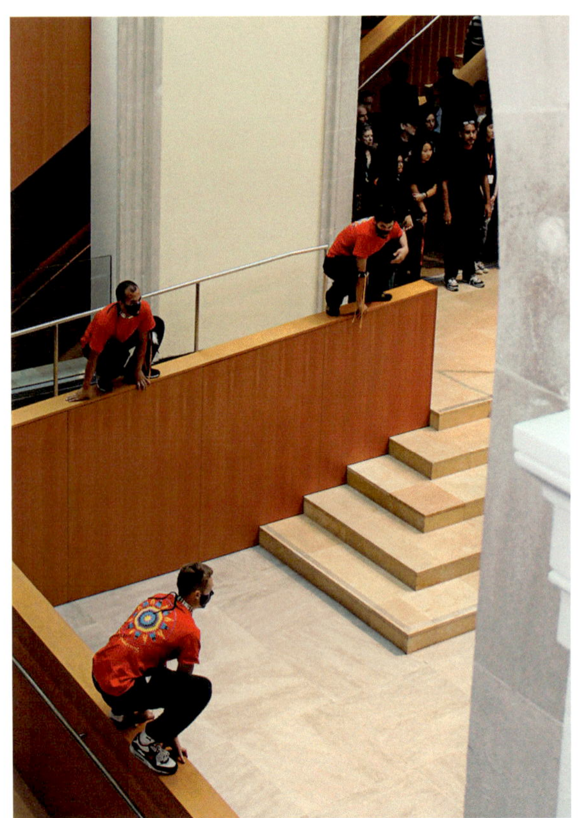

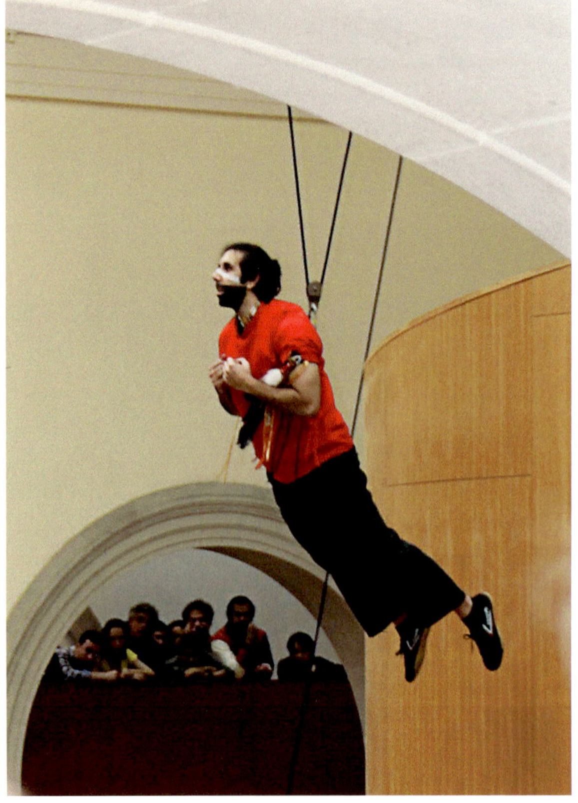

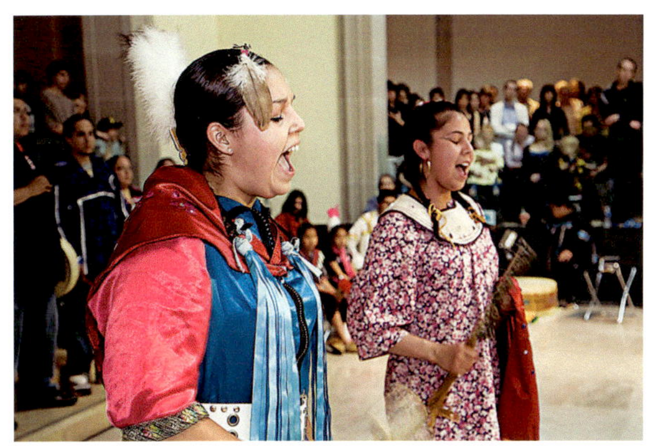

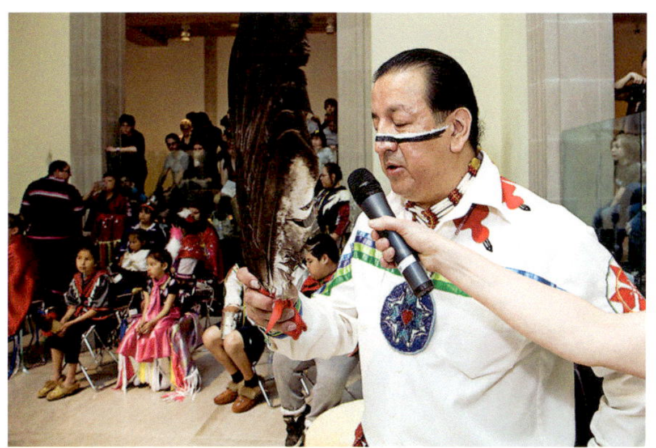

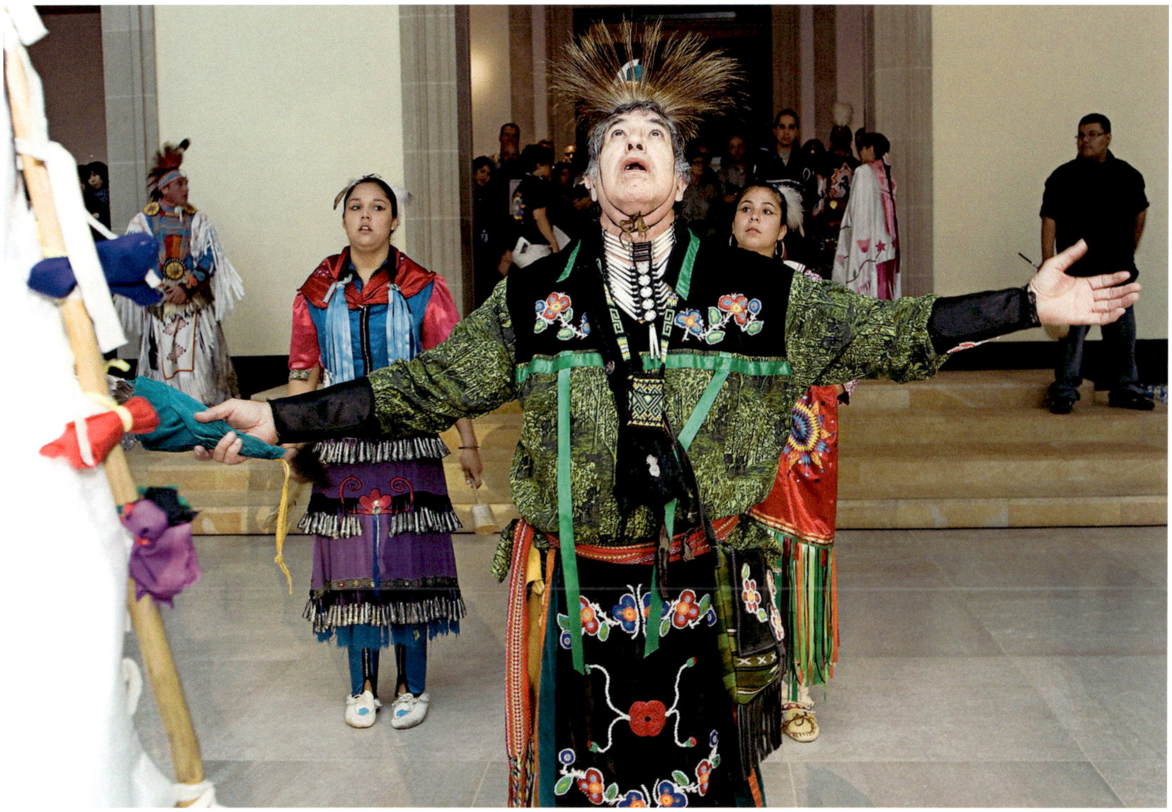

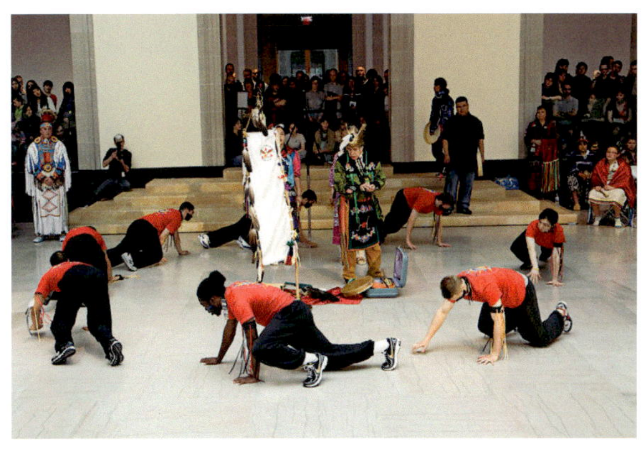

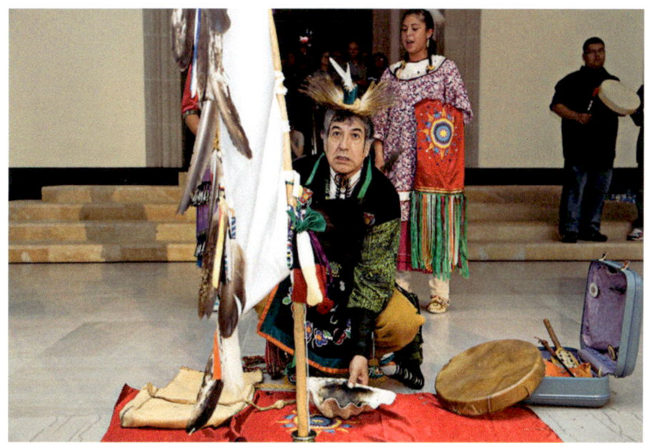

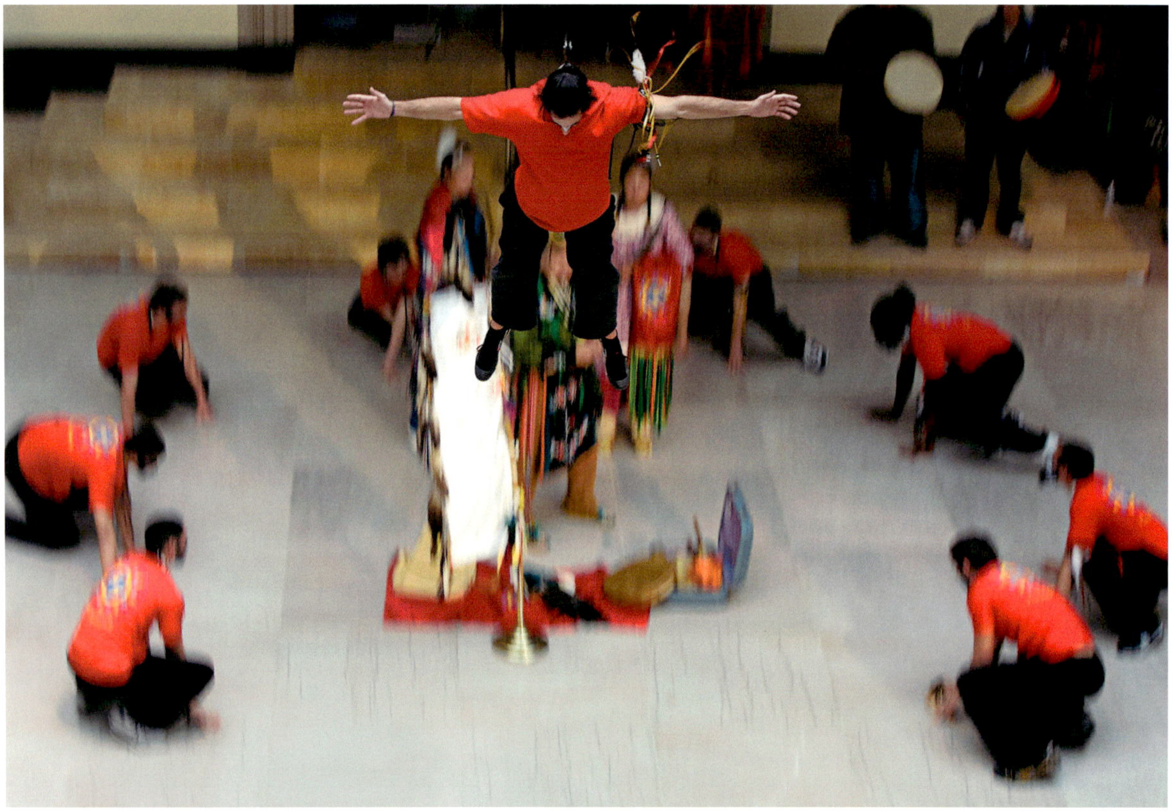

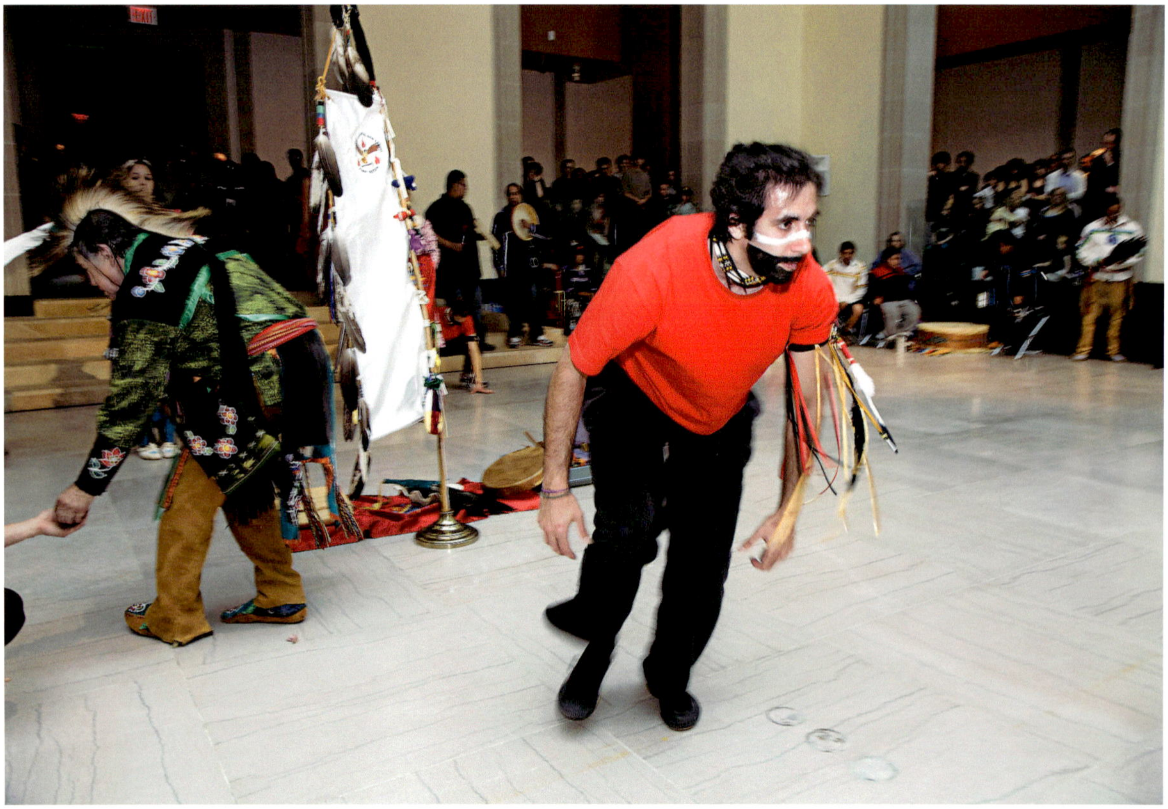

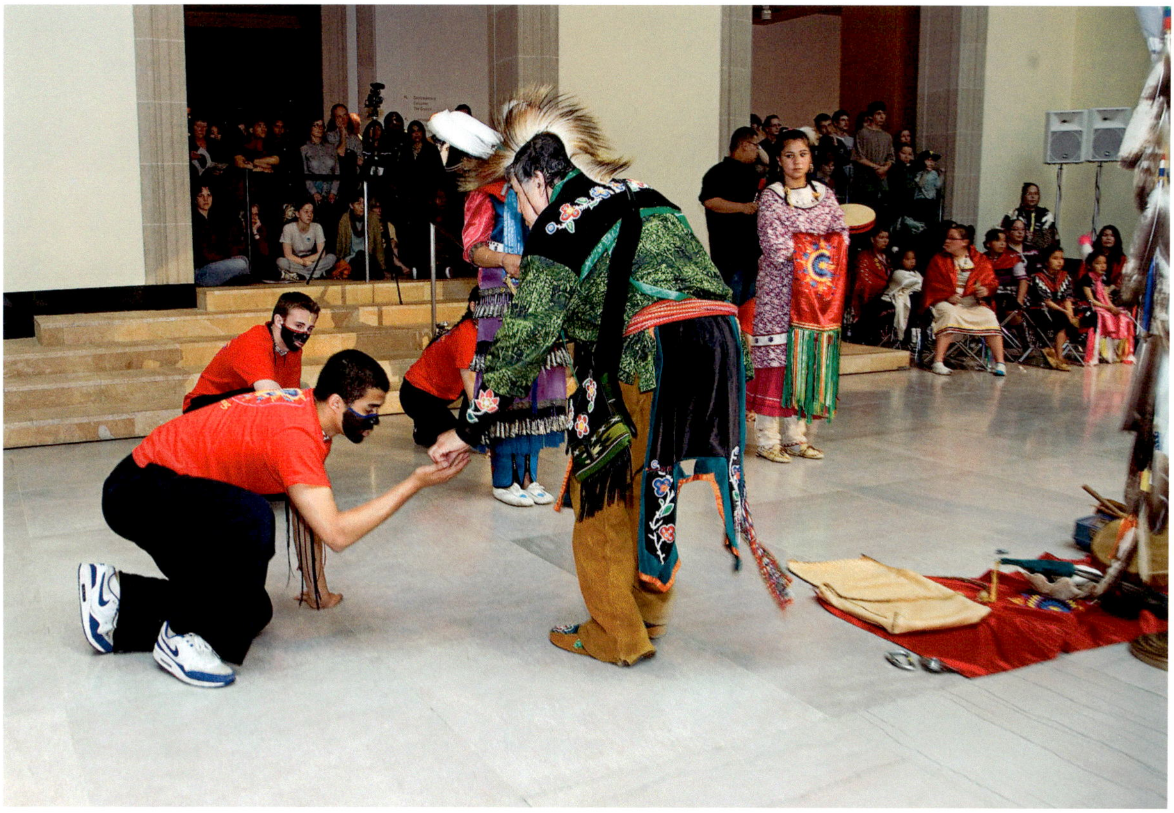

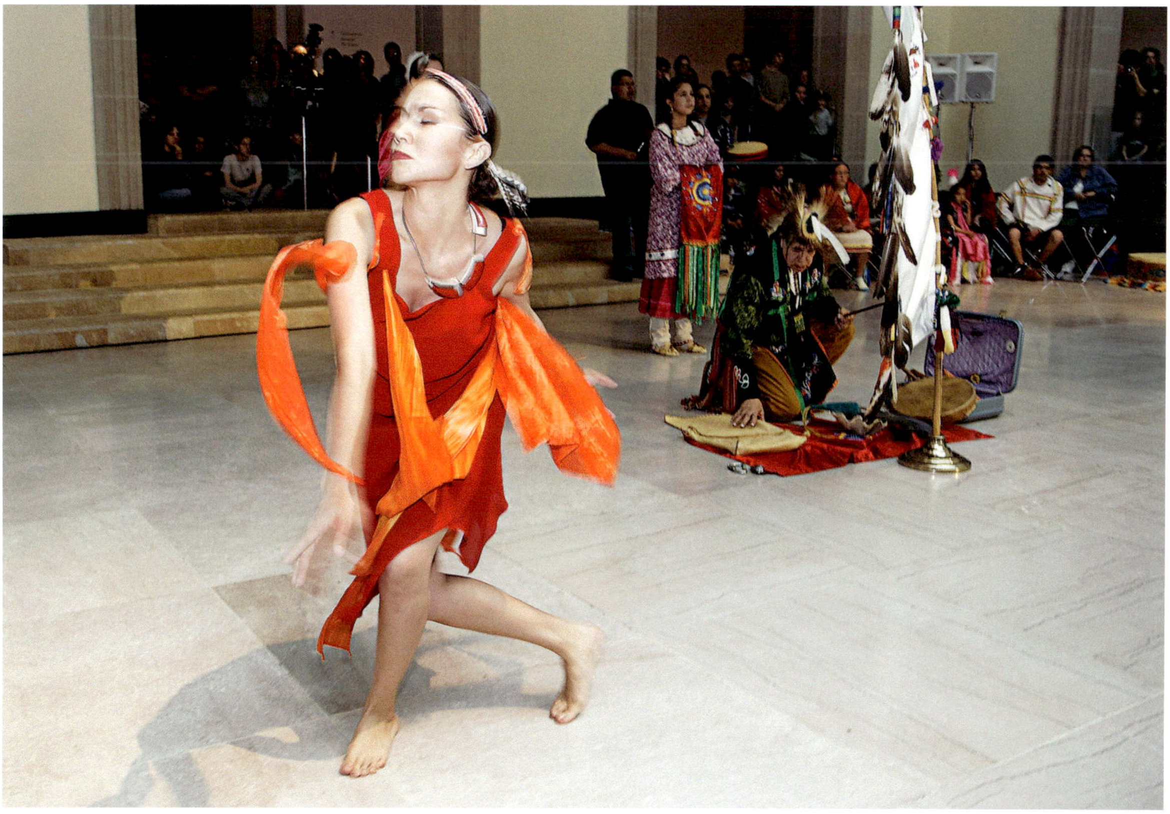

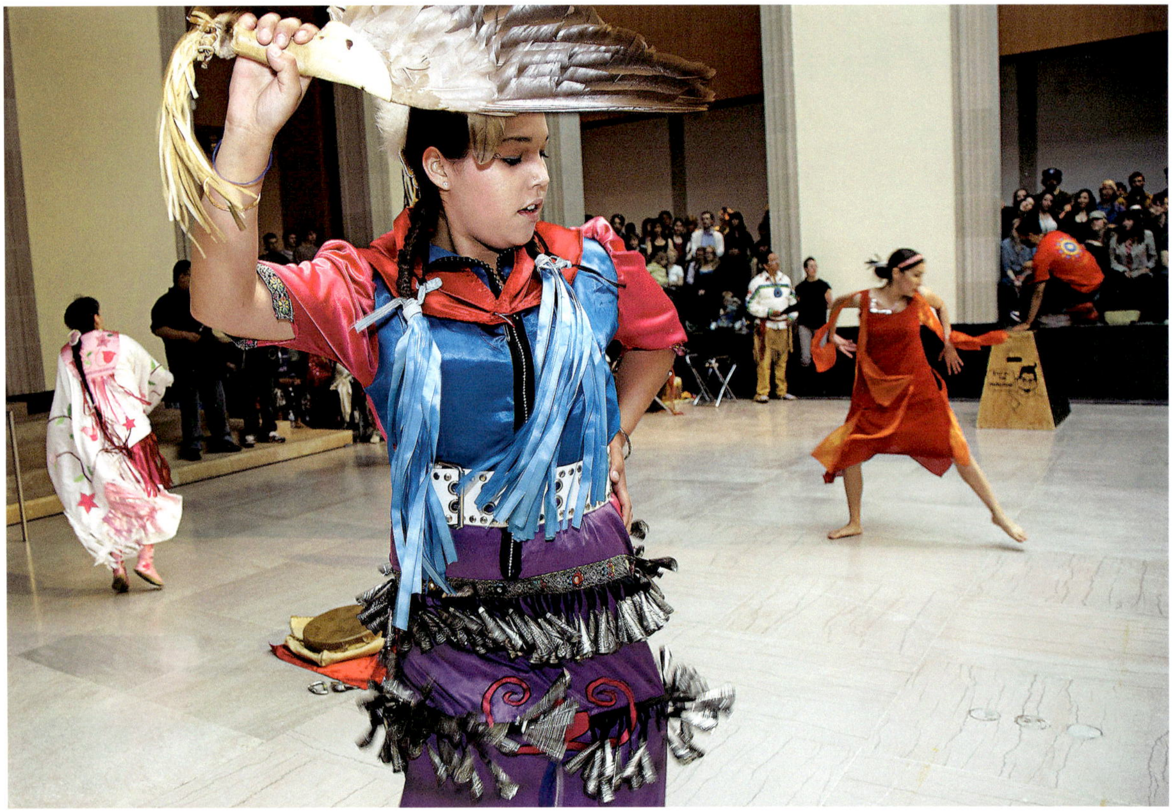

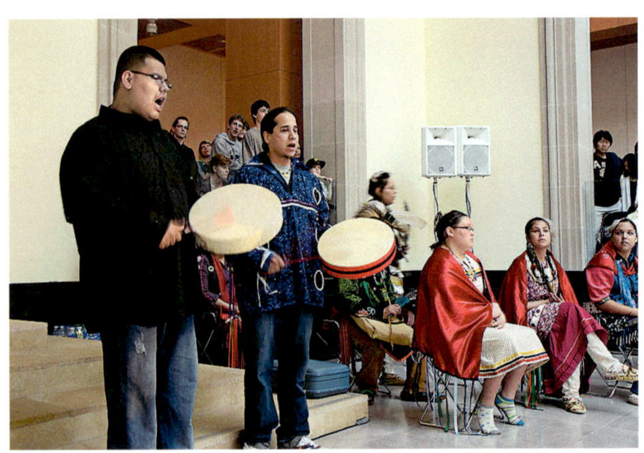
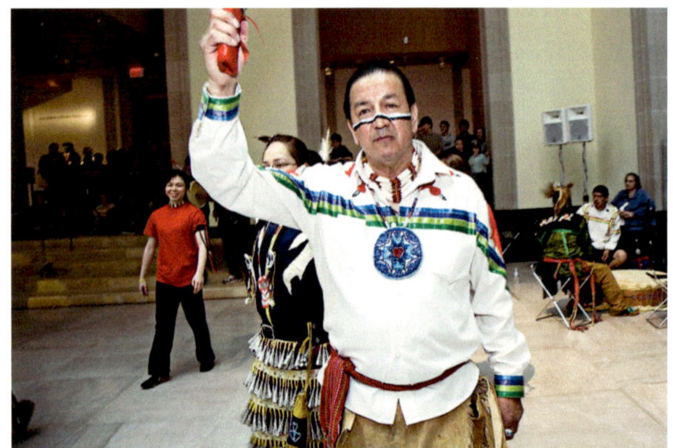
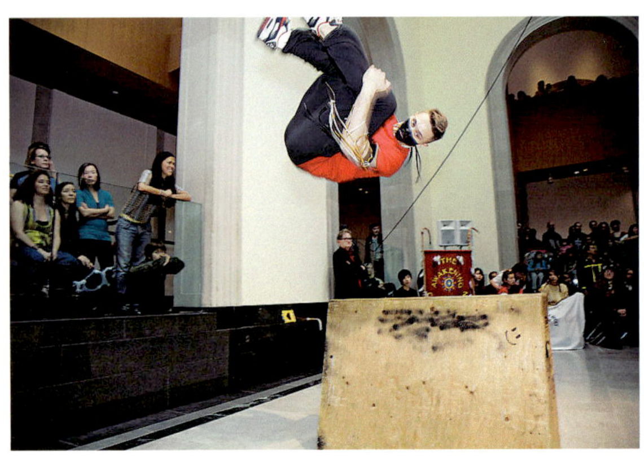
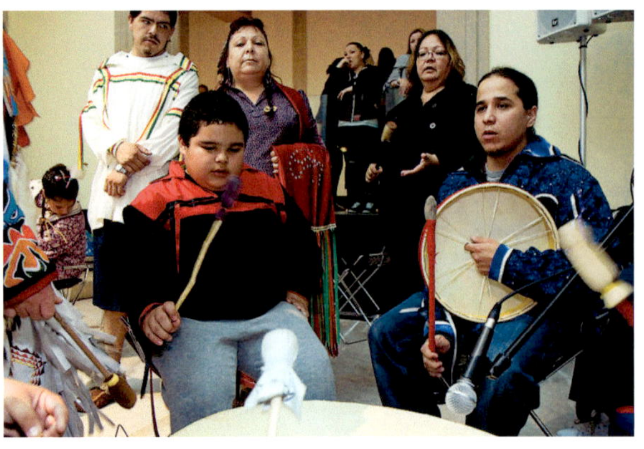

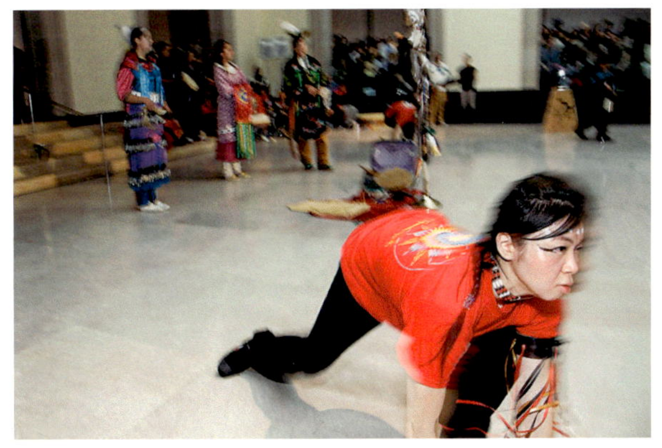
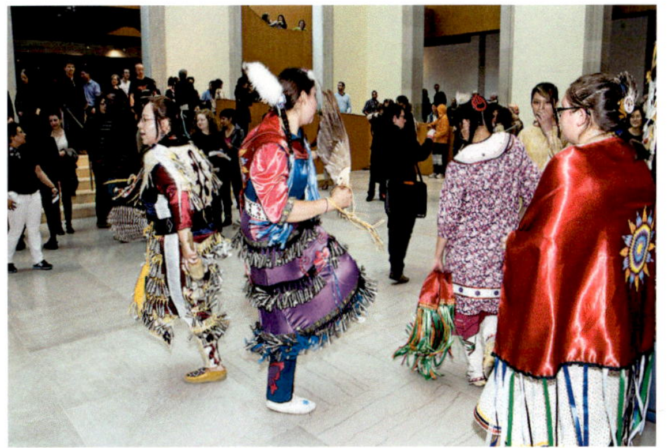
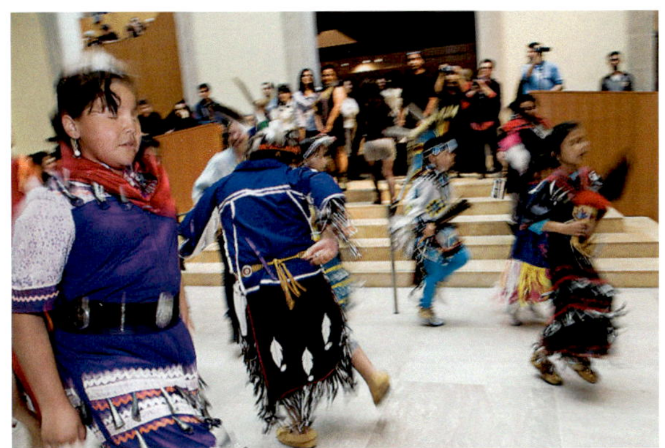
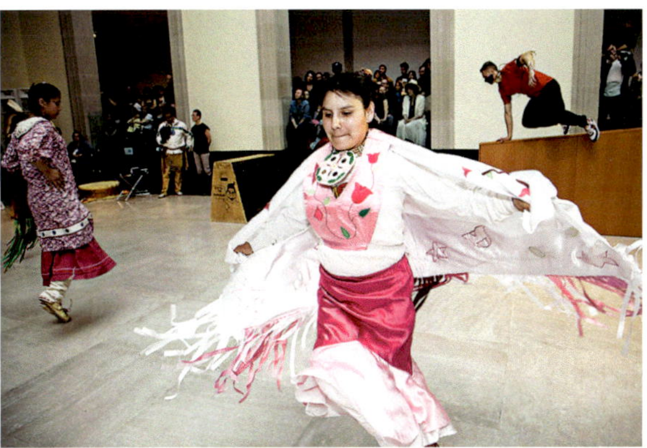

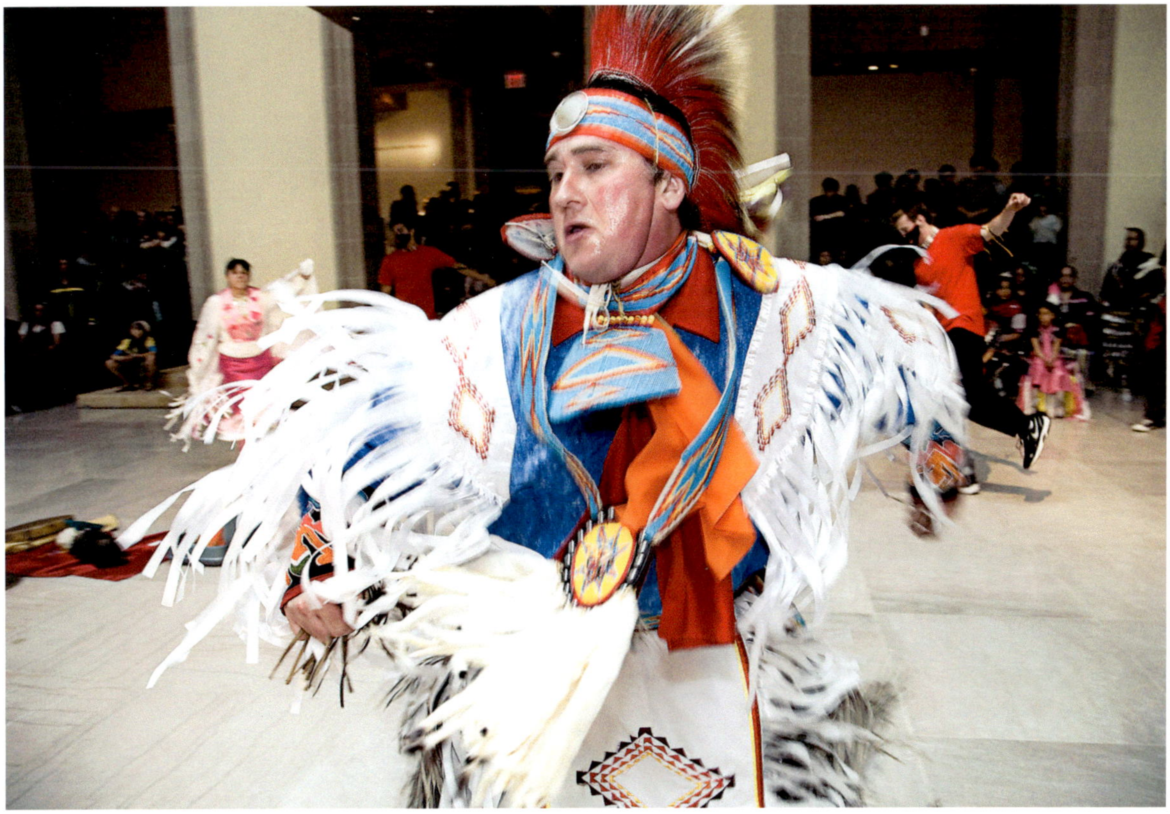

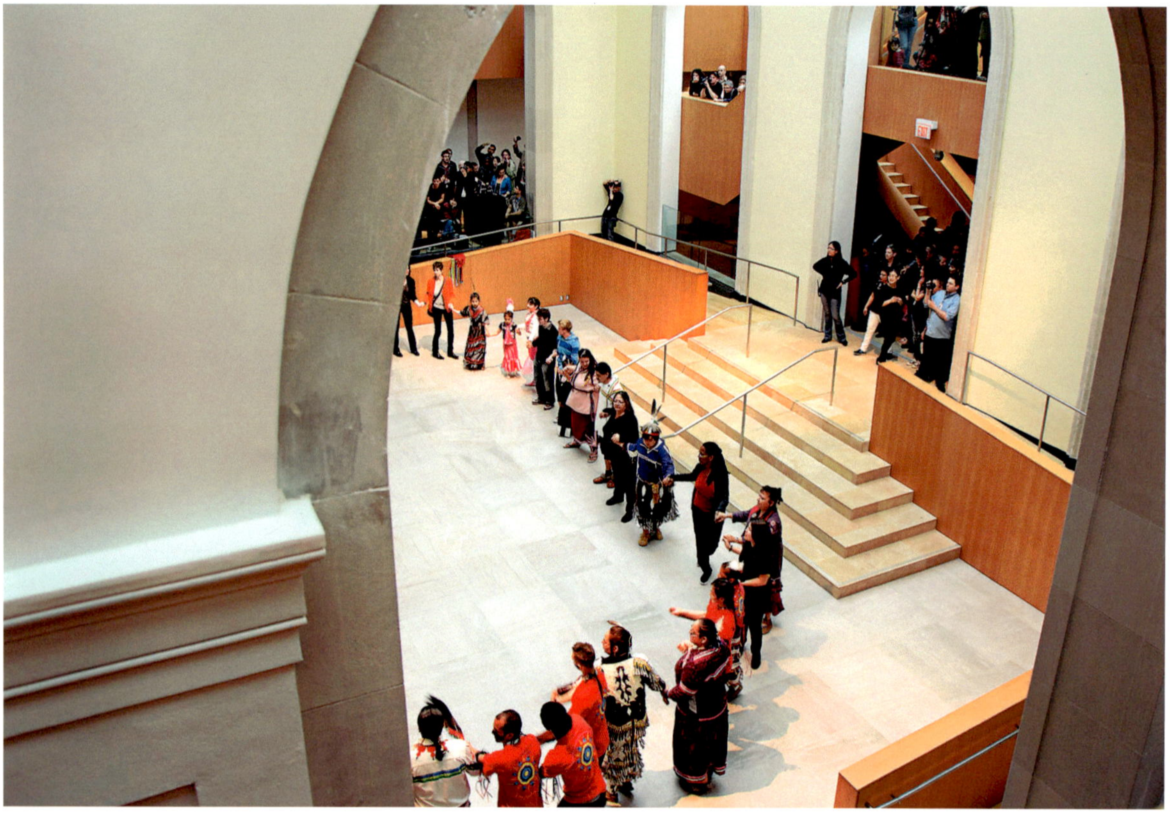

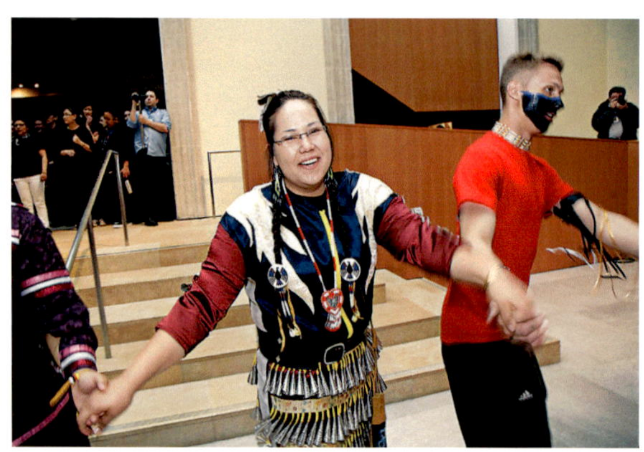
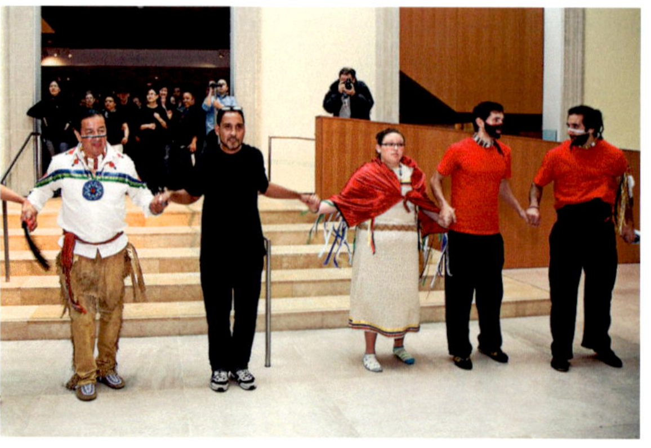
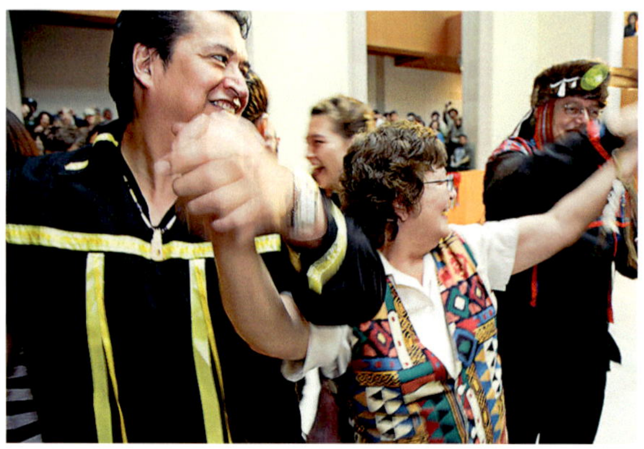
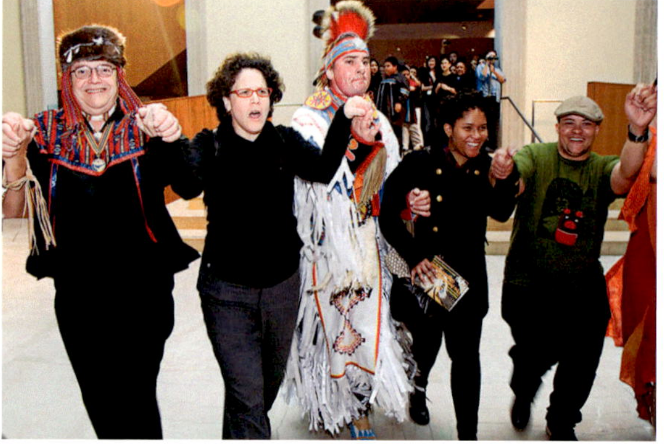

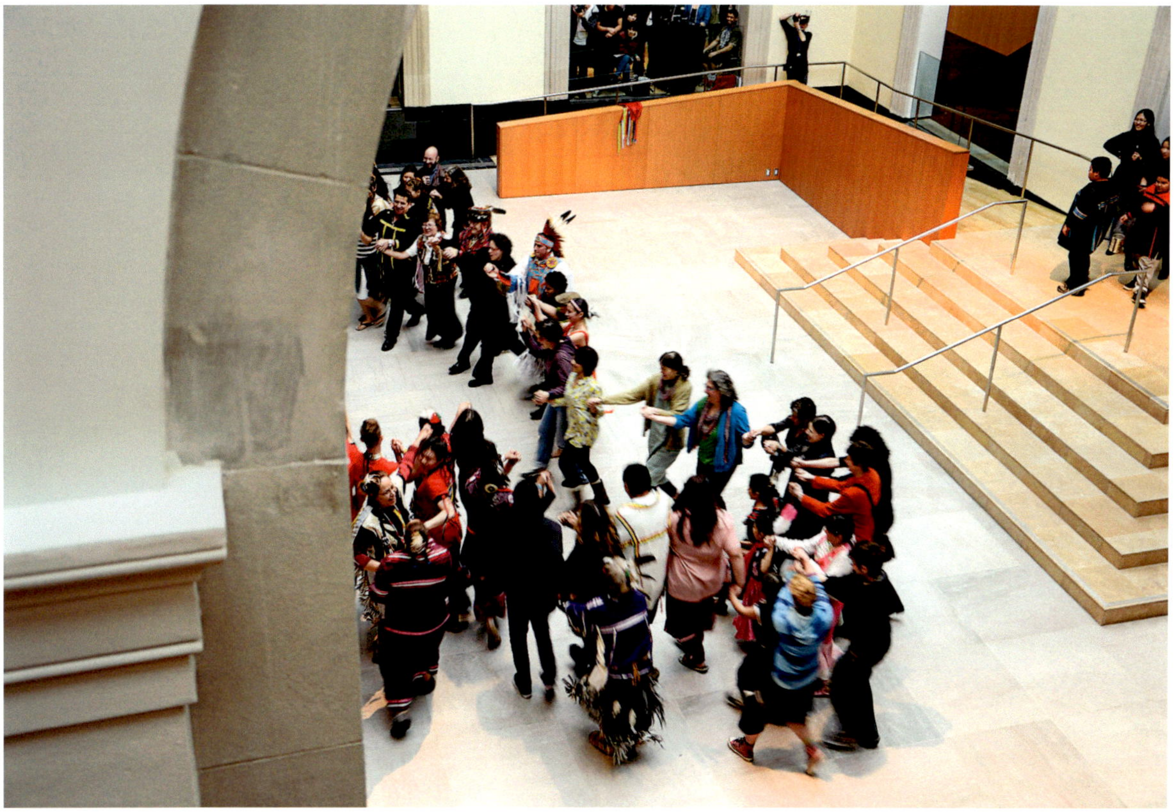

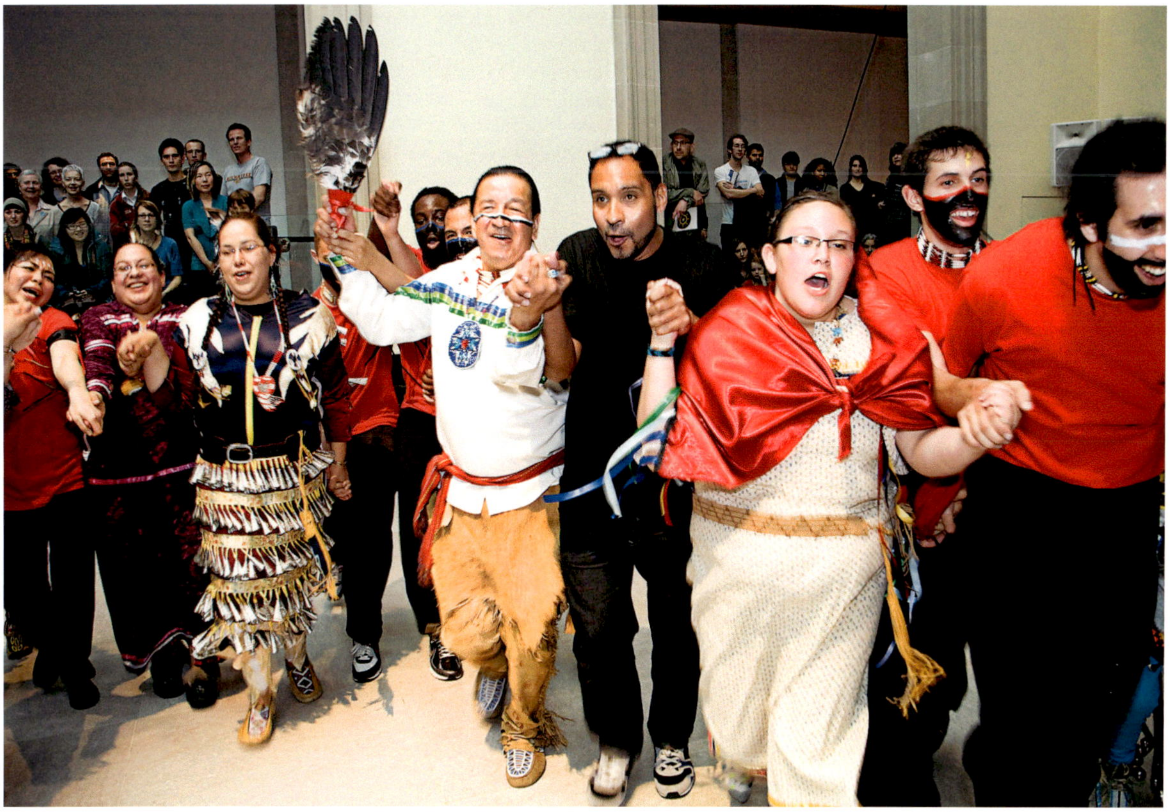

Contributor Biographies

EMELIE CHHANGUR is an artist and award winning curator and writer based in Toronto, where she works as the Assistant Director/Curator of the Art Gallery of York University (AGYU). Over the past decade, she has developed an experimental curatorial practice in collaboration with artists. Chhangur is interested in how exhibitions and texts perform to create unique interpretative experiences as well as in finding ways to enact activisms from within an institutional framework, believing that the contemporary art gallery must serve a social as well as aesthetic function. While she makes single channel videos and installations, which are shown nationally and internationally, questioning the nature and function of a contemporary art gallery is her primary art project at the moment.

LUIS CAMNITZER is a Uruguayan artist born in Germany in 1937. He immigrated to Uruguay when one year old and has lived in the USA since 1964. Professor Emeritus of Art, State University of New York, College at Old Westbury, he graduated in sculpture from the Escuela de Bellas Artes, Universidad de la República, Uruguay, and studied architecture at the same university. He has received numerous awards and fellowships, including a Guggenheim fellowship for printmaking in 1961 and for visual arts in 1982; the "Latin American Art Critic of the Year" award from the Argentine Association of Art Critics in 1998, and the Konex Mercosur Award in the visual arts for Uruguay in 2002. Amongst his many exhibitions, he represented Uruguay at the Venice Biennial in 1988, as well as participating in the Whitney Biennial in 2000 and Documenta 11 in 2003. His work is in the collections of over thirty museums. He is author of numerous books, including *New Art of Cuba* (1994/2004); *Arte y Enseñanza: La ética del poder* (2000); *Didactics of Liberation: Conceptualist Art in Latin America* (2007); and *On Art, Artists, Latin America and Other Utopias* (2010).

DR. HANS-MICHAEL HERZOG has been Artistic Director and Chief Curator Daros Latinamerica Collection, Zürich, Switzerland since 2000. Born in 1956, he studied art history, philosophy and classical archaeology at the University of Bonn, and was awarded his PhD in 1984 with a focus on Venetian Proto-Renaissance Sculpture. From 1987 until 1989, Herzog worked for the Bayerische Staatsgemäldesammlungen, München. From 1989 until 1999 he was Curator of the Kunsthalle Bielefeld. Critical writer on art and architecture, Dr. Herzog has been in charge of numerous exhibitions and publications, largely on international contemporary art. He has also been a lecturer at various German universities.

ADRIENNE SAMOS is a journalist, critic, and curator based in Panama City. She was founder and editor-in-chief of the cultural magazine *Talingo* (1993–2003), recipient of the Prince Claus Award; founder and director of Arpa (Art Panama Foundation); and founder of the publishing house Sarigua (2009–). She edited the anthology of essays, *Negociaciones: puentes estratégicos entre el arte y los públicos* (Panama: Ed. Sarigua, 2012). She has curated numerous solo and group exhibitions, most recently being two retrospectives of the work of Carlos Endara. She also acts as an advisor for the Cisneros-Fontanals Foundation and the Endara House Museum.

Biografías de los contribuyentes

EMELIE CHHANGUR es una artista, curadora, escritora de arte y ganadora de varios premios que reside en Toronto, donde trabaja como Directora Asistente y Curadora de la *Art Gallery of York University* (AGYU). Durante la última década ha desarrollado una práctica curatorial experimental en colaboración con los artistas con quienes trabaja. Chhangur está interesada en cómo las exposiciones y textos pueden crear experiencias interpretativas únicas y en encontrar maneras de promulgar el activismo dentro de un marco institucional. Apoya la creencia de que las galerías de arte contemporáneo deben servir una función social, así como una estética. Aunque su arte se manifiesta en forma de videos e instalaciones que se muestran a nivel nacional e internacional, su enfoque principal en este momento es el cuestionamiento de la naturaleza y función de una galería de arte contemporáneo.

LUIS CAMNITZER es un artista uruguayo nacido en Alemania en 1937. Emigró a Uruguay cuando tenía un año de edad y ha vivido en los EE.UU. desde 1964. Es Profesor Emérito de Arte de la Universidad del Estado de Nueva York, College at Old Westbury, se graduó en escultura de la Escuela de Bellas Artes de la Universidad de la República en Uruguay y estudió arquitectura en la misma universidad. Ha recibido numerosos premios y becas, incluyendo una beca Guggenheim para el grabado en 1961 y para las artes visuales en 1982, el premio al "Crítico de Arte Latinoamericano del Año" otorgado por la Asociación Argentina de Críticos de Arte en 1998 y el Premio Konex Mercosur en artes visuales para Uruguay en el 2002. Entre sus numerosas exposiciones, representó a Uruguay en la Bienal de Venecia en 1988 y participó en la Bienal de Whitney en el 2000 y Documenta 11 en el 2003. Su obra se encuentra en las colecciones de más de treinta museos. Es autor de numerosos libros, entre ellos *New Art of Cuba (El nuevo arte de Cuba)* (1994/2004); *Arte y Enseñanza: La ética del poder* (2000); *Didactics of Liberation: Conceptualist Art in Latin America (La didáctica de la liberación: Arte conceptualista en América Latina)* (2007), y *On Art, Artists, Latin America and Other Utopias (Sobre arte, artistas, América Latina y otras utopías)* (2010).

DR. HANS-MICHAEL HERZOG ha sido el Director Artístico y Curador Principal de la Daros Latinamerica Collection en Zurich, Suiza desde el año 2000. Nacido en 1956, estudió historia del arte, filosofía y arqueología clásica en la Universidad de Bonn y obtuvo su doctorado en 1984 con un enfoque en la escultura veneciana proto-renacentista. Desde 1987 hasta 1989 Herzog trabajó para las Bayerische Staatsgemäldesammlungen (Colecciones de pintura del estado de Baviera) en Munich. Desde 1989 hasta 1999 fue curador del museo de arte moderno Kunsthalle Bielefeld en Bielefeld, Alemania. El Dr. Herzog es escritor crítico sobre el arte y la arquitectura y ha estado a cargo de numerosas exposiciones y publicaciones, principalmente de arte contemporáneo internacional. También ha sido profesor en varias universidades alemanas.

ADRIENNE SAMOS es una periodista, crítica y curadora de arte panameña que reside en ciudad de Panamá. Fundó y dirigió la revista cultural *Talingo* entre 1993 y 2003, la cual fue ganadora del Premio Príncipe Claus en el 2001. También fundó y ha dirigido desde el 2001 la fundación Arpa (ArtePanamá), entidad dedicada a gestionar manifestaciones culturales y artísticas. Samos también creo la editorial Sarigua en el año 2009 y trabajó en la edición de la antología de ensayos *Negociaciones: puentes estratégicos entre el arte y los públicos* (varios autores, Ed. Sarigua, Panamá: 2012). Ha ejercido la curaduría de varias exposiciones, entre las más recientes, dos retrospectivas de Carlos Endara en Madrid (2011) y Panamá (2012). Escribe para varias publicaciones y es asesora de la Fundación Cisneros-Fontanals y de la Casa Museo Endara.

Artist Biography / Biografía del artista

HUMBERTO VÉLEZ studied Law and Political Science at the University of Panama and was awarded a scholarship from the *Fundación del Nuevo Cine Latinoamericano* to study at the *Escuela Internacional de Cine y TV de San Antonio de los Baños* in Cuba, founded by Gabriel García Márquez. In the early nineties, he produced social and educational videos for the province of Barcelona. He has been an artist in residence in Vienna (Ministry of Foreign Affairs); London (Triangle Arts Trust-Gasworks); Sheffield (Yorkshire Artspace); Southend-on-Sea (METAL); Paris (*La Cité internationale des Arts*); and the Art Gallery of York University (AGYU) in Toronto. In 2000, he presented his first solo exhibition, *Instalaciones* [Installations], at the *Museo de Arte Contemporáneo* in Panama and in 2011 a major survey of past performance works took place at the AGYU. He has created performances and installations for *ciudadMULTIPLEcity*, Panama (2003); Victoria Baths, Manchester (2004); *Centro de Arte La Regenta*, Las Palmas de Gran Canarias (2005); Tate Modern, London (2007); Centre Pompidou, Paris (2010); *Välparaíso: in(ter)venciones*, Chile (2010); and the AGYU (2011).

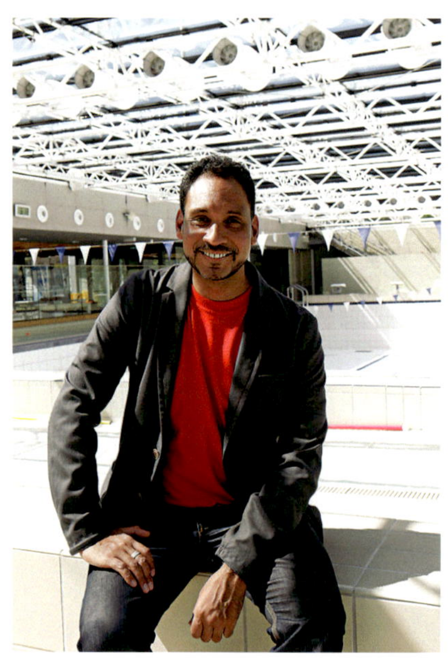

He has also participated in the biennals *Periferic*, Romania (2001); Central America (2002, 2004); Havana (2003, 2012); Shanghai (2004); Panama (2002, 2005, 2008); Liverpool (2006); Cuenca (2009); Venice (2011); and Montevideo (2012). His videos have been shown at numerous festivals, such as Sónar, Barcelona (1997) and the *Festival Ícaro de Cine Centroaméricano* (2003). He works as an artist, art professor, independent filmmaker, art producer, and is co-founder and director of *Visiting Minds*, an art and education project in Panama.

HUMBERTO VÉLEZ estudió Derecho y Ciencias Políticas en la Universidad de Panamá y fue galardonado con una beca de la Fundación del Nuevo Cine Latinoamericano para estudiar en la Escuela Internacional de Cine y TV de San Antonio de los Baños en Cuba, fundada por Gabriel García Márquez. Realizo videos educativos y sociales para la Diputación de Barcelona a principios de los años noventa. Ha sido artista residente en Viena (Ministerio de Relaciones Exteriores); Londres (*Triangle Arts Trust-Gasworks*); Sheffield (*Yorkshire Artspace*); Southend-on-Sea (METAL); París (*La Cité internationale des Arts*) y la *Art Gallery of York University* (AGYU) en Toronto. En el año 2000 tuvo su primera gran exposición individual (*Instalaciones*) en el Museo de Arte Contemporáneo de Panamá y en 2011 la AGYU presentó una extensa exhibición retrospectiva de su obra. Vélez ha realizado performances e instalaciones para *ciudadMULTIPLEcity*, Panamá (2003); *Victoria Baths*, Manchester (2004); el Centro de Arte La Regenta, Las Palmas de Gran Canaria (2005); Tate Modern, Londres (2007); Centre Pompidou, París (2010); *Välparaíso: in(ter)venciones*, Chile (2010); AGYU (2011); así como para las bienales *Periferic*, Rumania (2001); de América Central (2002, 2004); La Habana (2003, 2012); Shanghái (2004); Panamá (2002, 2005, 2008); Liverpool (2006); Cuenca (2009); Venecia (2011) y Montevideo (2012), entre otros. Sus videos han sido proyectados en un gran número de festivales, entre ellos el Sónar Festival, Barcelona (1997), y el Festival Ícaro de Cine Centroaméricano (2003). Trabaja como artista, profesor de arte, cineasta independiente y gestor cultural. Es co-fundador y director de *Visiting Minds*, un proyecto de arte y educación con sede en Panamá.

Acknowledgements / Reconocimientos

Dedicado a la memoria de mis abuelos, Francisca y Adolfo Valdés, con todo el amor.

GRACIAS A
la familia Vélez
la familia Valdés
la familia Fernández
Pitu, Carlos, Adrienne, Giovanna, José Luis y los amigos de Panamá
Andrew Pattinson y los amigos de Manchester
Hans-Michael Herzog

Dedicated to the loving memory of my grandparents, Francisca and Adolfo Valdés.

THANKS TO
the Vélez family
the Valdés family
the Fernández family
Pitu, Carlos, Adrienne, Giovanna, José Luis and friends from Panama
Andrew Pattinson and friends from Manchester
Hans-Michael Herzog

The artist and curator would like to thank the following people for their role in *The Awakening / Giigozhkozimin* and *Aesthetics of Collaboration*:
El artista y la curadora desean agradecer a las siguientes personas por su trabajo en *The Awakening / Giigozhkozimin* [El Despertar] *y Aesthetics of Collaboration* [La estética de la colaboración]:

Philip Cote, Rebecca Baird, Cotee Harper, Theo McGregor, Marc Merilainen, Elijah Stevens, Giovanna Miralles, Len Grant, Will Aldersley, Duke Redbird, Lida Kalisz, Dan Iaboni, Shawn D'Souza, Stephen Ling, Max Lee Fox Stussi, Curtis Randolph, Stan Silantev, Mandy Lam, Gerald Situ, Patrick de Perio, Simon Jackson, Leslye So, Gerome Wilson, Elder Garry Sault, Dan Secord, Cheryl Trudeau, Cole King, Conner King, Shane Junior Cameron, Carolyn King, Valerie King-Green, Veronica Jamieson, Faith Rivers, Karl King, Tina Sault, James Shawana, Stacey LaForme, "Double K," and all the Band Council members of the New Credit First Nation, Mya King-Green, Raini King-Green, Minga King-Green, Toni Green, Cathy King-Jamieson, Rachel King-Jamieson, Laura Jamieson, Mark Green, Autumn Henry, Tyrell King, Falcon King, Lauren King, Clarice King, Rina Kang, Natalia Gamaley, Claire Peng, Phat Le, Camille Rojas, Rachel Wong, Visien Li, Erin Liu, Jason Kung, Dasha Kuznetsova, Kira Xue, Mary Chiu, Marco Hernandez, Joanna Decc, Hailen Xu, Doris Isabel Pozo, Sophie Keresztessy, Sofia Ludwig, John Williamson, Larissa Sequeira, Maia Desjardins, Philip Monk, Suzanne Carte, Michael Maranda, Allyson Adley, Karen Pellegrino, Steven Laurie, Diana Morales, Faaiza Mansoor, Michael Beynon, Ken Ogawa, Fiona McDonald, Brian Davis, Danielle Greer, Craig Allan Marshall, Mia Nielsen, Syrus Marcus Ware, Michelle Jacques, Keri Ryan, Matthew Teitelbaum, Emiro Martínez-Osorio, Lisa Kiss and Jason Paré.

The Awakening / Giigozhkozimin was produced with the financial support of the Canada Council for the Arts: Artists and Community Collaboration Grant, the Ontario Arts Council: Aboriginal Art Projects, the Hal Jackman Foundation, the Ontario Arts Council: Investment Fund and in kind support from the Art Gallery of Ontario and the Tecumseh Collective First Nations Community Organization.
The Awakening / Giigozhkozimin fue producido con el apoyo financiero del Canada Council for the Arts: Artists and Community Collaboration Grant, el Ontario Arts Council: Aboriginal Art Projects, la Hal Jackman Foundation y el Ontario Arts Council: Investment Fund; y con el apoyo amable de la Art Gallery of Ontario y la Tecumseh Collective First Nations Community Organization.

© 2012 The Art Gallery of York University and authors
Art Gallery of York University
4700 Keele Street, Toronto ON Canada M3J 1P3
www.theAGYUisOutThere.org

Library and Archives Canada Cataloguing in Publication

Vélez, Humberto, 1965 -
   Humberto Vélez : the Aesthetics of collaboration / Humberto Vélez, artist; Emelie Chhangur,
author and curator ; Luis Camnitzer, author ; Hans-Michael Herzog, Adrienne Samos, interviewer.

Includes bibliographical references.
Text in English and Spanish.
Catalogue of an exhibition and public performance held at the Art Gallery of York University,
   13 April–26 June 2011, and 14 May 2011 respectively.

ISBN 978-0-921972-65-5

   1. Vélez, Humberto, 1965- --Exhibitions. I. Chhangur, Emelie II. Camnitzer, Luis, 1937- III.Herzog,
Hans-Michael, 1956- IV. Samos, Adrienne V. York University (Toronto, Ont.). Art Gallery VI. Title.

N6587.V45A4 2012   709.2   C2012-907424-1

Both *The Aesthetics of Collaboration* and
The Awakening / Giigohkozimin were curated
by Emelie Chhangur.

English descriptions of past works ("Works
Exhibited") written by Emelie Chhangur.
Spanish version by Humberto Veléz

"La estética de la colaboración," biographies,
quotations, and other incidental texts translated
into Spanish by Diana Catalina Morales.

Copyediting of texts in Spanish by
Diana Catalina Morales.
Additional copyediting by Emiro Martínez-Osorio.

Additional editing of "The Really Good-Citizen
Artist" by Selby Hickey.

"El grano de arena: Humberto Veléz en
conversación con Hans-Michael Herzog" was
originally published in *Errata# 4: Pedagogía
y educación artística* (April 2011). It is reprinted
here with the kind permission of the author
and the Fundación Gilberto Alzate Avendaño.

Commisioned by the AGYU, a version of "The
Really Good-Citizen Artist/El artista ciudadano"
was published in *ArtNexus 82* (September 2011).

Edited by Michael Maranda

Designed by Lisa Kiss Design, Toronto
Printed by Flash Reproductions
Bound by ANSTEYbookbinding

Distributed by D.A.P. / Distributed Art Publishers, Inc
http://www.artbook.com

Photography Credits
Courtesy Artway of Thinking: 8 (top middle left), 73
Fernando Bocanegra: 8 (top far left), 65–67
Suzanne Carte: 139 (top & middle right, bottom left)
Emelie Chhangur: 122–3
Clive Egginton, courtesy Yorkshire Artspace,
Sheffield: 75
Ovidio Gonzalez: 63
Len Grant: 8 (top middle, top middle right), 69, 81, 82
(bottom), 83 (top), 85, 99, 118, 125–6, 134 (top left),
141, 149–51, 152 (top left, middle, bottom right), 153
(middle), 154–5, 158 (top right, middle left, middle right,
bottom), 159–61, 162 (bottom left, bottom right), 164
(top), 165, 166 (bottom), 167, 168 (top, middle right,
bottom left, bottom right), 169, 170 (top left, top right,
bottom left, bottom right), 171 (bottom), 174
Byron Leiva: 8 (bottom far left), 89–91
Faaiza Mansoor: 153 (top right, bottom left, bottom
right), 158 (top left), 162 (middle), 163
Michael Maranda: 134 (top right, middle left, bottom),
138 (top left, bottom), 139 (middle left), 152 (top right,
bottom left), 156–7, 162 (top left, top right), 166 (top
left), 168 (middle left), 170 (middle), 171 (top)
Philip Monk: 121, 131, 134 (middle right), 138 (middle
left, middle right), 139 (bottom right)
Diana Morales: 4, 153 (top left), 164 (bottom left & right)
Cheryl O'Brien: 21–41
César Pincheira: 8 (bottom middle), 93
David Williams: 2, 8 (top far right, bottom middle left,
bottom middle right, bottom far right), 77–79, 82 (top,
middle), 83 (bottom), 95–97

The Art Gallery of York University is supported by York University, the Canada Council for the Arts,
the Ontario Arts Council, and the City of Toronto through the Toronto Arts Council.

 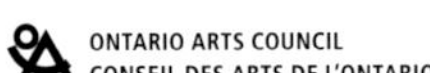 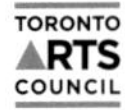 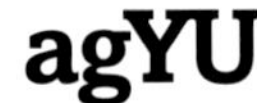